BANK
ROBBERS

BANK ROBBERS

C. Clark Criscuolo

ST. MARTIN'S PRESS
NEW YORK

Library of Congress Cataloging-in-Publication Data

Criscuolo, C. Clark.
   Bank robbers / C. Clark Criscuolo.
     p. cm.
   ISBN 0-312-11750-7
   I. Title.
PS3553.R516B36   1995
813'.54—dc20   94-36980
                                        CIP

First Edition: February 1995

10 9 8 7 6 5 4 3 2 1

For My Mother,
Lee Clark

ACKNOWLEDGMENTS

Members of the Sixth Precinct Detective unit for their cooperation in answering some pretty odd questions; the staffs at the U.S. Printing Office and the Social Security offices in New York for their help with Medicaid and benefits questions. Janet, Lynn, Linda, and Hope for their patience, honesty, and input; and as ever, Gregory.

BANK
ROBBERS

CHAPTER ONE

W<small>HERE</small> am I gonna get a gun?

". . . As I told you last week and the week before that, if the out-patient program is not on Medicaid's approved list, then we do not pay for it," Mrs. Simpson's voice droned.

"I understand that," Dottie said, gritting her teeth. "And as I told you last week and the week before that, I no longer have private insurance. I have no money. All I am asking is: What agency, or person, I can send these letters to, to get approval for this program?"

"Again, the program is listed as 'experimental.' We don't pay for experimental programs, and, osteoporosis is not on our list of life-threatening illnesses, therefore we don't review it."

"Oh, Christ! There's *another* list?"

"Yes, Mrs. Weist, and this disease is not on it—"

"Look, it's a special exercise program done in a pool to alleviate bone stress and—"

"It's experimental! It is not covered," the woman cut Dottie off. "And even if it wasn't an experimental program, osteoporosis is a *chronic* condition. We don't pay for treatments of chronic conditions."

"You pay for AIDS. Are you telling me AIDS is not a chronic condition?"

"AIDS is a life-threatening illness. Osteoporosis is not listed as a life-threatening condition."

"Well, it bloody well should be. My mother died of osteoporosis."

"Your mother died of heart failure, Mrs. Weist, you said so on your forms."

"She wouldn't have died of heart failure if all her bones hadn't broken," Dottie yelled, exasperated.

She watched Mrs. Simpson grunt and shake her head. "Don't raise your voice to *me*. You think you can come in here and use up all my time—"

"That's your job. I'm not asking for favors, I want a *name*! You jerk!"

Mrs. Simpson stood.

"Her name is Hillary Rodham Clinton and the address is 1600 Pennsylvania Avenue! Now get out of my office," she shrieked, and behind her, Dottie heard a cough. She looked over and saw a large guard, complete with gun, standing at the door, looking at her.

She glared back at Mrs. Simpson and grabbed the letters.

"I'll leave, oh, don't you worry," she said, stuffing them inside her purse.

"Good."

"My congressman will be hearing about this," Dottie warned.

"Send my regards," Mrs. Simpson yelled after her, as the guard wrapped a large hand around Dottie's upper arm, led her out of the little cubicle and down the hall.

She stared straight ahead, holding her head high with as much dignity as she could muster as the guard walked her through the filled outside waiting room. She was escorted down to the lobby, and the guard stood, watching her push through the revolving door. He crossed his arms over his huge belly and stared at her with a sneer, as if saying, "Go ahead, just try coming back inside this building."

Dottie stood in front of the large glass doors. She was not going to move until he did.

She focused in on her reflection in the glass, and was startled by the woman who stared back at her.

She looked so thin and pale. She'd been a size fourteen for nearly a decade, and now, after a seven-week stay in the hospital at the beginning of the summer, she was a size eight. Her baggy old dress made her seem even thinner and, worse, fragile somehow. She needed a haircut. It had been a while since she'd been able to afford one. For years she'd taken great pains with her hair, keeping it a reddish blond and cut chin-length. Now it was graying and overgrown. She had a sharp nose and dark-blue eyes that were exactly like her mother's had been. Her eyelashes were long and spiky, and curled up over puffy brows and drew attention to her eyes. She had flat Irish cheekbones which sat high on her face, and thin lips. She could still be considered a good-looking woman, but she looked so haggard in the glass.

She felt humiliated at having been physically ejected from the office. She had never been thrown out of a place in her life.

Her hip flashed pain through the right side and she'd only been at Medicaid for five hours. Five hours at their offices was a sneeze, as she well knew. She turned away from the building.

How dare they make her beg? She was not asking for welfare, she was not asking for a handout. She had worked hard all her life. The government didn't seem to have any exemption lists when they were taking the money out of her paycheck every week when she had a full-time job. But now that they had to pay some back out, well, suddenly she had to go beg.

Well, they were going to see.

Yes, they were going to see, she thought bitterly.

The government was going to *pay*.

From now on, the government was going to pay for *everything*.

3

She got on the train and went directly back to her apartment on Sullivan Street. She tossed her purse with all the medical letters on the kitchen table, and turned on the television. She strode into the bedroom and pulled Nathan's old address book out of a drawer. Dottie lowered the volume slightly on the television as she passed and sat down at the table in the kitchen.

She gently balanced her glasses on her nose, making sure the chain went around her neck, so God forbid she wouldn't drop them. That would be all she needed, breaking her only pair of glasses. Who the hell knew what she'd do then.

She turned the pages until her eyes stopped midway down at the N's.

Newhouse, Fred and Teresa.

That was the number.

When had she seen them last?

Christ, Agnes's wake. Fred had worn his usual baggy brown suit with a little paisley bow tie at the neck and a gray felt hat.

In the sixties it had looked sharp; in the nineties it looked like something that should have the smell of mothballs.

And Teresa, she had grown immense over the years. When they appeared in the doorway at the wake, her size made Fred seem scrawny. Teresa was the kind of woman Dottie saw over the years only when their husbands got together, or heard about through their mutual friend Roberta, who had grown up with Teresa. Other than that, she and Teresa had absolutely nothing in common. They'd never been friends.

When had Agnes's wake been? Dottie tried to remember. Well, she'd try the number. Fred would know a fence; honesty was not his long suit.

Her eyes looked up at the clock on the kitchen wall.

Two thirty-five.

She couldn't call Fred and Teresa till after three, that was what Nathan had always told her. She was edgy, and she stood up, looking around for something to occupy the time.

The kitchen was easily the largest room in the apartment, and had a serviceable but old refrigerator, a stained and pitted double porcelain sink, an equally serviceable four-burner stove. A large white porcelain table, ringed with a black stripe and scratched from years of use, sat in the middle of the room and served as both the only workspace and the dinner table. She remembered how many evenings she had slid the extension out and placed folding chairs around for her husband's poker games.

She and Nathan, Jr., would watch television in the big bedroom in back until he fell asleep. Then she would turn off the set and sit up and read. Most evenings she would fall asleep like that and would come out in the morning to find Nathan snoring on the couch, the porcelain table smudged by cigar and cigarette ashes, littered with overflowing ashtrays and juice glasses with stale beer in them.

How many years had she put up with that?

How many years had she excused herself from doing anything about Nathan's gambling? And what was her big stand?

That Nathan, Sr., was not allowed to play in the house since the child had to be up early, and his bed was the fold-out couch in the middle room. Dottie shook her head.

When Nathan died, she rearranged the apartment a bit, moving the television into the living room so she could watch it during dinner. Eventually she moved herself onto the couch, where she would fall asleep to the drone of the television. She walked into the living room and began making up the fold-out couch.

Well, she liked to think of it as a living room, even though it was mostly a kind of hallway connecting the bedroom in front, which overlooked the street, with the kitchen in back, which overlooked an air shaft. She carefully tucked in the top sheet on one side of the couch.

She had never thought it would come to this.

She winced and felt her stomach go on her again. She'd had a weak cup of coffee for breakfast and that was it. And at the hospital they'd given her this whole list of "calcium-rich" foods she was supposed to eat each day. Her stomach burned. She was lucky if she could afford the coffee.

She walked around to the other side of the couch, smoothed out the sheet, and folded it into a hospital corner on the end.

That stay in the hospital.

If that hadn't happened, then she wouldn't be in this situation . . . although, maybe, the hospital hadn't been that bad. After all, they'd fed her, given her clean clothes, and . . . she felt a wave of anger go across her chest.

There was something wrong when a hospital stay was the highlight of your year.

All she'd done was fall down crossing Fourteenth Street in the early summer. She'd woken up in St. Vincent's Hospital, to be shown ghostly X rays of broken-up pieces of bones all over the place. And this doctor, whose accent was so thick she could barely make it out, had given her some kind of explanation for all of this in big medical terms, but it all boiled down to this: Her bones were becoming too brittle to hold up her body.

And Dottie knew from experience it was not going to get better. She thought of her own mother, and all the time at the end when she had lived in the hospital. And she remembered the operations, and the pins in her hips and her knees, the broken wrist from trying to get out of bed. And all the weeks and months of broken bones until finally . . . Dottie couldn't think of it anymore.

Good God, dying of broken bones. She always thought

she'd die from emphysema from all those cigarettes she'd smoked in Joe's smoke-filled nightclub. Hell, if she'd have known, she wouldn't have quit smoking twenty years ago. But not to be able to walk . . . She remembered how high she could kick in a chorus line.

That was always the complaint about her performances: "Dottie, you got legs forever, but you can't kick that high! Makes the rest of the girls look like they ain't even trying."

She could kick so high she could kiss her knee without having to move her neck forward even a little. When she was a little girl, her one indulgence had been dancing lessons. First ballet, then tap and jazz . . . oh, the pairs of shoes and tights she went through.

Broken bones. It wasn't fair. She'd already spent too much time in hospitals with Nathan in the end. And yes, even though he'd lived to an old age—he was over seventy when he died—it had scared her.

The pain of being so close to her own mortality, that was what frightened her about Nathan's death.

No matter what she told people about facing death, the fact was that deep down she felt she was going to be the exception to the rule and live forever. And watching him die had been like being hit in the face with cold water.

Here she was, alone, with nothing! Nothing! Where the hell had all the years gone? Where was her life?

It was especially bad when she was alone in the hospital with all those foreigners sticking things into her, taking things out of her, rolling her here and rolling her there. She'd count every day waiting for the end.

And now she was on her steady diet of pills, and she spent her days waiting for the next round of broken bones.

It didn't matter anyway. No one was concerned with Dottie O'Malley Weist.

She looked back up at the clock.

Quarter to three. She just wanted to get this over with.

She had begun to feel as if she didn't exist anymore. She had lived alone for four years now.

After Nathan died she'd made an effort to get out, get involved with something. She'd signed up for a senior citizen's group which met every Thursday night in the basement of St. Anthony's Church.

Jesus! Had that been depressing!

A roomful of ancient women who spent each evening recounting the deaths of their husbands in, it seemed to Dottie, unnecessarily graphic detail. And when they had exhausted that topic, they would move on to the disgusting operations and ghastly deaths of friends and family.

Dottie soon stopped going to these meetings.

Slowly, a kind of eerie anonymity began to creep over her life. It was almost like being in solitary confinement, even though she lived in a city of eight million people.

For instance, she could recall one whole month going by without actually being addressed by another human being. Dottie felt her eyes begin to get itchy. She had to change the subject in her head . . .

And not to be touched by another human being—that she could count in years. Just to have someone hold her hand, or give her a pat on the shoulder, even . . . she began to hunger for that, and so for a while she would deliberately walk slowly and let busy people brush against her . . .

She finished making up the couch, and glanced up at the clock. Three on the nose. She moved over to the phone and dialed Fred and Teresa's number.

The television was still blaring as usual behind her. She'd gotten into the habit of turning on the set whenever she entered the apartment. She couldn't stand the silence of the place. She was thinking she should have turned it off before she dialed the number, but it was too late now, the line was ringing. She waited for the phone to pick up, and she sat, tapping a pencil.

"Hello?" A voice came on after the ninth ring.

"Is this Teresa Newhouse?"

"Who wants to know?"

"Dottie Weist, Teresa," she said as calmly as she could.

"Dottie? Weist?" the voice croaked back to her.

"I'm Nathan's wife? I saw you last at Agnes's wake, er, several years ago. Teresa, do you know who this is?"

There was a silence.

"Yeah. What you think, I'm stupid? What you want?" she demanded.

That was Teresa. Rude, with an edge in her voice that could cut through walls.

"I want to speak to Fred."

"He's dead."

Dottie exhaled. "When?"

"Five weeks ago."

"I'm sorry, Teresa. Is there anything I can do?" Dottie's voice softened.

She detected just the tiniest sob, and then there was a long silence; it sounded as if Teresa had put the phone down. Dottie waited patiently for Teresa to pull herself together.

"Dottie? You there?"

"I'm here."

"I gotta go."

"Sure thing. Look, you need some company maybe?" she asked. There was a silence.

"I ain't got nothin' in the house," the gruff voice came back.

"Well, I'd just like to pay my respects."

There was another silence, and she waited for Teresa to make some sort of decision.

"When you wanna come over?"

"I could come over now, this afternoon."

"All right. I'll be here," she said, as if it was a major concession for her to have to socialize with Dottie.

"Fine. I'll see you around four."

She waited and finally heard the click.

She prayed Teresa would be able to give her the number of a fence.

TERESA DeNUNZIO NEWHOUSE sat at the kitchen table and stared at the phone.

What the hell did *she* want to come up bothering her for? She took a deep drag on her cigarette and blew the smoke hard, so it shot out in a stream at an angle.

Miss High-and-Mighty.

And all the men, they would swoon over her like she was some kind of delicate flower or goddamn queen.

Well, Dottie O'Malley Weist was no queen.

Oh yeah, she knew her. She always had these airs, as if she were better than the world, but Teresa knew it was all an act. For instance, she wouldn't read the *Star* or the *National Enquirer,* like the rest of the world. Oh, no. She read "literature."

All those books she was always reading. The real thick kind, with the plastic library covers on 'em. She'd bury her nose in them and not talk to anyone else.

But Teresa knew what the truth was about those.

She wasn't really readin 'em.

She was just pretending. No one really reads those things. Says so right in all the newspapers all the time. Not with a kid and a husband to look after. It was just that she did it so *good.* Her eyes would actually move across the page as if she knew what all them words were, but Teresa had proof Dottie wasn't really reading.

Her lips didn't move.

And no one reads without moving the lips, this was a fact.

Dottie fooled everybody, except for her, Teresa.

She was a goddamned chorus girl, like the rest of 'em. Out there showing off her legs.

And Nathan, when he first brought her around . . . she'd gotten Teresa's best friend Margie kicked off the line, and Margie'd been with Nathan plenty. Poor little victim Margie hadn't even seen her coming.

And, wham, suddenly Dottie and Nathan are married?

No. Teresa shook her head.

And then she'd made Nathan miserable. "Get rid of her, Nat," Fred had always told him. "What you do for a living ain't good enough for her? Get rid of her. Have Teres' set you up with someone *nice*."

But Nathan, who was basically an okay guy, stuck it out with her. Jeez, Nathan Weist not good enough? If Teresa hadn't already been married to Fred, she'd have gone for Nathan herself. She'd have been as proud of him as if he'd been president.

Not that she hadn't loved Fred. Oh no, she had, and she'd have never given him up for nobody. Her eyes began to dribble tears again the way they had for five solid weeks, and Teresa wiped them with the back of her hand and then squashed out her cigarette in the tray.

Oh, God, Fred, she thought and then shook her head. She lit another cigarette to calm herself down. She sniffed and then tried to think of the things that had annoyed her about Fred. It made her feel better. If she thought about all the goodness in the man she'd go crazy from grief, so she'd surrounded herself with all the things he'd done that drove her nuts.

Teresa took a sip on her coffee and grimaced. It was cold.

Fred had been good to her, yes, but he had a lazy streak in him Nathan never had. Nathan would be at that club, cookin' in the back room with Ben Zimmerman at all hours of the day and night. But Fred, well, every day on the dot of two-thirty, she'd have to throw him out of the house. Two-thirty was her cutoff, because the kids would be in from parochial school and they had agreed that he should always be gone when they got in.

She'd brought her kids up right; it wasn't good for children to see their father lying around the house like a bum all day, that was the way Teresa had always felt.

And periodically she'd have to put Fred straight and she'd say, "I don't care what it takes, we got a three-hundred-dollar grocery bill. You bring it home tonight so I don't gotta go to Murphy's on a Hun'-two, where the produce looks like crap."

And out Fred would go, maybe do a little hustlin' or hijackin' or crack a safe, but he'd be back into the house at six the next the morning with the money.

Now there was a right guy, just like Nathan.

But did Dottie ever appreciate him? Naw.

This was not a right woman.

And now she was coming all the way up here to gloat over her widowhood.

That was just low.

Teresa felt her eyes fill again with tears.

TERESA still lived on 106th Street. Although it had been over twenty years since Dottie'd been to Teresa's, for some reason she remembered exactly which train to take.

The neighborhood that met Dottie's eyes when she left the station was frightening. Groups of dangerous-looking teenagers hung out along First Avenue, blasting music and screaming at one another with foul mouths. And the filth of the avenue, and the burned-out buildings—it looked like a war zone. Dottie couldn't think of anyone Teresa's age having to make her way through this destruction, and for a second Dottie felt that maybe she didn't have it that bad on Sullivan Street.

She kept glancing over her shoulder as she stood in the small hallway waiting for Teresa to let her inside. The buzzer rang and Dottie quickly opened the inside door and shut it, making sure it was locked behind her.

Dottie slowly climbed up the first flight of stairs in the tenement building. She stopped and took in a deep breath, resting on the second-floor landing.

She still couldn't believe she was fifty-eight. Deep down, Dottie was still twenty-four, that was the way she felt. When she looked in the mirror, it was like looking at herself with a mask on.

It amazed her that climbing stairs had begun to tire her quickly. Not only stairs, any physical activity at all. Dottie stared up at the next set of white stone stairs. Even the exercises they'd given her to do for her bones didn't help with some things, although she felt a lot better and was a lot more agile now than when she'd first begun them.

Dottie took another deep breath and started walking again.

Lord, not only was the outside terrible, she thought, but who could walk up all these flights each day? Especially someone of Teresa's weight. It must take her hours, she thought, as she continued up the steep steps.

"Dottie?" she heard Teresa's screechy voice echo down to her. "Dottie, you get in okay?"

"Yeah." Dottie exhaled as loudly as she could.

"It's the top floor," Teresa called down to her.

Dottie leaned on the banister breathing hard.

"What floor," she panted, "is that?"

"Sixth."

"Aw, God Almighty," Dottie muttered under what little breath she could catch.

By the time she reached the top floor, her throat was dry and she was gasping. Her hip was aching slightly. She slammed against the door and pushed it open with the entire weight of her body.

"What'd you do? Run up here?" Teresa asked, apparently stunned to see her so soon.

Dottie shook her head, just trying to get some breath to stay in her lungs. She shook her head, tried to speak, and staggered over to a chair and looked at Teresa, motioning for some water.

Teresa turned to the sink, took a glass out of the drainer and filled it with water. She handed it to Dottie.

She drank slowly, finally getting her breathing back to normal.

"How do you do that each day?"

"I don't. My daughter and her husband bring me up groceries twice a week. Way the neighborhood is now, I don't go out unless I gotta," she said. "You want some coffee or something?"

"Sure." Dottie said, and watched Teresa turn around. She heard herself gasp, as she really looked at the woman for the first time.

Teresa had lost an entire person of weight.

They were the same height, and now Teresa seemed to be almost exactly Dottie's size. Teresa turned back, looking at her suspiciously.

"Teresa, you're skinny."

"Yeah. I lost a lotta weight this past year, what with Fred being so sick and everything."

"Well, here we are, both skinny again. Like when we first met."

"Yeah," Teresa muttered softly and they both silently thought to themselves, 'and nobody's here to see it.'

Teresa moved over to the stove and lit a fire under a dented old teapot. She took out a small jar, and two cups.

"All I got in the house is instant," she said.

"That's fine."

"So, Roberta called from California and said you was in the hospital. You better now?"

"As well as I can expect."

"What do you have again?"

"Osteoporosis." Dottie watched Teresa shrug, unknowing. "It's a debilitating bone disease. Your bones get so weak they break easily."

She watched Teresa shudder.

"But you're okay now," she said, her back to her.

"No. It's wiped me out financially, and Medicaid won't pay for this new procedure that would slow it down."

Teresa let out a bitter cackle.

"Those bastards, they don't pay for nothin'. Jeez, I had to go in there beggin' for chemo for my Fred."

"Yes, and I'm tired of it. And I'm going to do something about it. Do you know they actually escorted me out of their offices, like I was some kind of common criminal? Well, from now on, the government is going to pay for everything."

"Yeah?" Teresa chortled.

"I have a plan, and I need your help."

"Me? I can't do nothin' for nobody," she said after a moment, turning around to look at her. Teresa peered down at her, her eyes narrowed. "What'd you want Fred for?"

Dottie looked her straight in the eyes. "I need the number of a fence."

Teresa's eyes grew round, and she looked quite stunned.

"You lookin' for an appliance?"

"A gun."

Teresa's face went neutral, the way Fred's always had when he was discussing business, but she didn't take her eyes off Dottie. Her hand shot out and grabbed a pack of

15

cigarettes on the counter. She pulled one out and lit it with a lighter. She exhaled hard.

"Gimme that again?"

"I need a gun."

"What, you gonna go shoot everyone at Medicaid?"

"No. I'm going to rob a bank."

Teresa's eyes stayed fixed on Dottie and she sat down at the table.

"Like the guy in the *News*?"

"The guy in Minnesota?"

"There was a nut in Minnesota too? Naw, the old guy from—hold on, I'll get the paper, it was just in it."

She watched Teresa open the closet door. Inside was a waist-deep stack of yellowing papers.

"I hate that stupid law they put in about recycling, I never know when to put the stuff out, what you tie it with . . ." Teresa was muttering as she sifted through the top of the pile, which was mainly comprised of gossip sheets, and magazines that followed celebrities.

Dottie shook her head at all of them.

"How can you read all that garbage?"

Teresa looked up, a bit surprised.

"What?"

"All those gossip rags? None of it is true."

"It's *all* true," Teresa informed her, holding up a copy of the *Star*.

"Yeah? What's that headline say?" Dottie asked, and Teresa looked at it.

"IS YOUR DOG A SPACE ALIEN?" Teresa read aloud.

"There, you see?"

"What? I took that test." Teresa said seriously.

"You—you don't even have a dog."

"So? My daughter's got a dog. You think I want some alien around my grandchildren? This test come out of a

16

university. Besides, even if it is silly, it's got all the good dirt on all them celebrities."

"Who cares about some celebrity?" Dottie sniffed.

"I do." Teresa looked confused. "I always read about everyone. I had someone famous in my family once," she said casually.

"Who?" Dottie asked, leaning forward.

"My great-aunt, for whom I was named. Teresa Salinotta."

"I never heard of her."

"Yeah, that's 'cause you don't read nothing important." Teresa sniffed, and they both let it drop.

"Here it is, here it is, McAlary's column: WHEN GRAND-DAD ROBS A BANK," Teresa read out loud and tossed the paper down in front of Dottie.

"I don't usually follow these stories, but this one . . . He was twenty in the hole, and he got his grandson's toy gun and robbed a bank way the hell out in Nassau County."

"Yeah? Did they catch him?"

"You kiddin'? The cops were all over him before he even left the building. And then the guy got so scared he began to have a heart attack, so all these cops sat there feedin' the *stunadze* heart pills, and doin' CPR on him till the ambulance showed. It was a big embarrassing mess. See? Looks like his wife's about to smack him in the photo," Teresa said, holding it up for Dottie to look at.

"What kind of time did they give him?" Dottie asked, leaning forward.

"It just happened. But they're talkin' eight to ten."

"Eight to ten, that's good."

Teresa frowned at her. "Yeah, well, maybe you should rethink the bank thing. I mean, some guy our age can't get away with it, you ain't."

17

"I don't want to get away with it. I want them to catch me. I want them to send me to jail."

Behind them the teapot began to whistle.

"You *wanna* go to jail?" Teresa got up, turned off the fire under the teapot, and poured the water into the cups. She felt herself grimace.

"Yes."

Teresa was silent. Dottie listened to her stirring the coffee powder into the hot water.

"You sure they said debilitating *bone* disease, not maybe debilitating *brain* disease, Dottie?"

"I'm not crazy!" she snapped indignantly, and Teresa looked around at her. "I'm not so stupid as to think I could actually get away with robbing a bank. Of course not, I'm not crazy," she repeated.

"Yeah, well, you ain't talkin' too normal neither."

"Listen, Medicaid wiped out every cent I had before they would pay for any of the hospital expenses. Then they humiliated me and refused to pay for treatments I need. Why the hell should I go begging for medical care, when they took the money?"

" 'Cause that's the way it works."

"Not with me, it doesn't."

"So this guy—from where?"

"Minnesota."

"Don't it snow all the time up there?"

"Yeah . . ."

"Ah, well, that's it, the guy just went nuts 'cause he couldn't get out of the house," Teresa joked and set the coffee down in front of Dottie.

"He didn't go nuts because of snow, he went nuts because he had leukemia and like me, had no insurance. And because he'd worked his whole life honestly, and they refused to pay. They told him he had to use up all his own money—sell his house, empty his bank account—before

18

they'd cover anything. But that would've wiped him out and, what was he going to do if they 'cured' him? Live in a home on welfare? It's crazy. He'd have no way of supporting himself, and besides, he wanted to leave something to his kids."

She watched Teresa's head rise and a flash of pain cross her face. Then she nodded very gently in recognition.

"So, he held up a gas station," Dottie said.

"They caught him?" Teresa held her cup, as she leaned against the counter, sipping at it, and stared at Dottie.

"Of course. And do you know where they sent him?"

"Jail?" Teresa asked sneeringly.

"Not just jail. Minimum security. I saw it on television. He was sitting in a nice clean infirmary. They were just handing him all the medication he needed, he was undergoing chemo—there were no triplicate forms to fill out, there was no begging. I mean, the man had clean clothes, was being fed hot meals. Do you know what I've been living on for the last four months? Bouillon cubes and toast. And at this facility there was a garden and a swimming pool and the second Tuesday of every month they have entertainers come, just like at Grossinger's in the Catskills."

"So it was a scam?" Teresa said.

"No, it wasn't a scam." Dottie said testily. "Look, they took the money out of his paycheck each month the same way they took it out of mine. It's just getting back what they owe me. No crap, no snotty clerks talking back to you, no guards escorting you out of buildings like some criminal. And that's why I need the gun."

Teresa frowned and sat down. "Ye-e-e-ah," she began and her eyes squinted as she went over it in her brain. "So let me get this straight: they send this nut in Minnesota to some country club, and pay all his expenses. But you ain't some guy. And this ain't some hick state. This is New York."

"No, but it's going to be even easier for me."

"How?"

"I'm a widow, my son was a war hero who died for his country. I've never been in trouble with the law in my life." Dottie counted them off on her fingers.

She watched Teresa purse her lips and nod up and down at her, and she then began to shake her head back and forth.

"You're like one of them crazy smart people, right?" she said, smacking the word "smart." "That's the stupidest thing I ever heard."

"No, it's not! It's a good plan. Hell, it is a *great* plan. Do you know where they sent Leona Helmsley? They had a *health spa* there. And that's where I'm going. And if they don't send me there, I'll do an interview on the six-o'clock news that would have the Pope himself writing the mayor." A hard smile went across Dottie's face.

"You and Leona Helmsley, huh?" Teresa shrugged. "Well, I could see some serious problems . . ."

"What?" Dottie demanded.

"For one thing, you ain't no bank robber. If I was a guard in New York City, seen some old woman with a gun, I'd just shoot you. And you ain't no Leona Helmsley neither. Sure, they send her to some fancy place, 'cause for her that's a big step down."

"It would be a big step down for me too," Dottie defended herself.

"Not the way you talkin' about it. You talkin' like you gonna win the lottery."

"Yeah, well, you're right, what might be a big step down for Leona Helmsley is a big step up for Dottie O'Malley Weist . . . All right, there is one tiny drawback." Dottie began to sneer. "They would put on my record that I'm a convicted felon. Oh, the stigma! I'm fifty-eight. It's not like I'm going to be in line for some fancy job where they would check my background. And on the up side, if I was a convicted felon, I wouldn't have to pull jury duty anymore."

"You show up for jury duty?"

"Doesn't everyone?"

Teresa rolled her eyes. "So this is your big plan," she said quietly.

"Yes. Now I need a gun. Teresa, do you have any of Fred's old numbers on you? I'll do all the calling."

"Yeah, damn right you do the calling. I don't deal with them people."

"Fine. You'll never need to know about any of this."

"I already know too much." Teresa shook her head.

Teresa didn't move. Dottie leaned forward and looked at her pleadingly.

"You gonna get yourself killed and then it'll be my fault," Teresa said.

"No. I swear."

Teresa looked at her again, and shook her head.

"You need a man," Teresa suggested.

"I don't need a man, I need a gun that can shoot," Dottie said tensely.

"They could both shoot," Teresa offered. "Maybe the sound's a bit different when they're goin' off," Teresa said and threw her head back into a bellowing gale of hoarse cigarette laughter.

Dottie's eyes narrowed and she stared almost in hatred at this coarse woman.

"Don't make fun of me," she said and felt her nose begin to itch, and her eyes begin to shed a small flood.

"Aw, come on, Dottie. Look, you come in here telling me that you, Miss Honest Citizen, is gonna rob a bank to get sent to the same jail as Leona Helmsley."

"Give me the number," Dottie demanded, deadly serious.

Teresa stared at her, offended at being ordered, and they were silent.

"I'll pay you fifty bucks," Dottie said.

"Seventy," Teresa shot back.

Dottie frowned. "Sixty-five."

"Seventy."

"I only have fifty on me."

"You give me the rest later."

"Done."

Teresa stood up and left the kitchen. Behind her Dottie could hear her rifling through a drawer. At last Teresa reappeared with two pieces of paper. She placed them down on the table.

"I got two numbers. I don't even know if they're still working. If they ain't, you don't owe me nothin'. If they are and you use my name or tell anybody where you got them, I swear, I'll go down to the Village and shoot you myself."

Dottie nodded and looked at her. She smiled shakily, and pulled five ten-dollar bills out of her purse, placing the money carefully on the kitchen table. In one sweep Teresa snatched the bills up and they disappeared in her apron pocket.

"I'll let you know what happens," Dottie said, standing up, and wiped her eyes, avoiding Teresa's stare.

"Yeah, when do I get the rest?"

"When I get the gun," Dottie shot back at her, pleased that she'd thought of it.

Teresa shrugged. "Fair enough. Just don't get yourself killed before I see that twenty," Teresa said sternly, and walked her over to the door of the apartment.

Dottie shook her hand and walked off down the stairs. Teresa leaned over the railing and waved after her.

"Good luck. Have fun," she yelled, smirking. "See ya on the six-o'clock news!" She shook her head.

Jeez, Teresa thought, what a nut.

She gave a sigh, and straightened up. Well, at least it had been the liveliest afternoon she'd spent in a while. She walked back into the apartment and looked up at the clock. Almost five. Her daughter and that *jedrool* she married would be here soon with the groceries, she thought.

They'd just better have "remembered" the carton of cigarettes this time, otherwise she'd be stuck having to walk down all those flights. As if at her age she should seriously give them up for health reasons! What, were they crazy? She'd already lived longer than she thought she would. And she'd have to walk down all those flights tomorrow again for that stupid doctor's appointment.

DOTTIE sipped on a cup of broth and looked at the number. She suddenly felt jittery. Jittery about the whole thing.

Now it could happen. Now it was real. Because she knew that all she had to do was dial a number and most likely she would be within reach of owning one illegitimate gun with bullets.

But, as Teresa had said, she was no bank robber. Was she really going to get a gun and rob a bank at the tender age of fifty-eight? Maybe she was deluding herself. Maybe she should just wait and see. Maybe things would get better, maybe she should just swallow what pride she had left and go back down to Medicaid and . . .

Her stomach gurgled and she looked at the empty cup of broth she had called dinner.

Right!

Go back down to Medicaid? Spend another day sneaking in and out of this building for fear of running into the super—or, heaven forbid, the landlord—because she owed so much back rent? She'd lost her last job, an off-the-books job in a small coffee shop on Fourteenth Street, when she was in the hospital. And no one now seemed willing to hire her at her age, off-the-books or on, even though she could do most office work. Social Security flatly refused to begin her survivor's benefits early, disability didn't even cover the rent, so it would be another two years before she . . . How was she expected to survive?

Right!

This time she was not going to sit around waiting for things to get better, waiting for some miracle, the way she had with Nathan. Oh, Nathan will be better, give him a month, oh, Nathan will stop gambling, give him a year; oh, Nathan will, Nathan will—but Nathan never did. She'd even scratched Nathan's name off the mailbox, that was how angry she'd been when he first died. She'd bent and bent and bent until she thought she was going to break, and what for? What the hell had it been for?

She was alone and desperate, and scared. And now she was out of time.

Hesitating to call about a gun? Was she crazy? She walked over and picked up the phone. She dialed the first number and patiently waited for the other end to pick up.

All she had to do was make sure she'd meet whoever this thug was in broad daylight, somewhere where there were lots of people and she'd feel safe.

A recording came on announcing that the number had been disconnected.

She placed the receiver back on the cradle and looked at the second number.

She inhaled deeply. All right, just do it.

She grabbed the phone quickly, dialed, and felt her breath get shaky.

The line picked up, and a voice, oddly familiar from memory, came across the line.

"Arthur MacGregor, Pawn and Repair. May I help you?"

She dropped the phone.

Oh my God, it was *Arthur.*

HE LISTENED for a moment after the click, trying to see if he heard any noises. At last Arthur MacGregor slammed down the receiver and glared at it.

Goddammit!

He watched his son turn around on his chair and frown at him. He was suspicious of anyone who called the shop.

"Pop?"

He just waved his hand at him, and watched Moe turn back to the repair bench.

Tapping his phone again, after all this time? Who did they think they were? He could call his lawyer about this. He'd been a legitimate businessman for seven years now.

Seven years . . . Arthur contemplated this. He had been pristine—a veritable saint. Seven years of steady, honest work, arriving with his son and opening the shop by nine in the morning, Mondays through Fridays. One hour for lunch at Gianni's, back by one, closed down by six. Hell, he didn't even jaywalk.

Seven years.

The seven longest, most boring years of his life, he thought contemptuously. But he'd done it! Nobody was going to send him back to prison. And now they were going to tap his phone again, after all this time? The United States government never ceased to amaze him.

He exhaled loudly and chomped down on the unlit cigar in his mouth, chewing the end so voraciously he could feel the fibers begin to dissolve. He rose from his desk and walked into the bathroom and spit a tarred mouthful of cigar juice into the sink and ran water in it. He walked back into what his son called "his office."

It was a windowless room that had originally been a second storage area behind a big backroom that now served as the repair area of the shop. The space was roughly a ten-by-six room—eerily, almost the same dimensions as the cell in which he'd spent nearly fifteen years at Auburn.

Even worse, his cell at Auburn had been downright homey in comparison. At least there he'd had a window and sunlight.

The walls of his office, which had been white once, had aged to an ugly brownish gray. The plaster was cracked here and there. It was dark, always damp, and smelled of mildew, although a string of plumbers of every nationality had been unable to explain exactly why it was so damp. Arthur had called the plumbers in when he had finally faced the fact that he had to be there every day.

It was a stipulation of parole. He had to show evidence that he was gainfully employed. At first each week he'd had to trek down to the parole office and sit in the waiting room with all the young gorillas. Men like the kind he'd spent fifteen years with.

They were hard, ignorant men, the kind who would do two years on the inside, learn absolutely nothing, not even how to be better criminals, and then get released. About eighteen months would go by and there they'd be, in the cafeteria again one afternoon. And they'd smile and wave at him as if he were their father and they'd just come home from summer camp. Arthur would watch them pick up their trays and move over to him. They'd plop down next to him and they'd say, "Hey, Pop, how's it been? Whatcha been doin'? You fill me in on what's been goin' on."

He could look at a man now and tell if his entire life was going to be spent shuffling between two places on the planet—jail and a parole office.

Arthur didn't mind the trips to the office. He had a twenty-nine-year-old parole officer who seemed to feel honored at having been assigned Arthur MacGregor. They'd sit in his office, and the kid would stamp his little booklet, hardly even bothering to look at his check stubs. He just wanted to talk about robbing banks.

It seemed they'd had a whole course in Arthur MacGregor at John Jay at one point.

So, he'd tried to fix up his little corner of hell, since he was honor-bound to do five years in it. Arthur had his desk and a large leather swivel, which was actually comfortable and gave him the only pleasure in the place. A green glass banker's light sat on the desk. Across from the desk was a small cheap bookcase, crammed with books. Books were also piled up on the floors. He was a insatiable reader, a habit he'd picked up his first time in jail and had carried with him. Two dark wooden chairs sat facing his desk for the odd customer, usually there to buy something under the table or sell it.

Behind his desk was a picture of Arthur taken in front of the store. It pictured him, Moe's mother, to whom he was married for a year, and Moe, about five years old. If you didn't know of the years Arthur had spent as a bank robber, you'd swear, from the photo, that he'd been a solid citizen all his life.

He rubbed his hand across the back of his neck and took several long, deep breaths. He had overreacted to a hang-up, and now he felt stupid, having ruined the end of his cigar over it. It seemed he was quick-tempered all the time now. He usually chalked it up to something that happens with age, but that as a ploy had not only begun to wear thin, he'd begun to take it as an insult as well.

He was sixty-one, not a hundred and one.

He sat down heavily in his chair and stared out to the main repair room at the back of the shop. He could see his son bent over the repair table, soldering a microchip on a board. He could see small puffs of smoke rise from over his shoulder and he could smell the acrid metallic burning of each solder.

Arthur looked at the phone again.

On the other hand, it could just have been someone nervous on the other end. Because, the truth was, he did do the occasional fence on the side.

But Arthur barely counted that.

That was nothing. Compared to what he'd been capable of . . . it was just to keep the boredom from killing him.

"Okay, Pop, it's ten of six," his son yelled in to him, and Arthur ground his back teeth together and could feel the muscles in his jaw tighten.

He was going to get the usual lecture. Moe was going to be a pain in the ass all the way up to Rye. As if the hang-up meant something.

A bank robber. The way Moe said it just hit Arthur in his gut. As if he were some kind of low-class criminal.

He was not *just* a bank robber.

He was Vincent van Gogh.

He was an artist. In all the years, and after the hundreds of banks he'd hit, no one had gotten shot, no one died, no one got maimed, no one suffered—except, of course, the Feds and the insurance companies. And as far as Arthur was concerned, having grown up on the wrong side of the American financial system, until they made sure that at least every small child was taken care of and had a decent meal each day, the greedy bastards deserved it.

"Just" a bank robber.

Maybe if he'd had more education he'd have been a great painter or writer or musician instead of a bank robber. But he'd only made it through the ninth grade. Not that he was stupid, or ill-read.

Ah, well. He didn't regret for one second any of his life, well, *almost* any of his life . . . You had to be a little crazy on the edge to be an artist.

28

For most people, safety was the number-one issue.

For Arthur, excitement was the number-one issue. From the minute he began planning a job till the minute he divvied up the take, he was in a constant state of excitement. Nothing, short of sex maybe, could come near to it.

Safety was like a death sentence.

His career in crime had begun quite honestly with a job he'd gotten in a repair shop.

The shop was owned by a man named Hymie Schwartz. He was a big, obese man whose clothes were always stained and greasy. He stank of cigar smoke and whitefish salad.

Hymie had hired him as an errand boy at first, and then, as the shop got busy, he'd been asked to help with the repairs. It started out slowly, "Put the back on the watch," or "Open up the bottom of the toaster." But as Hymie realized Arthur was good with his hands and a quick study, he was given more and more to do. And Hymie began to teach him everything he knew.

And that was considerable.

Hymie Schwartz repaired everything from jewelry clasps and radios and watches to lamps. All of the ordinary household appliances. And then some.

Like burglar alarms. And safe locks. He had a booming business as a locksmith.

Soon, another boy was hired to do the errands and Arthur spent his days learning all he could.

He put his whole heart into his work.

He began spending time at the library, reading up on the newest security devices. Soon Hymie was sending him out on simple locksmithing jobs, and allowing him to assist in the delicate matters of safe opening and burglar-alarm repair.

Arthur loved it. And, needless to say, the temptation to try out his new skills became too much.

He could still pick a lock faster than some people could use their keys.

He was the number-one wanted man on the FBI list for five years running. His credentials were impeccable.

All this snotty-nosed kid of his could see was some lowlife who'd spent his entire childhood either on the lam or in jail.

Maybe he had a point.

On the other hand, Arthur's father had always been around, and that had been no picnic. His father had been an abusive, lying drunk who smacked him around at least twice a week, whether he deserved it or not.

He stared back down at the desk again and began to think about this constant stream of tension he felt these days. In all his years he'd never felt this kind of degrading tension. He took pleasure in absolutely nothing. For the first five years he'd been there, the end of the day had given him a feeling of freedom. A kind of thank-God-this-is-over feeling, and there would be a spring in his step as he'd leave the dusty little shop. And Moe and he would drive back up to Rye, in Westchester. Moe would drop him off at his house and he'd bounce up the front steps, open the door, holler his hellos to Eva, his housekeeper.

He'd trot up the stairs, maybe lift some weights, or run on the treadmill, just to loosen up the muscles that were stiff from sitting behind a desk all day. Arthur was a large man, six feet two, with a barrel chest, sturdy, long legs, and a shoulder span a weight lifter would've been proud of. His body had always required physical activity.

Jeez, he couldn't imagine how people spent their lives behind a desk like that. He'd have just shot himself in the head if he'd spent his life cooped up in some office. He needed to be out in fresh air.

All right, so he might have been running around with a gun in his hand half the time, but at least he got to see the sunlight. And his hours were set to *his* needs, not to some lousy manager's timetable.

So Arthur would stretch out his stiff muscles and then he'd shower, shave, and most evenings hit Jack's Bar for a drink.

Jack's Bar had been a landmark in Rye. It had opened in 1951, and they blessedly hadn't changed the decor. It reminded him of the bars of his youth. And it was filled with some of the more lively if not shady characters of the town. And once in a while a woman would be at the bar and he'd buy her drinks, maybe have a few laughs for a couple of weeks or the night.

But Jack's had closed two years ago, and was now a video store. None of the other bars he went to seemed right. They either had blasting garbage the kids called music, so his head throbbed after ten minutes, or they were that kind of air-fern bar where people ordered nothing but Perrier with lime or white wine spritzers. He'd lost interest in finding a new place to go to.

Arthur stared catatonically at the scratched dark wood desktop in his office and gave a sad exhale. Because tonight he was going to do exactly what he had done the night before, and the night before that, and the night before that. Moe was going to drive him back to his big empty house in Rye and he was going give a tired yell to Eva, then tromp into the living room. And he'd make himself a bourbon, turn on the idiot box, and he'd lose himself in the same shows. Eva would silently place a tray of dinner in front of him and look concerned the way she did when she took the time to notice and was not rushing out the door to pick up one of her kids or something. And when he'd hear her bustle through the hallway and the door slam closed after her, he'd give a little sigh at how it would be to have someplace to rush off to, or people who needed you.

He was rarely invited to his son's house. Only tolerated for holidays or special occasions. Moe's wife, Doreen, had never cared for him and, unbelievably, had told him once that she didn't think he could be trusted around his own grandchildren. As if he were some kind of pervert or something!

And he'd shot off his mouth, informing her that yes, she was right to be frightened, as he couldn't stand the little dears anyway, which was an utter lie, but he felt he had to say something to the bitch.

So he'd sit alone in his living room and sooner or later he'd turn off the lights and sit in the dark, watching old movies or boxing if he could find it. And he'd drift off, and half the time he'd wake to the sound of Eva arriving in the morning for her day of work.

There was the sound of a throat clearing, and Arthur looked up from the desk.

"You ready to go, Pop?"

"Well, what are *you* waiting for?" he snapped gruffly.

He watched Moe turn and pull on a windbreaker at the same time. Moe had good shoulders and well-formed legs. But his son was soft around the middle from what he called "the good life." Arthur had been hard as a rock when he was Moe's age. He remembered where he was when he was Moe's age.

He'd just done the first year at Auburn. And the more he thought of it, the funnier it seemed, that he was looking on a prison term as "the good old days."

He was going crazy.

He flicked off the light on his desk.

DOTTIE hung up the phone before she had to talk to him, or hear his voice say her name.

It was cowardly, she knew.

She flicked off the television set for the first time in years and allowed the quiet of the apartment to try and soothe her as she paced back and forth. Out of the corner of her eye she could see the edge of the big armoire.

She couldn't stand it anymore.

There was no reason for her *not* to look at it.

She stomped into the dusty bedroom and pulled a chair over to the dark wooden thing. Tottering slightly, she grabbed on to the handle of the armoire to steady herself. That would add consummate insult to injury, if she fell getting the bloody thing, she thought to herself.

On top of the old armoire, covered by a greasy film of dust, she took down a ragged manila envelope. She brought it out to the kitchen, placed it on the table and stared at it.

In one sudden movement she swept the envelope up, opened it, and shook out the contents. Yellowed newspaper clippings fluttered down onto the tabletop. Torn magazine pages, folded into squares, and several letter-sized envelopes dropped down after them, sounding small whacks against the tabletop as they hit.

She sat still, as his face, oh God, the way she remembered him, met her eyes, in mug shots—she winced—reprinted grainily in the newspapers. Terrible photos they were of him, too. She carefully unfolded several magazine pages and laid them out in order on the table.

There was a picture of Rivington Street, the way it had been with the laundry and filth. Dottie saw the building he used to live in and found her eyes glued to a window almost dead center on the third floor. She stared and stared at it, as if, by staring at it long enough, she could see inside. Then there were other pictures of Arthur at various times during his life.

A picture of his father appeared on the third page of the magazine layout. Her eyes looked again at the black-and-white photo of Arthur MacGregor, Sr. The fierce look on his face still made Dottie shiver. His father had scared her. He had been a lunatic.

She let her eyes gaze back at Arthur, Jr.'s, face, *her* Arthur.

She read some of the copy, snickering here and there. It made him out to be some kind of genius, as if robbing banks took any real brains.

Her eyes glazed over for a moment, and she remembered that when she'd made her plan, the thought had crossed her mind that Arthur MacGregor, ironically, would have been the one person to ask about this . . .

She began smoothing out the newspaper clippings. There were many from his last big trial. She looked at the pictures of him sitting next to his lawyer in court and frowning.

She knew that look.

Her eyes scanned some of the copy. She suddenly felt stupid about having kept this record of him all these years.

Her eyes hovered over one of the envelopes. She stared for a long time at the brownish ink, and the almost shaky letters that formed her name. Her eyes looked up to the corner, at the horrible return address: Ossining Federal Correctional Facility, Ossining, New York.

Slowly she opened it up, slipped the pages out of the envelope, and began reading.

"Dottie," it began in his squiggly handwriting. She remembered at the time being furious when she read the letter, thinking that he was swaggering and boasting about being in jail, but now, as she reread it, she was struck by the language and hints of terror and the tenderness of how young he'd been. It suddenly dawned on her that she'd been wrong. This letter had been written by a very young man who was very frightened and trying desperately not to let on.

At the end was a long passage about getting out and being with her again at "home."

Home. Her eyes blurred and the tiny room came into her head.

It was a dirty little room in an SRO just where Little Italy turned into Chinatown. There was an old Murphy bed that wheezed when it was pulled out, and made a clanging, squealing racket when you lay on it. A cheap rug, so filthy you could barely make out the large tea-rose pattern, was spread out over most of the floor. The rest was an odd floral linoleum, cracked in places where wooden floorboards shone through.

A half-pint refrigerator that never worked sat in a closet. On top of that was an old Waterman stove and oven which had no controls on it and smelled of leaking gas. You just lit the stove with a match and prayed there'd be no explosion.

The oven had two settings, burned and raw.

Mostly she remembered a window with a yellowed pull-down fabric shade that overlooked a rectangle of backyards. The rectangle was divided up into boxes by gray wooden fences, some half-falling down. Streamers of laundry hung across the entirety of it, and from the window, especially during the summer, you could hear the noises from all the buildings. Opera played, women shouted gossip across the buildings, children played and hollered in the dirt below—occasionally there was the sound of a saxophonist practicing.

In winter, when the window was shut, all was quiet except for the hiss from a radiator that sat beneath the sill. She used to lie across the Murphy bed and stare out that window, for when the bed was opened, there was really no room to walk, and so she liked to imagine that it was a large, luxurious window seat, or a boat. And when she imagined it was a boat, she would roll up a newspaper to use as her telescope, and she would roll back and forth, just enough to hear the springs creak beneath her, and she'd imagine the boat was rocking.

Had she really been that young? So young that she was still playing childhood make-believe games as she was lying naked, waiting for him?

She closed her eyes at the memory of the warm feeling of fullness in her hips as she rode the bus home to her parents' apartment on the afternoons she had made love to Arthur.

Arthur.

They had been happy. . . . Until Dottie spent an afternoon at her younger cousin's wedding. She had listened to the toasts and talk of babies, and a honeymoon, and suddenly it seemed of the utmost importance, to stand up in front of a church full of people and let everyone know that this was the person for you. It made it important. It made it honest, so you didn't have to sneak off after work and walk past all the winos and the derelicts, and slink up the stairs of some sleazy SRO, avoiding the manager's lecherous grins and winks. They deserved better than that, for what they had. It was the first time she let it matter to her, not having a wedding ring on her finger.

And when she was back in Arthur's room, she'd ripped the fancy wedding clothes off, crawled into bed, and wept. She had ached to bring Arthur around to have dinner with her family—her parents, her brothers, their wives and children—but she knew what would happen. The first thing they'd ask is what Arthur did for a living. What could he say? I'm locksmith's assistant? At his age? That was another thing she'd brushed under the rug. How come someone as smart as Arthur was nothing more than a shop assistant?

She knew her brothers and father would glance back and forth at one another and shake their heads. That would be just the beginning; it would get worse. Then would come the questions about his education.

She could just see the look on her mother's face when he told them he'd dropped out of school in the ninth grade. And even though Dottie thought that what Arthur had accomplished was admirable, her family wouldn't see it that way. All they'd see was someone with a very limited education, very limited ambitions, whose father was a child-beating drunk. One of the men her father said gave all Irishmen and Scots a bad name.

Almost every characteristic she'd ever been warned against was, on the surface, at least, embodied by Arthur MacGregor.

And they'd all be as polite as they could, and shake his hand at the door. And once the door was shut, they would fall on her. Her brothers would obnoxiously ridicule him. Her mother would tell her that whatever she did in life, she had to marry someone who could take care of her, who had a good education, who had a clear goal in life; not some uneducated locksmith's assistant from the Lower East Side who appeared to have no idea what to do for a living.

Her father would flat-out refuse to let her see him again.

And that was how Arthur found her, huddled under the covers, crying and crying into the pillow.

That was when they had their discussion about marriage and ambition . . . and Arthur had been hurt and offended and stormed out of the room. When he hadn't come back by seven o'clock, she'd gotten dressed and left.

Days went by and she didn't see him or hear from him. Then it was a week, and then a week and a half. She went over it and over it in her head, arguing with herself until dawn each day what she could say to him or do, or if she should take it all back. But she couldn't . . .

Two weeks later, Arthur finally reappeared. He was sitting on the stoop of her building. It was late afternoon. In a tense tone he announced that he had talked his boss, Hymie Schwartz, into letting him and his two new partners sell some new security systems. And that, if he worked hard—and that meant weekends and evenings—and if she didn't give him grief about the hours, he might be able to have enough money for a place for them and a nice church wedding within the year.

She threw her arms around him in front of everyone for the first time, because it was going to be all right. They were going to have a life together. And everything went fine . . . until the day Arthur and his "partners" were arrested for a string of jewelry-store robberies on Canal Street. And Arthur was led out of Hymie's shop in handcuffs in front of the whole neighborhood.

She remembered getting sick behind the courthouse when she went to bail him out. And she remembered being ashamed and horrified at having to sit in a courtroom each day watching him and the lawyer, who had just about told them from the word "go" that Arthur was going to do time.

But what hurt the most was that he'd so successfully hidden all this from her. The lie had been perfect. She'd never suspected a thing. And that was what cut through her soul. How could he lie to her? She didn't lie to him. God! She'd bared her whole soul to him. Hell, she'd bared her whole body and her soul and . . . and how dare he do this to them!

And that was why she got sick behind the courthouse.

BANG. Right between the eyes. It was like being shot.

By the time the judge handed down the sentence, she knew she couldn't trust him again, or wait for him or live this kind of life.

So, Arthur MacGregor did 24 months and Dottie

O'Malley married the first person who looked at her—Nathan.

She met him the first night she'd started as a dancer at the club. He was off stage right, arguing with the man who'd hired her, demanding to know where the girl he'd sent in had gone to. And Dottie came on and started a series of kicks, and out of the corner of her eye this skinny little man of about forty, who looked a little like Frank Sinatra, stopped arguing in mid-sentence. His eyes just about popped outside of their sockets and his jaw dropped.

Her family approved. He was older, he was mature, he was part owner of the nightclub. Sure, he gambled now and then, but . . . Dottie'd had enough trouble, and no, Nathan was never going to be the great love of her life. That had been Arthur. But she thought Nathan was steady, and honest and consistent, so she resigned herself to the trade-off of passion with peace. She wrote Arthur a good-bye note and set up her life as a housewife.

And it was fine until the day Arthur showed up again.

She hated who he was and what he did and the fact that, regardless of what he claimed, she did not believe that he was going to turn into a solid, voting, tax-paying citizen for her or anyone else. But what she hated most of all was the fact that he slid in one afternoon and took her to bed so easily, as if the marriage didn't exist or the baby, or the time he'd spent in prison. And she hated herself because for some reason, Arthur MacGregor could have her anytime, anyplace, and anywhere.

But she'd been strong and ended it.

It had been a warm night out, so warm she was wearing a sleeveless dress, that last time, and she was being pressed against a parked car, in a dark, tiny street on the Lower East Side.

Not really a street, but an alley.

There was that deep, whispery voice in her ear, making her shiver up and down, his breath and the slight brush of his lips, and his roaming hands, gently caressing the outsides of her arms, her waist and hips, reaching under her skirt and up her thighs. He'd always been very free with her body. She'd gone weak in the knees. So weak she couldn't do anything about it.

He'd made sure he kept his eyes on hers, so when she'd try to look away from him, he'd move his face again, so she'd have to look at him. That face . . . those deep eyes, with lids that drooped slightly at the outer edges, those heavy eyebrows . . . His nose sloped down razor-sharp and then gently formed two pillows of flesh at the nostrils. His jaw was square, leading into a strong chin which, at the center, was formed into two small mounds of flesh echoing his nose in perfect symmetry. His cheeks were separated from his mouth by two slashes of skin that turned into dimples under the cheekbones when he smiled.

Pleading with her.

Oh, God. She stopped thinking. After all this time Arthur MacGregor still took her breath away.

But after a month of seeing him behind Nathan's back she had had an attack of the Morals.

And that night she'd found the strength to push him away, and tell him that she was not going to see him anymore.

Or talk to him, or touch him.

"Don't turn me away, Dottie. You don't mean it. You can't do what we do to each other and not mean it. Oh, how I love you. I'm going to take care of you." His voice was whisper-low and he'd pulled her back against him.

They began to talk to one another at the same time, in pleading whispers, for and against running away together.

But she won in the end.

Won, she thought, and it struck her that it was an odd way to look at it. Yeah, she'd *won*.

She now had a son. And she couldn't just up and leave her own child, and she couldn't take him—no matter what Arthur said—and she couldn't go around thinking that seeing Arthur on the sly would be all right.

She grimaced to herself.

That wasn't the reason she hadn't run away with Arthur, and she knew it. And she was too old to lie to herself about it.

The truth was that deep down she knew she'd never be able to trust him. She'd have been a nervous wreck every time he left the apartment, worrying about what he was up to, when he was coming back, or *if* he was coming back, or how many years he'd be in jail this time.

She remembered Arthur laughing at her.

"You're never going to be able to keep it up. Dottie, you're never going to be Donna Reed. Nathan might be safer, but he's just not that smart—"

"Oh, and you're so smart? This, coming from a man who just did twenty-four months in jail?" she'd snapped.

"What does that have to do with anything? Either you're smart or you're not, but I'm the one you should be with and you know it. I swear, I have something honest I can do—"

"Like what?" she cut him off.

He was silent, and, teasing, gave her a ponderous look.

"Well?" she said, her eyebrows raised.

"Well what? You can't expect me to answer right off the bat, can you, woman?" he said in that half-Scottish, half–New York accent of his.

"Right off the bat? Right off the bat! You've had twenty-four months to think about it, for Christ's sake!"

His eyes had grown wide and twinkled at her, and his

mouth, when she got angry with him, turned up into an amused grin, like a small child watching some wonderful and mysterious thing.

"—Maybe I could go into forgery." His eyes danced.

"There, you see!" she bellowed and actually reached up and hit him on the shoulder.

"Come on, Dottie, you have to give me a chance . . ."

She'd looked away from him, stepped back, and crossed her arms in front of her so he couldn't touch her.

"I can't do this anymore. I am married—"

"To Nathan Weist?" He chuckled incredulously.

"Yes."

"It'll never last—"

"Oh, yes, it will, he's a good man—"

"He's twenty years older—"

"No."

"How much older is he then?"

". . . Eighteen," she lied.

"Oh, well, I can see where those two years would make a whole hell of a lot of difference—"

"It doesn't matter what age he is, Arthur, he's steady—"

"He's a gambler, for Christ's sake, Dottie."

She could tell by the grin on his face that he wasn't taking this seriously, and that made her blood boil.

"He's a nightclub owner—"

"He won it in a poker game."

"So? He works at it. He's there every night—"

"And how many hours is he in that backroom with Ben Zimmerman?"

That had given her pause.

"How do you know all this?"

"Ben's brother's doing five in Sing Sing. Come on, Dottie, I don't believe you're any more in love with this man than—"

"I have a child with this man."

His face had hardened in a flash at the mention of the child. And he'd looked harsh and impatient and angry.

"I don't believe this man can do to you what I do," he said low, in a whisper.

She looked away, knowing exactly what he meant. "He does."

They were both silent, and she glanced at him.

"You're a liar, Dorothy O'Malley." His voice was hard.

She remembered spreading a sneer across her face, and inside going cold.

"You better think about what you're saying," he said, "because some people never have what we have, and you don't throw it away because someone made *one* mistake."

He turned his back on her, took a step away, and for one moment she knew he was absolutely sure of himself.

"I'll be at the Ambassador Hotel at three tomorrow," he said matter-of-factly.

He took another step away from her, and stood. She could tell he was just waiting for her to reach out to him and say it was all right, that she'd be there with her son and her suitcases.

"I won't be there, Arthur," she said as strong as she could and she watched him stop. He never did turn around.

"Well, I will. And . . ." His voice had begun strong and then faltered, and she knew he was suffering and taking short breaths that were making his wide shoulders go up and down, almost as if he were shaking. "If you need more time, you can . . . you can just be sure"—his voice was harsh, and then it broke—"I'll wait."

She watched him walk down to the corner and disappear.

The following afternoon she went to see a two forty-five showing of the movie *Can-Can* and wept through the entire show. A man across the aisle kept glancing at her, then up to the screen puzzled, as if asking, "Are we watching the same film?"

43

She wept through several weeks, stunned to realize that Nathan didn't seem to notice. No. That wasn't true. He'd noticed. After a week or two he even said something.

"You upset about something?"

"Just . . . I don't know," she'd muttered as she scrambled eggs over the stove.

And that was it.

Although, now that she thought about it, she realized that Nathan began to stay out of the house more and more, until he barely seemed to come in at all.

She spent three months in this half-crying, half-furious state, and finally decided that she couldn't live like this anymore.

Okay, he'd lied to her once, but she would, against her better judgment, give Arthur MacGregor another chance. Because it was human nature to err, and no one should be thrown away because of one mistake, and because she couldn't bear the thought that she'd never have him again. He had insisted that he was going to find something honest to do, and even though she read every report of every robbery in the newspapers, she'd find some way of trusting him. The fact that his name hadn't come up in any of the news media she took as a sign that maybe he was back at work as a locksmith.

She would track him down and tell him straight out that yes, he had her, and her son, but that if he ever pulled another stunt like that, she'd kill him. And she was not kidding.

So she hired a baby-sitter for the following afternoon, when she knew Nathan would be out of the house anyway, and decided to start on Rivington Street, at the hotel where he had a room . . .

She lay in bed all that night thinking about it and thinking about it, only pretending to be asleep when Nathan got in

44

around five. She was surprised at how much she ached to have Arthur again.

And at one the next day Nathan was sitting at the table reading the paper and she turned around with a plate of breakfast and dropped it on the floor.

There was Arthur MacGregor's face staring back at her. The headline in the *Daily News* read: HAVE YOU SEEN THIS MAN?

And his ensuing robbery spree confirmed that she had been absolutely right not to go with him. She felt for the flash of a moment that she had made the right decision and she was victorious.

And then it broke her insides.

And she hated it that Arthur'd forced her to face the fact that she didn't love Nathan, and she hated even more that, as it turned out, he had been right about him.

After those first couple of years the gambling did get worse, or maybe she just focused in on it more, but whatever, they were in a constant state of poverty, until at last he lost his share of the club and wound up as a waiter in a steak house on Fourteenth Street. Dottie got a job working as a secretary for a small company in Brooklyn that supplied parts for typewriters. And that was all right; the money was at least steady, and there was enough from his paycheck even after he paid his weekly into the shylock for them to get by.

So she'd kept everything to herself over the years, and often she would think back on it. Toward the end of Nathan's life four years ago, she'd begun to surround herself with memories of those hot afternoons with Arthur, even though she knew she'd never see him again, or maybe he wasn't even still alive.

And now, of all the fences Teresa knew, this was the number Dottie had to be given?

Was God trying to drive her crazy?

She turned off the light and walked back over to the couch.

Well, hell could freeze over before she'd call Arthur Mac-Gregor for anything.

CHAPTER TWO

AHEM.'' Dottie cleared her throat.

The kid sitting next to her on the park bench still didn't take any notice. She looked over at the small dots of black foam covering his ears. The music on his Walkman was turned up so loud it sounded like bees buzzing through the earphones.

She suddenly nudged him. "Ahem," she said louder.

His eyes popped opened and he looked at her, startled.

"I'm looking for something," she said coolly, looking the other way, at several old men sitting near her on the bench. Out of the corner of her eye she watched the kid take off the headset and stare, frowning, at her.

"What?" he asked, and moved his neck back so his chin became double.

"I'm looking for . . . a piece," she said as roughly as she could, and watched his expression turn to confusion.

"Of what?" He looked scared.

"You know," she said uneasily.

She watched his eyes dart around, and look back at her.

"You looking for *sex?*" he shouted at her.

The old men sitting next to her stopped talking. Dottie went pale and for a split second it seemed as though everyone within earshot had frozen and was gaping at her.

"*What?* What!" Dottie barked at him.

"Look, lady, what is it that you want from me?" the kid asked, staring at her.

"A gun," she said through clenched teeth.

"A gun," he said almost in relief. Then his lip turned up in an insulted sneer and exposed a set of stunningly straight and stunningly white teeth. His eyes stared at her, angrily.

"I am a *law student*!" he barked. "Je-e-e-sus!"

She watched him jump off the bench shaking his head, and he began walking away quickly.

Dottie stiffly rose, trying to hold back tears. She stared straight ahead, trying not to look at anyone directly, and gritted her teeth. She began rigidly walking out of the park. She stared ahead of her, down the main walk in Washington Square, at a group of black men huddled around.

They were probably medical students.

She began to move faster and faster. She just wanted to run away. God, yelling out loud that she was searching the park for sex, that was just so humiliating. Not to mention it was the second time in twenty-four hours someone had insulted her like that, first Teresa and now that rude kid.

Did she look desperate? Did she look that lonely? God, she could bear anything but that, to be some woman people felt sorry for. And even if she did look that way, where the hell was human decency? Where the hell was the human compassion not to make some demeaning crack about it— as if being alone were a crime! And even if she was lonely, what the hell was she supposed to do about it? As if she was going to find someone to date? It was just cruel.

She needed a gun.

She looked back to the park. Maybe she should try an-other park? She felt herself begin to waffle about doing this again. A shot of anger went through her. No, she was going to go through with this, and Arthur, like it or not, was the fastest way to get this done with. So what was she going to do? Was she going to call him and actually speak to him this time? Would he sell her a gun? No questions asked? Like his regular clients?

That would give him a laugh, she thought bitterly. She could see him . . . and then another thought occurred to her. She stopped walking and stood still in the middle of the sidewalk.

What if Arthur looked terrible?

Like the man who had the physical-therapy session right before hers when she was in St. Vincent's. The man had had a complexion the color of old newspapers, and liver spots dotted his face and hands. The skin on his hands was so tissue-paper thin that Dottie could see his veins pulse. He had no hair or teeth, his eyes were all watery. They would lower the man into a wheelchair as she arrived and then they would cover him with blankets or, sometimes, more disturbingly, tether him to the chair—as a safety precaution, they told her. She would watch them wheel him off.

What if Arthur looked like that?

She shuddered.

That memory her being pressed against the car by him in the dark street, and how young and handsome he had been . . . did she really want to see how old he'd gotten?

Maybe she could find someone to pick the gun up for her?

Could she trust Teresa with something like this?

It would maybe cost her another fifty.

She winced.

Maybe if she had Arthur wrap it up like a steak or something, maybe Teresa would . . .

And what if Teresa got caught?

If she wasn't popular with Teresa now . . . she could see her with that mouth of hers being carted off to jail screaming and cursing the name Dorothy O'Malley Weist. No, if she wanted a gun, she was going to have to go pick it up herself.

That meant facing him.

Did she want him to see what *she* looked like these days? She stopped in front of a clothing boutique and stared at the odd garments in the window.

Clothes.

She couldn't show up in her old clothes. She'd lost so much weight in the hospital and kept it off with the silly exercises they had her doing with weights. They were supposed to build up her bone density or something. Her eyes looked at her reflection. She turned sideways. She stared at her hips and how the dress was belted tightly around her middle. It made her waist seem tiny.

No, she didn't look nineteen, but she had a pretty waist again and hips, and even her legs had gotten back some of their shape, and her skin had tightened up.

As a matter of fact, she looked good. Damned good.

She would need to buy a new outfit. Something light green or red. Red would put color in her face. She'd need new makeup.

And that would make it possible for her to face him.

She did have four hundred dollars left in the bank, and if she was going to jail, what the hell was she saving it for?

She knew she was talking herself into this, and that it was insane to spend her gun money on clothes.

All right, Dottie thought, clearing her head, another point in favor of getting dressed up to see him was that, if she looked good . . . maybe she could get him to lower the price.

That ploy had worked on men for a millennium. Christ, it had worked for Cleopatra, for Helen of Troy, and Queen Isabella had gotten half a country out of it.

Of course, it hadn't worked for everybody.

Marie Antoinette came to mind.

No, that was too mercenary. And she'd never been the kind of woman who either thought that was proper or thought she could actually get away with it, so that idea was out.

But if she spent the money, then she could see herself, in one of those Chanel-type suits that always made her look good, opening the door to the shop—she imagined there would be a bell that would ring. And the moment she saw that certain look on his face, the openmouthed gaze, and watched his eyes and mind wander over her body . . .

Dottie felt a sad pain go through her. Her getting all dressed up wasn't about getting him to lower the price of a gun.

It was about him looking at her and then, once he looked at her, maybe he'd . . . maybe he'd . . .

Stop her.

Every once in a while over the last day that thought had charged through her. For someone to give a damn enough to stop her.

The hell with it. If she was going to jail, she was going with her hair done.

She began walking quickly up Eighth Street. There was something calming about finally making up one's mind. She wasn't going to be stuck sitting on a bench in Washington Square park like a spectator in life.

She was going to have a wonderful day buying clothes and have her hair done and make herself feel as lovely as she could, like a female version of an ancient Greek warrior preparing himself for battle . . . or possibly death.

And it was a battle she was fighting.

And once she'd gotten her clothes and had her hair done, she was going up to the Bronx and take Arthur MacGregor by storm—or get a gun.

★   ★   ★

"YOU CALL me Mother Teresa one more time and I swear I'll smack you." Teresa crossed her arms over her chest and stared at her son-in-law. She watched his eyes dart over to Tracy, and she could tell Tracy was rolling her eyes.

"And I ain't your mother . . . Now, explain to me again why someone your age gets amnesia every time they're supposed to buy a carton of cigarettes."

"It's just that the doctor said—"

"I been smokin' since I was twelve and I ain't gonna give it up now."

"Mother, you spent a whole month in Sloan-Kettering watchin' Pop die, didn't you learn nothing?"

"Yeah, I learned they got benches out front where youse can smoke; now where the hell are my Marlboros?"

Again the redheaded pain in the ass she called her son-in-law stared behind her. They had been standing in the kitchen of Teresa's apartment for twenty minutes now, arguing. Teresa refused to be taken down to her doctor's appointment until she'd cleared up this crap about her cigarettes.

"Tracy," he said pleadingly, and Teresa turned to her daughter.

Tracy had Teresa's black hair, which she kept permed and crimped and teased out into volumes. She was skinny as a rail, even under the heavily decorated sweat suit she was wearing. Her nails were long and painted a bright shade of pink to match her lip color. Her lips were now pursing and twitching back and forth the way her father's had when he got angry. She was twisting a large diamond engagement ring around her finger. Her daughter had changed since she'd moved out to the Island. Now all her clothes were by big-name designers, and every time she talked of things it was always what brand name they were, that she and Brian had a big fancy house at some big fancy address . . . and East Harlem was not good enough anymore.

"Why the hell do you wear sunglasses in the house, huh? You got a problem with your eyes?"

Tracy's smile twisted into a frown and she pulled off the pair of designer glasses and glared at her mother.

"Brian didn't forget your cigarettes, I told him not to put them in the cart, all right? You wanna blame someone for not killing your lungs for twenty-four lousy hours, you blame me."

There was a silence.

"Whatsa matter, Brian don't have no thoughts on his own?"

"Aw, Christ! There she goes again," she heard Brian yell out behind her. "I can't win with your mother!"

Teresa's eyes narrowed.

"The doctor told you months ago to stop smoking. What is it, you wanna get sick and die? It's not enough we just had to watch Pop?"

Well, maybe Tracy had changed, but, Teresa thought, she still fights below the belt.

"You want cigarettes? You walk down those six flights for 'em from now on, 'cause we ain't bringing 'em," Tracy said, staring straight at her.

Teresa grabbed her purse, and glared at them.

"Okay, fine. I'll go out in this neighborhood for my own cigarettes. And when someone stabs me, I'll just tell 'em it's because my daughter couldn't remember to bring me my cigarettes." Teresa turned and walked into the hallway.

"That's another thing, you shouldn't be living in this dangerous neighborhood by yourself," she heard Tracy call after her, and she listened to the clacking sound of Tracy's high heels against the stone hall floor. She was going down the stairs as fast as she could.

The sounds of Brian locking the apartment door echoed above Tracy's heels.

"Now don't start in about that!"

53

"Yeah, I am startin' in about that. Fred's comin' into town next week and we're gonna sit down and discuss you movin'—"

"I ain't movin'."

"It's dangerous and stupid to live here, especially now that Pop's gone. Fred's got a extra room in his house down in Florida. His wife says she'd love to have you, and you could get to see little Fred and little Joe—"

"And neither of youse would be stuck driving in my groceries twice a week," Teresa tossed in nastily. She heard a grunt from Tracy, who was right behind her.

"And we're gonna fix it up for you, nice. Really nice. You're going to *love* it," Tracy said harshly through clenched teeth.

Teresa turned and stopped sharply. Tracy, who was right behind her, knocked into her, startled. She put her hand up to her chest.

"Now listen to me. I ain't moving, I ain't giving up smoking, and I don't care what you or that *jedrool* brother of yours got planned for me. This is my life, not yours, and I'm gonna live it where the hell I want, doing what I want." Teresa gave her daughter one last look, hard, just to make sure it sank in, then turned around and started down the stairs again.

"Now I'm gonna be late for my doctor's appointment," Teresa snapped, knowing full well she was the one who had held them up.

ARTHUR sat staring over the books and the receipts. His eyes shifted over to his watch.

Ten-fifteen.

It was Wednesday, and every Wednesday was like this. It seemed so slow, as if the hands of his watch were weighted down, so for every minute it registered, it seemed he actually had to live through an hour. Or maybe Wednesday signaled that he'd made it halfway through another week of this misery.

In all his years, he never thought he'd end up like this.

Bored to death in some dark, dank little hole he called an office.

He looked at his watch.

Ten-seventeen.

Great.

Time was just whizzing right by.

He went back to the ledger and added in a receipt for solder, and another one for coaxial cables. He tapped the numbers into a small calculator on the desk.

Maybe he'd do something this weekend. Actually leave his house. Maybe he'd take a ride downtown to Manhattan. Maybe find some of his old haunts, just to blow off steam.

Blow off steam. With whom? Everyone he knew was either dead, in Florida, or in jail.

When he'd first gotten out of jail this last time, he'd traveled down to Florida, to Sarasota, thinking he might just buy himself a condo and retire there.

It looked like a wheelchair-testing division. So Arthur figured maybe it was just not the right part of Florida, up north, so he traveled deep into the state almost to the tip, till he got to Miami.

He was shot at on the first day.

It reminded him of what they said Chicago had been like during the twenties.

So Florida was either depressing or dangerous.

And at this point he had a theory that Florida had become a prison without bars. They were keeping it a secret, so you didn't know that an entire peninsula of the United States was actually a penitentiary.

And the crime you were sent there for?

Being old.

And Jesus, the nuts down there. His first day in Miami he'd watched all these people sitting on the beaches in the beautiful sunshine, wrapped up like mummies or lepers.

He'd sat next to this man who was covered in a sheet, a golf cap, and a blanket. And the one piece of the man still sticking out was his nose, which was spread with this white gunk. Under all the blankets, Arthur assessed that the man was probably near ninety.

"Say, pal," he'd asked, "why is everybody covered up down here?"

"Because the sun is bad for you and you might get skin cancer."

And Arthur'd looked at this guy, who was telling him this through his sheets, and two thoughts occurred to Arthur.

Number one, if you're so afraid of the sun, why the hell would you move to *Florida,* "Sunshine Capital of the World," and two, if he was eighty-eight or ninety, he would not be worried about skin cancer, for Christ's sake, he'd be happy just breathing.

Arthur looked at his watch.

Ten-eighteen.

Yup, his life was just whizzing by.

ALL RIGHT, Dottie thought, so he has a braid and green hair. So what? Look at how she'd mistaken the kid in the park. She couldn't go around prejudging people.

No.

She couldn't.

And besides, the sign on the door read "Haircuts $10." That was her price range.

She had temporarily given up on clothing, since none of

the stores seemed open at this hour of the day in Greenwich Village.

She forced her eyes to look back up into the mirror at the young man standing behind the barber's chair. She smiled as broadly as she could at him.

He was picking up strands of hair and frowning and shaking his head. He put both hands, one of them holding a pair of scissors, on his hips. He shook his head so his braid swung out from side to side and the light bounced off the ten small hoop earrings which adorned one ear lobe, and Dottie wondered if there was an actual name for that part of the outer ear.

"I really prefer, um, a conservative cut and color . . ." she said shakily.

"Well, I ain't gonna give you a Mohawk." His voice had a heavy workingman's Queens accent.

"Oh, that's good, I'm more of a page-boy type," Dottie said half-sarcastically. "Can you do something to make it soft, and color it?"

He stepped back, frowned, moving his head from side to side.

"Not for ten bucks . . . fifty."

Dottie stared hard at him in the mirror. Every time she turned around it cost her fifty dollars. She watched his face looking at her hair. He was just so scary-looking.

"You do know what a page boy is?"

He grimaced at her, and put his hands on his hips.

"I am a professional."

Professional what? was what was going through Dottie's mind.

"So?" he said, after a moment.

She closed her eyes, exhaled loudly and said, "Okay, do it." She felt as if she were about to be operated on.

★ ★ ★

ELEVEN-TWELVE.

Too early to have lunch. Arthur sighed, shifted in his chair, stretched one leg and lifted it onto the corner of his desk, swung his other leg up and crossed it over the first one. He took his unlit cigar out of the ashtray and held it between his teeth. He opened the book and leafed through it until he got to the first page.

"Chapter One, I Am Born," he read.

Aw, Jeez, he thought, and placed the book back down onto his lap. His eyes scanned the bookcase and the piles of books on the floor. If only he had something exciting to read.

He supposed he could reread *Lady Chatterley's Lover* for the fourth time this month, but it made him so . . . lonely.

Eleven-thirteen.

TERESA stared over at the nurse, and took the lid off her cup of coffee. She sipped and winced. Coffee-shop coffee was the worst, but it was the only thing between her and falling asleep in the damn waiting room.

She still didn't understand why they made these appointments so early in the morning. Jeez, eleven was the crack of dawn as far as Teresa was concerned. She'd never been an early riser; hell, there were some years she and Fred didn't make it to bed until almost eleven in the morning.

And, it seemed to her, that once they saw you coming, and you were over a certain age, they tried to get you up earlier and earlier. Some *jedrool* actually told her that all old people are up early.

Hah! Fred would've belted him.

She took another sip of the terrible coffee.

This was the second time in two weeks they wanted her in for tests.

She felt a flutter of nervousness go through her, and then dismissed it. Tracy and that jerk of a husband, Brian, had left almost an hour ago, but she was still having a fight with them in her head.

So they were going to move her down to Florida to Fred, Jr., and his wife, a woman she'd met maybe once.

Pains in the ass.

Teresa DeNunzio Newhouse leave East Harlem? Leave New York? The city she'd grown up in? The neighborhood she'd grown up in?

They had to be kidding.

They wouldn't be pulling this crap on her if Fred were still alive. No. Fred would straighten them out, fast.

Fred. She felt her eyes begin to dribble again. What were they in such a rush for? Fred's body was barely cold and already they wanted to ship her off down to some hellhole with sand and water—to do what? They knew she didn't like the beach.

No. Fred would've let them have it.

She felt a tear spill hot down her cheek, and immediately wiped it off.

Maybe it didn't matter anymore. Maybe it didn't matter where she was anymore. She'd had a good long life with Fred. God, she'd loved him. So what did it matter where she lived? It was over.

Teresa took another sip of coffee, and frowned at the wall.

Feeling sorry for herself? Over what? Whenever she started feeling sorry for herself she always thought of one person she knew who was worse off . . .

Dottie Weist.

Teresa at least had good things to look back on, not like crazy Dottie Weist, who had nothing and was now running all over New York like a *stunadze* looking for a gun. Teresa was grateful she wasn't Dottie.

Dottie's marriage had been bad, her health wasn't so good . . . And her boy dying in the army, trying to take over some island somewhere, that had been just tragic.

She remembered Nathan, Jr. He'd looked just like Nathan, same skinny little thing, running all around Joe's. And he'd been smart, not Nathan-smart, Dottie-smart, always reading all them books.

From the time he was seven, Teresa hadn't been able to understand a thing that kid had said, he'd been so smart.

She remembered his funeral, when they finally got his body back from Grenada.

She knew then it was going to end badly for Dottie.

So, she should be grateful. Grateful to have a good marriage to look back on, grateful her kids were alive and well . . .

The hell she was! The little bastards were planning on shipping her down to Florida like some suitcase. Leave New York? Where she'd been with Fred her whole life?

Naw. That wasn't right. And she'd be damned if she'd have a mess of kids she'd diapered, and whose noses she'd wiped, order her around. No. This they could not do.

She felt her heart sink as she thought of the showdown—she didn't care that they were calling it a meeting, it was a showdown—with all her children next Wednesday.

Because the truth was that they paid her rent and they paid for the electric and the gas and the phone, and had ever since Fred had gotten sick last year and all their savings had gone to the hospital before Medicaid would pick any of it up. And the fact was that if they decided to move her down to Florida, then that was it.

She had to think of something, fast. Otherwise she was going to be some permanent guest living in another woman's house and having no control over her own life.

The image of Dottie Weist sitting up in her kitchen the previous afternoon came into her head. She gave a wry chuckle into her coffee cup.

Now that would call off the kids. Holding up a bank, she thought, amused. She could see the look on Tracy's face at having to go and bail her mother out. Hell, smoking cigarettes would look like a deal if it was either that or bank robbery.

Teresa gave a little chuckle and felt the corners of her mouth droop.

Naw, she wasn't that desperate or lonely.

"Mrs. Newhouse?" The nurse behind the desk motioned to Teresa and she got up.

"Yeah?"

"The doctor wants a sonogram of your breast done."

"Whatever," Teresa grumbled.

The woman handed her a piece of paper. "This is the address; it's right across the avenue and two blocks down."

"All right," Teresa said and took the paper. She stared at the woman "Eh, this isn't the thing that hurts, is it?"

"No."

"Thank God for small favors," Teresa grumbled and walked away.

ARTHUR had lingered over lunch an extra forty minutes. Just walking back into the dark hole at the back of the store made his chest hard and tense.

Christ, he'd seen mushroom farms with more light and less dampness than his office, so he'd opted to sit up front for a while. He answered some phone calls; then his mind went back to the hang-up the night before.

He looked at his watch. It was two-thirty.

If it was someone interested in buying under the table, he'd bet he'd call back at around the same time of day. In just about two hours.

And if he didn't get a call then, it was the Feds, tapping his line again, and he was going to be ticked off.

PLANNING to rob a bank was getting expensive.

Dottie'd already laid out over a hundred dollars, and she didn't even have a gun yet.

At least her hair looked good. Yes, the kid had been scary-looking, but he had really worked hard, and her hair was still not baby-soft, but it was softer than it had been, and light red, and cut to her chin with soft bangs.

She walked slowly across Third Street, to the one store where she knew she could buy a cheap dress. She didn't want to go there, but she'd already spent way too much money.

As she got to the door of the shop she wavered. Maybe she could alter one of the size-fourteen dresses into something presentable? Maybe if she bought a nice belt? No, that wasn't going to work, and she knew it. All she felt she could reasonably spend on a dress was sixty dollars, and that was thirty more than she felt she ought to, what with the fifty dollars she'd given to Teresa plus the fifty for the haircut, and she still owed Teresa twenty dollars.

Dottie stood in front of the tiny thrift shop. Reduced to this—buying used clothes. She opened the door and unenthusiastically went to the racks of suits and dresses.

In twenty minutes, Dottie was standing in front of a

full-length mirror at the back of the store, staring hard at herself.

It was shocking.

She was wearing a pink Chanel-type suit that fit as if it had been made for her. It didn't look as though it had been worn before. She turned sideways, staring at her hips and her waist, how the skirt slimmed her stomach and emphasized her long legs. How the color made her face almost glow.

She looked pretty. She *really* looked pretty, she thought, stunned. She just stood still, staring at the reflection of a woman she hadn't seen in at least ten years. A small smile began to draw across her lips as she looked at the suit, and herself all fixed up, the way she had liked to look. She'd always taken pains with her appearance. She'd forgotten what it was like to take care of herself like this. After all the ugliness of the past year, she never thought she'd stand in front of a mirror again and like the person who was staring back at her.

Jesus, did she need this.

"Are you going to take that?" a voice sounded behind her, and without taking her eyes off her reflection Dottie watched herself nod.

TERESA finished dressing and took her bag and walked into the waiting room.

She'd wasted the whole damn day on this nonsense. It was almost five o'clock. This clinic was really soaking Medicaid, she thought. This was the third time in two weeks they'd given her a mammogram, taken X rays, taken blood, and poked and prodded, and now this crap of a sonogram.

At least the sonogram didn't hurt, she was thankful for that. It was humiliating, having her breast treated like a slab of meat, that was true, but at least there were no needles involved. She turned and was walking out to the elevator.

"Mrs. Newhouse, oh, Mrs. Newhouse, wait!" a woman's voice called out, and Teresa turned around.

"I can't have nothin' more poked into me today, *capisce*? I had enough a this crap!" Teresa shot off at the scrawny woman in a white lab coat who had given her the sonogram.

"No, no, Mrs. Newhouse, no more tests today," the woman said gently.

"Well, that's a relief," Teresa barked at her and turned for the elevator.

"Are you planing to go back and talk to your doctor now?"

"Which one? The Arab or the one I don't know where he comes from?"

"Uh, which one sent you here?"

"A nurse at Metropolitan Hospital sent me here; I don't know which one."

"All right." The scrawny woman looked upset. "I'll find out who your physician is and have them give you a call. It's important that you talk to a doctor."

"Yeah? Somebody finally gonna explain what the hell you've been poking around so much for the last two weeks?" Teresa began. "I mean, you wanna soak Medicaid, youse go right ahead, just so long as I can go home"—Teresa looked at her fiercely—"unless you know something I don't?"

"We're not at liberty to divulge results. But when you talk to your doctor . . ." The woman was talking at her and looking jittery.

Teresa suddenly felt a chill go through her and she grabbed the little woman and nearly lifted her off the floor.

"What the hell's going on here?" she said, her voice loud and panicky.

"I really can't say—"

"Look, you know something, you spit it out! You don't just run after someone and be all mysterious and scare the hell out of them." Teresa's voice was beginning to rise loudly. She could feel the woman shaking inside her white coat.

"Look," the woman said, lowering her voice, "we saw something on the mammogram and then on the sonogram we don't like. I urge you to call your doctor immediately."

"Don't give me this crap, I been around hospitals plenty recently, I just buried my husband five weeks ago. I know when you doctors aren't saying something. Now what is it?"

"You have a—a density—"

"Speak English, goddammit!"

"You have a lump. I think it's cancerous. I think you may have breast cancer. I don't know what stage it's in."

Teresa went numb, and her eyes darted wildly all over the woman's face. She suddenly felt as if all the oxygen had been sucked out of the hallway and she was going to pass out.

"I'm sorry," the scrawny woman said fearfully.

Teresa let go of her and took a step backward. She was pale and her mouth was moving without a sound, and her eyes just kept moving from the woman to the walls, to the lights, to the chairs; she couldn't focus in on anything. And deep inside her head, images of the hospital and Fred and the way he had died in such pain from cancer was rerunning itself mercilessly.

"WHAT? I HAVE WHAT?" she screamed out and her voice echoed off the walls.

DOTTIE walked up the stairs of her building and noticed a spring in her step. She went to the mailbox. Her smile dropped as she pulled out the only envelope. It was a bill from Con Ed with the words FINAL NOTICE stamped on it in red. Oh, Christ. It would be in two weeks. And this was it, the beginning of the end, Dottie thought. The phone was going to be cut off by the middle of next week.

Now, heavily, she trudged up the stairs to her apartment. She took the key out and let herself into the apartment. She dropped the keys down on the table and stared at the phone. She had to pull herself together.

Determined, she opened the bag, carefully laid out the suit and went into her bedroom. She opened the armoire and took out a cream-colored silk blouse, walked back into the kitchen and pulled the jacket of the suit over it. It would be perfect. She carefully hung the hanger from the bedroom doorknob.

Okay, she was ready.

She had decided that it would be best not to identify herself over the phone to him, so she spent a good ten minutes trying to disguise her voice.

"MacGregor Pawn and Repair, may I help you?" A young man's voice came over the wire, and temporarily threw her. She cleared her throat. She was not going to hang up this time.

"May I speak with Mr. MacGregor?"

"Speaking."

She began to feel her stomach go on her, her hand was sweaty and shaky as she held the receiver to her ear.

"Mr. Arthur MacGregor, Senior?"

"Hold on," There was a muffled sound of someone putting his hand over the receiver, and she heard the voice call, "Pop, pick up line one."

She took in a breath and held it. Her free hand wandered over the bag with the makeup in it.

"Mr. MacGregor."

Her knees went weak, and her tongue got all tied up and

for a moment she didn't think she was going to be able to go through with it.

"Mr. MacGregor here," he repeated.

"Arthur MacGregor?" It came out breathy and low, but it came out.

There was an odd pause, and she heard him exhale.

"Yeah, that's me." His voice sounded odd, as though he was busy thinking of something else while he was talking.

"I'm looking for a certain item."

There was another odd pause, and an exhale. He cleared his throat suddenly, his voice became crisp and business-like.

"What kind? We carry all kinds of things."

"I would rather come in and discuss it with you."

"Can you be here by six-thirty?"

"Where are you located?"

He gave her the address. Arthur Avenue in the Bronx.

"So around six-thirty I'll be expecting you," his voice said in a businesslike tone.

"Six-thirty on the nose, Arthur," she said without thinking, and then froze.

There was the sound of an exhaled "Huh?" on the other end, and she panicked and immediately hung up.

Not only had she said his name, but she'd used exactly the same phrase she had always used when they were making plans to meet.

She put her head down on the table and covered herself with her arms.

She'd blown it.

HIS EYES were bulging at the phone on the desk. His mouth had dropped open. Was it possible? After all these years?

Was that what the hang-up had been the night before?

67

Or maybe it was someone who sounded just like her . . . and used the same turn of phrase?

Oh, why bother playing that game? He knew who it was. It was Dottie all right. He'd known it right after the first sentence. And that had been Dottie on the phone the night before. She hadn't had the guts even to answer him, she'd just hung up.

That would make sense. It relaxed him a bit because he'd just been working the hang-up over in his mind.

He looked through his office doorway and stared at his son's back. He was hunched over a keyboard attaching a cable. Arthur glanced at his watch. It was almost five-forty. He'd have to hustle Moe out of the shop before six-thirty and make some excuse for not car-pooling it home to Rye with him that night. This was going to be ugly. The kid had spent the entire ride last night lecturing Arthur on the evils of fencing.

He looked around the outer room. He looked at the tables filled with pieces of computer terminals, keyboards, VCRs and televisions, and watched Moe replace the board and then test the machine.

He had good hands, his son.

Just like he had. He watched his son look up at the clock on the wall. He turned off the computer he was repairing and stood up and stretched. He yelled out to Nyles, the Jamaican kid they'd hired, that it was almost six and he could knock off for the night. He turned and frowned at Arthur, and walked into the office. Moe was the spitting image of Arthur at thirty.

"Hey, Pop. You ready to leave?"

"Naw. I got some work to do."

Frown.

"I thought we agreed you weren't going to do anything on the side anymore."

"What are you talking about?"

"Pop, I'm not stupid. I know when calls come in for you you're up to something, and we agreed that you weren't going to do that anymore."

"This isn't for a fence."

Moe rolled his eyes and placed his hands on his hips. The thought that he could probably still take Moe crossed Arthur's mind.

"I don't get it. It's not like you need the money. You're rich as Rockefeller, it's like you just do this to get your rocks off—"

"Hey, let's clean it up?"

"Oh, come on. You know what I'm talking about here. Now what are they?"

"What?"

"Whatever it is this woman is coming up for."

Arthur leaned forward. "She's coming up to see me. I grew up with her."

He watched Moe's eyes narrow. "That's a good one, Pop. Look, I know you're bored and I can see you sitting here thinking about the good old days—although why you think robbing banks and spending years in jail was such a great way to live—"

"I enjoyed it. I was good at it."

"Then how come you got caught?"

Arthur leaned forward. "If you look at the number of jobs I pulled versus the number of sentences I got, I got caught maybe two percent. That's not bad, since it is an occupational hazard. I am waiting for an old friend. I'm going to take her out to dinner down the street, all right? Now why don't you go home to Doreen and the kids and get your mind out of the gutter?"

He watched his son shake his head and look disappointed. Arthur stifled a small sigh as Moe turned and walked over to the office door. He looked back at him.

"Okay, Pop, I'll go. But I'm warning you: I see so much

as one piece of jewelry I can't identify and I'm out of here. You may think prison is a hot place to be, but Mom raised me, and I got a wife and three kids and a dog and a cat and I'm not losing everything because you can't rob banks anymore. You hear me?"

Arthur nodded and waited for him to sweep out of the back room. Moe left the doorway, and after a minute, he heard him pick up the phone outside. After some low murmurs he hung up. Arthur heard the front door open and close behind his son.

Arthur walked through the repair area in the back and into the front of the shop. He turned off all the lights except the big neon signs hanging in the window and stared across the street.

The little punk was sitting in his car, parked in front of the bakery, acting as if he were too smart to be seen.

Nobody trusted anybody in this world anymore, Arthur thought, and walked back to his office. He reached into his bottom drawer, took out a box of cigars and bottle of bourbon and a shot glass. He poured himself a shot and took the glass into the front of the store.

He surveyed where he wanted to be. He sat down behind the old cash register, which he knew from experience would keep him out of sight when she walked in the door.

Take her out to dinner. Hell could freeze over.

He sat in the dark behind the counter, smoking the cigar and drinking his shot and thinking about anything besides that phone call, because if he thought about it he'd explode. So he kept his eyes on the car across the street and thought about how hard he'd tried to give that kid the best life he knew how. He'd sent Moe to good schools and college, where he learned the fine art of computer electronics, and his mother had made sure she'd raised a solid citizen.

And Arthur could barely stand the self-righteous son of a bitch.

He'd taken Moe in when the company he worked for went bankrupt. And Moe had given him grief ever since. Of course the money Moe brought in with the electronic repairs was much more than Arthur had ever expected from the business.

There was a certain symmetry to that; he'd only bought the shop as a concession to Moe's mother when she was pregnant. He personally never had much interest in owning a business. But in the end it had worked out well. It made parole easy, it gave him a comfortable life, and also gave him a way to launder what he'd been able to hide from the Feds, of his treasured loot without being conspicuous.

And Moe's repair service really gave the shop the aura of being totally legit, but the crap he got when it came to his sideline . . .

Yeah, Arthur knew it was stupid he was still fencing things. Moe was right, he didn't need the money, and actually the money that he did get out of it at this point wouldn't come close to covering the expenses if he was caught. But old habits die hard.

He chomped down on the cigar and watched the tip glow brightly. He watched the red neon light bounce off a row of saxophones hanging in the window and bathe the shop in warm red color.

It was almost romantic. He shuddered, it was too good for her. So he got up and flicked on all the overheads and squinted in the glare.

That was worse. He angrily turned them all off again, and sat back down on his chair. He couldn't believe it was Dottie . . .

Think of something else.

His eyes darted up to the front window again. He saw

Moe start the car, and then, oddly, he saw the figure of a woman quickly duck into the car, and his son drove away.

Arthur sat very still for a moment. It didn't look like Doreen's silhouette . . . Well, he wasn't going to jump to conclusions.

Arthur tapped his cigar ash into an ashtray he'd brought up to the glass counter. His eyes briefly fell on the contents of the top shelf of the case.

Diamond rings. Rows of them. Would've made him drool when he was young.

He stared at his watch, and then looked at the door.

So now she was coming to him to buy something on the sly, a ring or a fur coat.

No call. No explanation of what took her thirty years.

What had he ever seen in her anyway? Arthur blew out a ring of cigar smoke and watched it dissolve in the air. And his mind helplessly wandered back to Rivington Street.

He'd been young and prime, and it had been summer on Rivington Street.

During the dog days of July and August you could literally see all the inhabitants of Rivington Street. The kids, and merchants with carts and stalls on the streets. And you could look up through waves of drying sheets, hanging like banners from fire escapes or from one building to another across the street. The fire escapes were thickly padded with mattresses, pulled out onto the metal landings through bedroom windows. People would sleep outside on the landings when the apartments got too stifling hot. And on either side of the fire escapes old women in apartment windows, resting their elbows on pillows, formed a wall of eyes, policing the kids on the street below. And there were arguments and brawls in every language imaginable, from Yiddish to Chinese to the heavy brogue of the newly immigrated Irish. And down at the corner you could see the true hoods who ran the games in the alleys, and shook down the dock workers and the newsstands, the men Arthur unapologetically admired.

And Dottie had been just another kid visiting—oh, what was her friend's name? Arthur tapped his index finger against the glass countertop. He could see the girl's face . . . a little brown-haired girl who lived on the second floor of Arthur's building. A big family it was, and they all had perfect Irish first names and a perfect Italian last one . . . The one whose mother would ask Arthur to fix their old radio that was falling apart. Something Spinoza.

Eileen Spinoza.

Dottie didn't live there; no, she lived in the better section of the East Village. But she'd been around . . . for how many years? Playing with the Spinoza kids in the streets, until he that one summer.

And then, suddenly, Dottie had a figure, and you took notice of her. Well, she'd always had a figure, just maybe he'd never noticed it. But that year, whenever she passed, it set him on fire.

And during that summer he'd spend whole days praying Mrs. Spinoza's radio would go on the blink, as it often did, and she'd yell up the fire escape for him to come fix it. He'd take his little tool kit given to him by Hymie Schwartz and trot down, and if he was lucky, Dottie would be there.

She'd stand over his shoulder and watch him, and ask him questions. She was smart, smarter than the Spinoza kids. As he would explain what he was doing, she would lean against him, and he'd eventually give her the job of handing him the tools as he needed them. He'd make sure she'd have to reach across him to get them. And he'd take a very long time, sometimes literally taking the whole thing apart, whether it needed it or not.

And then he'd lean his head back. He could feel her breasts and stomach up against his shoulders and back, and by then he could hardly talk anymore, his heart was going so fast, and he was aching in his hips.

"And that's how you replace a tube," he'd manage to breathe out.

And she'd be very slow to answer, "I see, I see."

And then some kid, usually Eileen's younger brother, Doyle Spinoza, would start making all kinds of snotty comments and Dottie would immediately step back from Arthur.

He hated that kid.

He made sure he always went to Nicholson's for his afternoon smoke so she'd see him—that and because old man Nicholson was crooked as the day was long and had sold him cigarettes at two cents apiece since he was twelve without even thinking about it.

So he'd stand on the corner, boldly smoking his cigarette, and watch the little kids splash around in the open fire hydrant in front of Nicholson's. And down the street you could watch the bigger boys play games of stickball, and the girls playing intricate clapping games and rhythmically singing:

> *"Miss Mary Max, Max, Max*
> *All dressed in Black, black, black*
> *With silver buttons, buttons, buttons,*
> *All down her back, back, back."*

And he'd keep one eye out for Dottie O'Malley and another out for his father, the drunken bastard, who'd come and whack him down the street if he saw Arthur was spending money on cigarettes—not out of any parental care that Arthur was smoking, but because he always assumed Arthur had stolen the money from him.

But the money was from the jobs Charlie the Cheat and

Joe were taking him on as lookout. He was making good money, which he stashed in the one place he knew his father would never look: his mother's Bible.

And after the first heist, a small jewelry store in midtown, as part of the celebration, Charlie and Joe took him over to Brooklyn. To the Navy Yards, and Sands Street.

All along Sands Street were bars and whorehouses that catered to the sailors, longshoremen, the dockworks, and a gang called the Navy Yard Boys who would roll the drunks who passed out in the street.

They got him drunk, drunker than he'd ever be again. He remembered throwing up in the street, and then laughter and being pushed into a building, into a room where a sad-angry looking woman was.

She took him to bed, telling him to make it fast, and the only reason he got through it was that the vision of Dottie came into his head, and he closed his eyes and got on with it.

And the next morning, dizzy and sick and lying in cold water in a washtub in the middle of the kitchen in the apartment on Rivington, he decided to make his move on Dottie.

So he waited until the weekend, two days later, when Dottie would stay over at the Spinozas'. He'd gotten her to say she'd meet him up on the roof to see the pigeon coops. It didn't matter that he didn't own any of the birds himself. He had sat so still in the dark, waiting for her to come up on that roof.

He remembered the moon was full and big and it almost looked like day out. He was standing behind the pigeon coops and listening to the birds coo. It was soft and breezy up on that roof. It almost seemed pastoral to Arthur.

Or at least it was as pastoral as Rivington Street could get in August.

And he heard the creaking of the rusty iron roof door and pressed himself against the chimney behind the coops and watched her step out onto the roof. He could see her dress, this kind of filmy cotton blowing in the breeze. When she walked in a certain direction it became almost transparent and he could see the outline of her thighs and the whiteness of her panties through it. And when she passed by he'd pulled her against the chimney stack and kissed her as hard as he could.

She pushed him away and whacked him one, right across the jaw.

"Get the hell off me. What are you, crazy?"

"Don't give me that. I see how you watch for me at Nicholson's grocery. I seen you run an entire two blocks trying to make sure you'd be there when I stop by. And I see the smart-ass way you answer me, and how you always lean against me when I'm fixing that radio."

"Don't flatter yourself. I hate you, Arthur MacGregor."

"And I hate you, Dottie O'Malley."

And he'd pulled her into him again and whispered in her ear that he wanted her and how he wanted her and how he cared for her, not that he ever imagined he wasn't going to get whacked again for what he was saying. He felt her begin to shake as he kissed her up and down.

She wrapped her arms around his neck suddenly, kissed him hard, and he knew that it was all right. She shook as if it was the most special thing in the world to be touched by him.

He took a swig and finished his shot of bourbon. He watched the empty space Moe's car had been in. He almost wished the kid would have stayed out there so he could make this short, and not have to think anymore about her.

And, oh, God, that room he had near Chinatown. And the years he'd come in from work and she'd be there waiting for him.

He tapped the cigar ash into the tray, and the image of her lying back in the Murphy bed overwhelmed him. And a ritual they'd had, when he'd get up to run out and get them something from the deli on the corner because the stove in the apartment was too dangerous for words. The ritual went like this:

When he would dress he would glance up at her, startled sometimes to see a kind of resentment. And suddenly, covering his body from her sight seemed to be an act of treason. Her eyes would get dark and flash at him grimly. It seemed unfair that he was performing this perversity in front of her. He'd turn away, and feel oddly ashamed and thrilled at it. Then he'd give her a kiss and leave.

Thud, thud, thud, jumping down three flights of stairs, his feet maybe landing on the center step on each flight, and he'd hit the lobby running. He could make it back to the room in ten minutes flat if there wasn't a line at the deli.

He'd run up the three flights, taking the steps three at a time, and he'd have to pull himself up by the banister on the last flight, he was so winded.

Then he'd stand very still when he got to the third-floor landing to catch his breath because he still had some dignity left, and he wanted her to think he'd taken his own sweet time strolling down to the corner. So he'd stand and breathe, and make sure he wasn't winded and his heart wasn't pounding when he opened the door.

He'd carry in the brown paper sack with sandwiches and beer and he'd place them on the chair by the bed and he'd kick his shoes off and begin unbuttoning his shirt. And he'd wait because he knew it would drive her crazy.

Sharply, he'd hear, "Come here." And he'd feel an amused grin go across his face at the cutting tone of her voice and he'd obey, and slide back down, fully clothed, into the warm sheets.

He'd watch the top of her head, touch her soft hair, and

he sometimes felt as if he were hovering back, behind his own body, staring down at her.

She would have a serious, thoughtful look on her face, as though she were doing some sort of very delicate, close work to which must be paid extraordinary attention as she undid the buttons of his shirt.

"Sit up," she'd command, and again he'd obey, and she'd pull the shirt off him and toss it scornfully out of the way. Then she would unbuckle his pants, and unzip them with the same serious expression, and sometimes there would be a soft thud from his belt buckle if his pants fell on the rug and sometimes a metallic clank if his pants landed on the linoleum. And if he'd bothered to put on socks and underwear, they would get tossed aside too. She'd still pay close attention, with the serious look on her face, and smooth the sheets out over both of them. And finally, when her work was done, he'd watch a contented smile cross her face, and her head would lift and she'd gaze happily at him, as though she'd washed some unspeakable horror off his body, and he was now clean and decent and pretty.

It was all upside down when they were in that room. Indecency seemed to become decency, and things he'd been taught to be ashamed and afraid of seemed honest and upright and something to be proud of.

It was only when they left the room that life seemed to become one lie after another.

But it wasn't simply sex that he remembered, it was . . . details. It simply astonished him, for example, the unspoken thoughts that would cross her face. And what astonished him more was that these unspoken thoughts, which would whiz by as expressions, were something that was as plain and understandable to him as if she'd spoken them aloud.

It was amazing that someone, a woman—a female—

would feel anything about him at all, but to be so warm and honest and readable was something Arthur decided was very rare. And some days he felt that he knew he was the first man ever to have a woman like this. Just the care she gave to him and the detailed way which she seemed to feel about him from moment to moment was something extraordinary.

He'd listen to other men speak about their women, and it always seemed impersonal. None of them really seemed to take notice of them. There were men who joked about their women, and other men who spoke of them merely as tits or pieces of ass, or the other kind who had a boiling resentment of them, almost as if women were something dark and evil and utterly untrustworthy.

And he couldn't figure out for the life of him why Dottie seemed so different from those women the men he knew spoke of. Some days he suspected it was just that he was in love with her and so all these moods and expressions, no matter how small, were of intense interest to him. And other days he felt, that no, maybe it was that she *was* extraordinary.

It was memories like these that drove him mad for a while.

Because she had made it matter that he was alive on this planet.

There was someone to whom his existence was important. And no one had felt that way about him since he was seven. That was the year his mother died.

And that was a revelation to him, after the years with his father—the drunken rages, and the watching him, from a slightly ajar closet door, as he tore the room apart looking for things that maybe didn't even exist. And the years Arthur'd spent huddled at the bottom of the bedroom closet trying to pretend he was a box or maybe one of the shoes he was sitting on—any inanimate object—so he wouldn't be discovered and get whacked by this madman because there was no one there to stop him.

Until Dottie, he'd thought of himself like that. A piece of furniture, he was, not even a human being. And when he'd grabbed her that night he'd figured maybe God would let him steal a kiss. A kiss that he could have as his own.

And she gave him herself.

And she promised to wait.

And she *lied*.

And Arthur was thinking back on all this when the door to the shop opened and he saw her outline as she came through the glass-and-wire-mesh door.

He couldn't help but lean forward as she moved into the soft red light from the neon, almost looking like firelight from a fireplace, and still he didn't let her know he was there, just like that night on the roof.

"Hello?" Her voice was shaky, as she took several steps inside the shop.

He wanted to hurt her.

"Hello?" she said again, and he watched her look around. He could make out on her face that she was frightened.

And he could make out that she still was one of the best-looking women he'd ever seen in his life, and still had a figure he could spend entire days exploring.

Not one of his other women had ever affected him like she did.

And that made him even angrier about what she'd done to them.

"Is anyone here?" Her voice sounded panicky.

He watched her blink, and then her face fell and she turned around and put her hand back onto the doorknob.

"What do you want, Dottie?" he said loudly and sharply and he watched her jump, startled, and spin around.

"Arthur MacGregor?"

"That's me, remember, Dottie?" he said harshly.

He watched her look hurt and back herself into the wall next to the door.

"How have you been, Arthur?" she said after a moment.

"What do you want from me?"

He watched her face stop looking hurt and begin to look angry.

"A gun, Arthur."

That threw him. He sat still for a moment, watching her. Her eyes didn't waver.

He stood up and walked around the cash register and stared up and down at her, and when he looked back up to her eyes, he realized that she had done the same to him, and that her breathing was shallow as she looked over his body.

He felt good about the dim lights at first but now he wanted to take a good look at this woman who'd thrown him over for a nobody.

He shot one arm beside her to reach the light switch behind her, and for a split second she almost ducked, as if he were going to hit her. He played with it, as if he were having trouble, all the while making sure he was pressed up against her.

She was shaking like a leaf.

Snap. The lights went on and he stepped back from her a foot, and they both blinked at each other in the harsh light.

"I liked it better the other way," he said nastily and snapped the light off, and he leaned against her just for a second too long, just so she'd get the point, then stepped back.

"I didn't come here for you to appraise my looks. I want a gun, Arthur," she repeated.

"Why?"

"You ask all your customers why they want guns?"

She had him on that one.

"No." He walked around the counter, sat back down on his chair near the register. She walked over and placed her bag on the glass counter.

"So?" she prodded.

"So why do you want a gun, Dottie?"

"It's dangerous where I live."

"It's dangerous everywhere these days."

"You got a chip on your shoulder."

"You noticed."

"I never did a thing to you." She was jittery. Her eyes were looking everywhere but at him.

He gaped at her.

"You said you'd wait for me. You didn't wait for me."

"Are you gonna sell me a gun or what?"

"Twenty-four months, Dottie, twenty-four lousy months, you couldn't wait."

She stepped back and felt her eyes begin to fill. He could see the reflection of the water along the lower rim.

"For what? Until the next time, Arthur? And how many years was the next time? How much time did they give you then?"

"I—"

"Twelve years, right? But you only did one and then you broke out and were on the lam for how many years?"

"I—"

"Five years, Arthur, and then they caught you and they sent you back, with another robbery conviction, which was twelve more years, plus the twelve from the sentence you never finished before, plus two for being a bad boy. Twenty-six years, out of which you served fifteen. And that was what I was supposed to wait around for? Sell me a gun, Arthur."

"Yeah, that was what you were supposed to stick around for. Maybe if you had, maybe—"

"Oh, don't even say it! I'm not stupid. You'd have given it up? You? You, who have books and articles written about you, of all the crazy things?"

"Maybe I could have."

"You would've been worthless. And you would've wound up taking it out on me. Otherwise you would've quit when I asked you to that last time. Sell me a gun, Arthur."

"And I could have become a nine-to-fiver, tax-paying, voting, solid citizen, right? You would've lost interest in me immediately. You like what I do."

"No, I never did."

"Then how come you seem to know all about me? You followed it just for the hell of it?"

"No." She straightened up, and stared at him silently. He could see in her mind she was trying to come up with some explanation for her being able to recite his whole life history with such accuracy. He'd had a Pulitzer Prize–winning journalist who was not able to get those facts as straight as she had them.

"It was just . . . difficult not to notice; you were in the papers all the time." She floundered.

He gazed at her, and let his eyes meander down the suit she was wearing; he could see her straighten up her back as his eyes lowered, almost as if he were touching her.

"I would've found something to do and taken care of you. And you gave your word you were going to wait."

They were both silent.

"Now why would an upstanding citizen such as yourself want a gun, Dottie?"

"I got mice."

"You gonna shoot some little tiny creatures?"

"These are big, annoying mice."

"Don't you think shooting them is overdoing it?"

"Sell me the gun, Arthur."

He exhaled hard, and frowned at her.

"You're right. You don't mean nothing to me and you never have."

Her face looked as if she'd just been slapped. Good. He wanted to hurt her.

He reached behind the cash register and pulled out a small handgun. He placed it on the counter.

She blinked at it.

"How much?"

He leaned forward and stared at her.

"Don't you want to look over the merchandise first?"

She swallowed and picked up the gun, holding it with two fingers by the handle as if it were some rotten piece of meat.

"Cock it."

"I beg your pardon?" She gaped at him.

"The gun. Cock it. Let me see you."

He watched her blow out a breath and glare at him. She wanted a gun, fine. He was going to make sure at least she had some idea where the safety was.

She turned it around and around and he finally took it from her and cocked it. He held it up to her.

"Now it's cocked. Now you can shoot."

He pulled the cock back with his thumb, listening to it click back into its original position.

"Now the safety's on. Now you can't shoot it. You try."

"It's okay, I know how to do it."

"Well, I just don't want you to get stuck with the safety on when those mice come around."

She glared at him. "How much?"

"One twenty-five."

She swallowed.

"Does that include bullets?"

He looked at her incredulously.

"No, that includes the gun. You want bullets, you go get bullets."

She exhaled loudly. This was a lot more complicated than she'd imagined.

"Well—" She shook her head. "How much if I buy bullets from you?"

"You know in New York City there's a one-year mandatory for carrying an unlicensed gun?"

"That's not what I asked."

"I know. Another twelve for a box."

She frowned, and then looked up at him.

"How about . . . if I only want six bullets?"

He felt the corner of his mouth turn up into a grin at the naïveté of the question.

"You're not buying grapefruit here. Bullets come by the box. The box is twelve dollars."

She stared at him a long time.

"All right, I'll take the box." She was angry, and she opened her purse and took out the cash.

He took it, and then handed her the gun.

"Don't I get a bag with that for a hundred and twenty-five dollars?" she asked sharply.

He glared at her, then turned around quickly to stifle a chuckle. And then he got angry again. Not only had he been thrown over for a lowlife, but Nathan was using her to get a gun on top of it? He didn't know what Nathan was up to, but whatever it was, he wanted to slow it down. He needed something to bide the time.

He grabbed a paper bag and spun around and tossed it at her.

"There, now get out," he ordered.

"What about my bullets?"

"Come back tomorrow night, at seven."

"What?" she nearly shrieked. This was barely going to leave her enough money to get back downtown. "You don't have the bullets here?"

"You know I don't keep guns around for my personal use. I don't believe in them." His eyes were steady on hers. She grabbed the gun, pushed it into the bag with a crackle from the paper and shoved it inside her purse.

"You want bullets, you come back at seven tomorrow night."

She glared at him and walked to the door. She turned around and watched his eyes staring at her legs, and she felt a small tingle go through her in the dim shop, lit entirely by red neon.

"I hate you, Arthur MacGregor."

"I hate you, Dottie O'Malley, and I always have," he answered and listened to the sound of the door slamming and the rattle of the mesh gate on the glass.

He waited until he thought she was a couple doors away, then he quickly slipped the keys out of his pocket and went to the front door. He silently opened it and peeked out. She was down the block, almost at the corner. He slipped out, locking the door behind him, and pressed himself into the little vestibule. He watched her cross the street, and look around lost. He stayed there until she turned and walked onto Arthur Avenue proper.

Dammit! He had no car.

He darted across the street, keeping far back, just around the corner, keeping his eyes on her. He watched her look around when she got to the corner, and then suddenly he watched her step into the street. Dammit.

He whirled around and looked down the street. He could see one cab. He stepped into the street and his arm shot up. He cranked his neck around, and relaxed. She was still standing there and there were no cabs in sight. It seemed an interminable amount of time between the light and the time the cab pulled in front of him. He got in and sank down in the seat and stared at her through the window.

"Where to?" the cabbie demanded.

"Just run the meter and wait here a moment. Turn your 'Vacant' sign off." The cabbie shrugged and obliged him.

At last a cab pulled up in front of Dottie and he watched her gingerly get inside, clutching the purse as if it were some bomb that could go off if she loosened her grip.

"Hey, pal," Arthur said, leaning forward, "you see that cab the lady just got into?"

"Yeah."

"Follow it."

"It's your fare." The cabbie gave a shrug and pulled the car up to the corner.

They both watched the cab drive past them toward downtown.

The cabbie pulled the car into the intersection and stepped on the gas.

"Try not to be conspicuous about it," Arthur added and was glad when he felt the cab instantly slow down.

The lights twinkled over the river as they hit the East River Drive, and Arthur had developed a certain admiration for the cabbie's tailing ability by midtown. He guessed he might be a cop.

Dottie's cab turned off on Houston Street, and they followed it across and onto Sullivan Street.

"Slow it down and pass them," Arthur said easily, and hummed to himself.

His eyes bounced up to the rearview and he watched her get out, look both ways, and almost run into the building.

Good, he thought. That little tidbit about the mandatory sentence had sunken in.

"Stop the cab."

He opened the door, and the cabbie turned around quickly.

"Keep the meter running, I'll just be a minute," Arthur said and threw a twenty at him.

He kept his eyes on the front of the tenement building.

Nathan, it seemed, had never amounted to much, and that gave him a certain smug satisfaction.

But sending a woman to get a gun . . .

He opened the front door, reached into his pocket and unzipped the monogrammed leather case. He took out a pick and in one second was inside the hallway.

He went over to the mailboxes and looked for the name "Weist." He bent down, squinting, and suddenly realized that the name "Nathan" had been scratched from the mailbox. He felt his back suddenly arch.

He silently walked up the stairs, got to the landing, and turned. Arthur walked to the door at the end of the hallway and put his ear up to it.

He heard the sound of her walking around inside, and then he heard the television snap on. He listened and listened, and then he felt his chest tense up at the noise from the television and the sounds of her moving about. He stepped back and stared at the door in almost horror.

Good God, it was true, he thought, she's alone in there.

He stared at the case of tools in his hand. He could get in there if he wanted, and for a brief second he wavered in favor of opening the door.

And then what would he do?

He knew what he wanted to do, strangle her just a little and then . . .

And then he got angry again.

Why the hell should he give her pleasure?

She hadn't waited for him. And what was worse, she'd thrown him over for a lowlife gambler, not even someone with his standing in crime. Although, he thought vainly, there weren't too many people who could match his talents.

And maybe it was stupid that he was still angry after all these years. But she'd broken his heart when she wouldn't go with him, and only because of her lousy middle-class Irish Catholic morals. He'd never had any use for morals. Or maybe he was still so angry because she'd turned out to be the unattainable woman.

He was not used to not being able to get anything he wanted.

But the fact she had her own mind on these things, that was what he'd loved about her as a girl. She was smug and sassy and haughty, and didn't take any crap from him.

But no. She hadn't trusted him and had played it safe with Nathan, and she'd denied him a whole lifetime of being with her and having her . . .

Still, he was now very uneasy about his stupidity in selling her the gun.

He turned and walked down the stairs. He could be back down here by seven in the morning, he thought.

The cab was still standing there when he got back outside. He zippered the case on the way over to it and he slid it back into his pocket, got in and slammed the door.

"Where to?"

"Rye."

"New York?"

"Yeah, you know where it is?"

"If you got the fare, I know where it is."

Arthur pulled a hundred-dollar bill out of his pocket and gave it to the cabbie.

The cab pulled away, and Arthur looked at her front door in the rearview.

This situation needed casing.

CHAPTER THREE

A<small>RTHUR</small> was whistling "I Get a Kick out of You," and pondering why he could never do a job when he wasn't in disguise.

He pulled the thin black jacket out of his closet and laid it on the bed. It had thick padded shoulders and changed his shape appreciably. His middle was padded by one of those false theatrical stomachs. He pulled on the pair of extra-large black pants and belted them.

He opened the armoire and looked at himself. Between the jacket and the padded middle he looked to be a hefty size forty-two.

He walked over to the dresser and took out his kit. He opened the bottle of spirit gum and smeared some across the back of the two pieces of fake mustache and carefully placed it on the white marble surface of the dresser. He smeared more of the gooey liquid on each piece of his mustache and waited for it to dry. While he was doing that, he took out a tube of clear mascara and deftly stroked his eyebrows, making them appear heavy and bushy.

The phone on his night stand rang and he walked over and picked it up.

"Pop?"

He winced.

"Yeah? Wha—?" He murmured.

"Did I wake you?"

"What time is it?"

"Seven-fifteen."

"Aw, Jeez."

"You oversleep?"

He was such a nosy little bastard, Arthur thought.

"Yeah. Listen, I don't feel so good, you go ahead. I'll be there later."

There was a silence on the other end, and he knew Moe was going through all sorts of creative reasons why Arthur was not going in today.

"Pop?" His voice was stern. "What is going on?"

"Jesus, nothing. I got in late, is all."

"From your date?" he said, punching the word "date" as if it were the great white lie.

"Yeah. You don't believe I could have a date with a woman?"

"No."

"Moe, go to the store, I'll be in later. Let me get back to sleep," Arthur said and hung up.

If that kid wasn't there in twenty minutes, that meant he'd bought it.

Downstairs he heard the door open and Eva's heavy footsteps in the hallway. He'd be gone in the next ten minutes anyway. He'd leave Moe to deal with her, a zaftig woman of Polish descent whom Arthur doubted an army could get around.

He walked back over to the dresser and took out a faded shirt. He pulled it over his head, and down over his padded middle. He looked back in the mirror. His figure bore no resemblance to his real body.

He took the pieces of mustache off the dresser. Carefully he pressed one on one side, lining it up with his real mustache perfectly. He did the same on the other side, then took a small mustache comb out of the makeup case and brushed some of his real mustache over the fake hair pieces so you couldn't tell where the real hair ended and the fake hair began. He looked at himself in the mirror. He now had a mustache with heavy handlebars. He took the jacket and pulled it on, then took a cap out of the drawer and put in on. It covered his hair, or rather, covered the top of his head where his hair had thinned considerably. The hat made him look as if he had more hair than he did, and was big enough so it could be pulled down low on his face. He searched in the bottom of the armoire for the geriatric cane which completed the character, and then stood with the cane in front of the mirror. He hunched over and took a few steps.

Stanislavsky would've disapproved of his need to look in the mirror. Arthur was a big fan of Constantine Stanislavsky, he had read and reread *An Actor Prepares* many times over the years.

Of course, by the end of his career, these disguises had become utterly meaningless. The cops knew who'd done the job. Arthur went back to pondering why he felt the need to go into a heist in disguise even at the end when it didn't matter.

Maybe it was superstition.

Maybe he was a victim of habit—it wasn't the kind of habit normal people had, but it was habit all the same.

Or maybe it was that heightened sense of excitement he got when he dressed in these outfits.

Whatever it was, it was giving him the tingles, staring at his reflection.

It was as if he were pulling one last job.

That had to be it. The rush, and the anticipation of the danger, and the chase. Once he was in disguise it was as if a signal went off in his brain that got his juices flowing. And he secretly felt that people had come to expect it of him and looked forward to it.

Toward the end, he'd once dressed up as an Indian—the

kind from Calcutta, not the Midwest—and got applause in a bank in Weehawken.

He closed the armoire door. He picked up the brown paper bag he'd swiped from the kitchen at about three in the morning, and stuffed a change of clothes in it, the way he'd done over two hundred and seventy times.

This whole incident with Dottie had gotten him pacing and out of bed for two hours that night.

With the change of clothes in the bag he walked out into the hallway. He peered down the stairs, and silently descended.

He quickly walked to the front door, seeing no need to alarm Eva by facing her in this getup.

"Going to work, Eva," he yelled over his shoulder.

"Have goot day, Mr. MacGregor," Eva, in her heavy accent, yelled back out of the kitchen to him.

He slipped outside and walked down the mossy green brick path, and around to the garage.

The air had that nice autumnal snap to it, and he found himself whistling as he trotted down to the garage. He always looked on fall as the beginning of a new year for some reason.

He opened the garage door and walked inside. He threw the bag with the clothes next to him as he slid in behind the wheel of his car. He started up the Ford, backed it out and onto the street.

He exhaled and felt flush. He hadn't realized how long it had been since he'd spent a weekday anywhere but the back of the pawnshop. He adjusted the rearview and then noticed the ear-to-ear smile going across his face.

Hell, this was the first morning in years he couldn't wait to get out of bed.

His eyes looked down at his watch. Seven-thirty.

Christ, he was going to be late, he thought, and drove to the corner.

He hoped Dottie had not turned into an early riser.

TERESA rolled over onto her side of the bed. Where the hell was Fred? Why had he left her here all alone? They were talking about cutting her up. She felt her body contract into the same fetal position she'd been in all night.

Fred.

She'd been fighting the memory of the first time she'd seen him for hours now because she was already scared, and she didn't think grieving on top of it was going to make her feel any better. Teresa closed her eyes and again tried to think of what her options were. Fear bolted through her.

Fred. Where the hell are you? She closed her eyes.

The first time she'd laid eyes on him she knew.

He was the one.

Whose wedding was it? It was a big one, with ten bridesmaids all wearing heavy blue brocade dresses with petticoats so stiff, the outside of the skirts brushed both sides of the door when they entered the reception. They had spiked heels, dyed to match the dresses, white gloves, and little pillbox hats with sheer blue netting. The men all wore tuxedos with thin lapels of black shiny material, and their hair was slicked back. A tenor sang "Ave Maria" in church during the ceremony, and the aisles were overflowing with flowers—white lilies and baby's breath.

She'd been sitting about midway down on the aisle with her girlfriend Rosie when she watched Fred pass. There was a buzz as he walked down the aisle. And people up and down pointed as he passed. Teresa couldn't take her eyes off him, with all the whispering and pointing. She remembered leaning into Rosie and asking her what the deal was. She didn't know, so Teresa was left with her imagination.

She sat back up and just watched him, every move he made.

He was trim and tall, and had on a gray sharkskin suit, a silk shirt and pencil-thin tie. His red hair was slicked up into almost a pompadour, and he was the sharpest-looking guy in the whole place. He waded through to the center of the second pew, and bent down to speak to a woman in a large hat. As he bent down, his eyes fell on Teresa, and she could see his lips stop moving. His face went lax and his eyes kept staring at her and staring at her, and for one moment they both seemed to stop breathing. Something jolted him back and he looked forward and sat down.

She waited patiently through the full service, her eyes pinned to the back of his head. Once or twice during the ceremony he turned to sneak a peek at her, and their eyes met again. She held his stare. And then everyone got into cars and drove out to Brooklyn to one of those big wedding places for the reception.

She'd just been handed a glass of champagne when he walked through the door. People were crossing over to shake his hand. Teresa watched his eyes wander about the room as he shook hand after hand. Just as she was about to turn away, he spotted her, and to her amazement he slowly began to walk across the floor to her, not taking his eyes off hers.

Some idiot dropped a sugar cube into her glass as he approached. She didn't even realize the champagne had foamed up and over the side of the rim, until he stood in front of her. His eyes never left her face.

"Your champagne's spilling," he said, and she blinked, as if he'd spoken another language.

"Your glass is overflowing" he said, and she suddenly snapped to and looked at the mess. It had run down her arm and onto her bag. Someone handed her a napkin and she wiped her bag, barely looking down.

"Fred Newhouse, I'd like you to meet Teresa

DeNunzio," someone said, and then she felt an awed voice whisper, "His father was Dutch Schultz's right-hand man."

She never took her eyes off Fred, he never lowered his eyes from hers. She knew by the way he was looking at her that he was waiting to see a reaction, and then waiting to gauge that reaction.

She drew a proud smile across her face and narrowed her eyes slightly, just so he wouldn't think she was impressed by this information. Slowly she extended her hand to him.

"My great-aunt was Al Capone's mistress. Pleased to meet you, Mr. Newhouse."

Teresa exhaled with a sigh, took in another deep breath, and clasped her two hands together and tightened them into her stomach.

And for all their famous family lineage, they'd never been more than marginal—that had been the only letdown for Teresa. That she'd somehow been gypped out of the fame this match had promised.

She reached up and turned off the light and stared at the green glow of the clock dial on her nightstand.

Of course, never having gotten to be famous was now the least of her worries, she thought, as she stared at the sunlight coming in the window. She pulled the covers over her head and just shook.

THAT CRACK about turning the lights back off really hurt, Dottie thought as she sipped her coffee. She waited for the toaster to throw her toast on the counter, the way the damn thing had done since she'd gotten it in the late seventies.

And the crap about the bullets.

It was Thursday morning. That meant she couldn't get the bullets till that evening, which meant she couldn't rob a bank until Friday.

It was the waiting until nightfall that would be the hard

96

part. She had an appointment at the clinic at St. Vincent's that day and had hoped to be in jail instead because they were going to test her bones, which probably involved some sort of pain.

Dottie stared at the two three-pound dumbbells she'd used that morning for her exercises—every other day she was supposed to do so many repetitions, lifting the weights to improve her bone density. She picked up the weights and placed them carefully in the corner, alongside the ankle weights she used for leg presses. She took out the bottle of Tums and meted out her morning ration of calcium. She stood at the sink and chomped on the pills.

And she had to go pay Teresa the rest of the money, now that she actually had the gun.

She looked at the gun on the counter.

God, he'd been so cold and mean . . .

All right, she thought he'd be less than cordial in the beginning, but somehow, with the newly done hair and the nice outfit . . .

She'd really deluded herself, she thought angrily.

She mechanically held out a saucer, just to the side of the toaster. The toast shot up, hitting the bottom of the cabinet, and fell onto the center of the plate she mindlessly held out.

There had been this fleeting moment, as he'd pressed up against her, when she thought he was going to grab her and kiss her and tell her it was all right. And she'd tell him what she was going to do.

And he'd stop her.

And he'd help her because it mattered.

But he was just mean. A mean *old* man, he'd become. She couldn't emphasize the word "old" too much in her brain. All her effort to impress him. Some old, old man. Well, Arthur MacGregor didn't look so great himself.

For starters, he'd lost a lot of hair. She glowered smugly.

And he was shorter.

And when he'd brushed up against her, his body had been so . . . so . . . a tingle went through her. Whom was she kidding?

He even looked good without hair, the bastard.

And now she was going to have to go back up there, and let him be nasty and insulting again. After the way he'd acted, even if he was nice this time, she would not now tell him anything.

And then it struck her that it was going to cost her even more money! She didn't have anything to wear. No, it wasn't vanity, it was that she wasn't going to give him the satisfaction of knowing she was needy. She was not going to humiliate herself. Even if it cost her every last cent.

She spread some margarine over the toast and bit into it.

All right, so he hated her . . . The worst part was that, deep down, maybe he was right for hating her.

She *had* promised to wait for him. Maybe he was right, he might have been something else if he'd had her to come home to at night.

She laughed out loud.

Arthur MacGregor was born and bred a career criminal, and some woman cooking stew in an apartment was not going to change that, no matter what he said or what he promised.

She looked over at the clock. It was almost ten and her doctor's appointment was at one.

All right, if she was going to rob a bank tomorrow, and have to spend an entire weekend in a jail, she'd better find a precinct she liked. That thought had occurred to her in between crying and anger bouts at four that morning. She could rob any bank in any neighborhood, so long as the precinct house they took her to was clean and neat and the food was hot. She'd have to devise a way to see the inside of the precincts. She was looking for something like . . . the jail on "The Andy Griffith Show."

A clean little jail, with meals cooked by someone's Aunt Bea.

She could walk into station houses on her way to St. Vincent's for her tests.

She walked into her bedroom and over to her closet. She pulled out a dress and put it on. She hadn't had a pair of pants on for ages—none of her jeans fit anymore, and they were too expensive to replace. She took out a dress and pulled it over her head. She belted the baggy thing. After wearing an outfit that fit, it was depressing to have to go back to these sacks.

She looked at her face in the mirror. How could she have deluded herself into believing Arthur was going to turn into some knight-errant and come riding in and save her from all this?

"I liked it better the other way." Snap, he'd turned off the lights, then leaned against her. She could feel how warm he was, and it had been so long since she'd felt anyone against her. It welled up inside her, this hunger, just simply to feel the touch of another human being, warm flesh.

He broke her heart, is what he did.

Cold-hearted bastard.

Well, she was going to pull herself together. She was going to find a police station she wanted to spend the weekend in and would case the inside of a nearby bank.

She stared at the pictures on her dresser. She stared a long, hard time at her son. He'd looked exactly like Nathan. When he was little she'd look into his face, hoping to see more of herself in him, but it never happened; he resembled Nathan.

She looked at the last photo he'd had taken when he was alive. He was in an army uniform, and looked so reedy. Maybe it was his Adam's apple, jutting out just above where his tie was knotted at the collar, which gave him such a gaunt look. His brown hair was chopped shorter than he'd ever worn it, and his head seemed so small under the big visored hat of the uniform.

He seemed like a child playing dress-up in a man's clothing.

He'd be over thirty now if he'd lived. Maybe she would've been a grandmother. Maybe she would've spent her afternoons wheeling a stroller around, and wiping little noses and digging in the sand.

God, what a waste. Dying on an island most people couldn't find on a map, in a battle no one remembered, for a reason no one could explain so it made sense.

If he were alive, maybe he would be close in age to Arthur's son.

That thought didn't give her any satisfaction, and in fact made a small lump form in her throat, as it seemed very unfair that she, who had been honest and straightforward, should be in this position, while Arthur, who'd been totally, unabashedly criminal, should have a fine son and a business, and live well in his old age.

A cold-hearted selfish bastard was all Arthur MacGregor was.

Sometimes God made no sense to her.

She walked carefully back into the kitchen and over to the sink. She filled a glass with water and began counting out the pills, two of these, one of those, half of the blue one, another one that looked like Contac. She swallowed them and picked up her purse. Again she looked at the gun. She walked over, picked it up and looked around the kitchen. Dottie opened the utensils drawer and put it inside.

The thing gave her the creeps. Well, by Friday night she would hopefully be under arrest and on her way to being convicted of armed robbery.

Maybe she was mad . . . crazy mad, not just angry mad.

She opened the door and walked out into the hall.

What a cold-hearted bastard Arthur MacGregor was.

ARTHUR picked up Dottie's trail on the corner of Sullivan and Bleecker around ten o'clock. He bought a paper to distance himself from her and hung back a half-block length as he followed her east along the street.

In Washington Square Park, she talked to a cop. Arthur watched the cop point and seem to give her directions. He watched Dottie walk off east.

She veered over east on Fifth Street, and got past Broadway before she came upon what she was looking for.

Her first police station. She grimaced and swallowed.

It was horrible-looking! A sooty brownstone, with an ancient wooden police precinct sign over the door. And the windows were so dirty you barely could see through them. She had actually tried to see into a window, and found that a forest-green shade had been pulled down almost all the way.

Well, if she was going to do it, she had to know what it looked like inside. She opened the grimy front door and walked in.

Inside, it was even worse. The station house was gray and smelly, and the thought of trying to eat a meal in that filth made her shudder. She walked over to the desk and gave the officer behind it a weak smile.

"Yeah?" he said, not looking up at her.

"I," she floundered, "I—" His eyes bounced up to her with that kind of police suspicion. "My . . . I've lost my dog," she said quickly and strongly.

The man's eyes lowered and he pushed a form in front of her. She sat down and had just begun filling out a name when the front door flew open and two officers dragged in a man who was screaming at the top of his lungs. He was filthy beyond measure. His hands were cuffed behind him and he suddenly broke loose and began slamming into people like a battering ram. Blurs of uniforms ran past Dottie as officers piled on him, knocked him to the floor, and began punching him. He was pulled across the floor on his stomach toward two big double doors. Two cops ran ahead and held the doors open.

The noise coming from down the hall sounded as if it were the door to hell itself. Screams and moans and clanging metal echoed into the outer office.

"What's down there?" she asked shakily.

"Holding cells," the officer murmured and took her form. "We'll let you know if anyone sees your dog."

She walked out of the station house so fast her heart was pounding. She would never be able to survive that. God, what if they were all like that? No, she just had to find the right neighborhood, that was all. Some nice, quiet, wealthy neighborhood where the police spent their time writing out parking tickets.

So, Dottie thought shakily, as she walked quickly west, the East Village was out. She was not even going to look at banks in that area.

She stopped for a moment to calm down. She was afraid. Maybe Teresa was right. Maybe this was insane. Maybe she wouldn't be able to survive in jail, and she should stop now.

Maybe she should try the employment agencies again . . .

She took a deep breath as a wave of humiliating memories about that washed over her. Like the personnel manager who had called enthusiastically about her resume and 'wanted to see her immediately.' And, twenty-five minutes later, standing at the door to his office, Dottie watched his face fall and his eyes go blank. She was not even asked inside. Interview after interview had gone the same way: She was overqualified, she was underqualified, she wasn't *right* for their firm—what they meant was "too old."

Too old. At fifty-eight!

Dottie began walking again, faster and faster as the image of the man screaming came back in her head. She took frightened strides. She had no choice. She wouldn't settle for anything less than a nice, small, clean precinct; at the very least she would look for something she'd imagine would have decent food.

WHEN SHE walked out of the building, Arthur snapped to. He'd been leaning against a car across the street, trying to figure out what she needed in a police station.

God, those places gave him the creeps. Even to this day, after years of comparably honest living, he still cringed like a guilty man whenever he was in close range to one. He dropped back at first, and then realized that he'd better step up the pace.

Dottie was running down the block.

At Sixth Avenue he watched her look around. Finally, she spotted a patrol car parked near Waverly Place. He watched her walk over to it and lean down, talking to the officers.

Arthur hung back far.

He watched her nod as an officer pointed west, down the street. She seemed to thank him and resumed walking up the street. She walked across Fourth Street, crossed Seventh Avenue, and Arthur watched her turn down Tenth Street. She kept going west toward the river, and Arthur, who was trailing by about half a block, stopped short.

What was she doing?

She had gone inside another police station.

The momentary thought that she might be ratting him out for selling her the gun crossed his mind.

* * *

"MY DOG'S LOST," she said to the officer.

The officer looked up from behind the desk. "Here, I'll give you a form," she said and handed Dottie the same form she'd filled out at the other station house. Dottie stood over the desk writing, and periodically she would stop and look hurt, so she could look around the room.

A cheery banner hung on the opposite wall and read WELCOME TO THE SIXTH PRECINCT. There was a case of medals and trophies. It was clean. And it was light, the building was brand-new, it seemed, and it was a lot smaller than the other one.

"What kind was it?"

Her eyes darted over to the woman.

"What?"

"Your dog?"

"Oh, it was a mutt."

"Aw, and they're usually so sweet," the officer said and began a several-minute diatribe on mutts versus purebreds.

This was definitely the jail she wanted to spend the weekend in, Dottie thought and she smiled at the officer. There was another double door off to the side, and it was propped open. There was no screaming or yelling. She could imagine eating a meal in here. She could imagine that the cells were nice and clean.

She finished filling out the form and pushed it back to the woman.

"Well, to be honest, we don't usually get any information on these things, but if we do . . ."

Dottie smiled at her broadly. "You've already made me feel so much better, just knowing this precinct is here, you have no idea."

The officer smiled and with that Dottie went back outside.

She turned and stared at the clean pebbled facade—there

were even flower boxes planted out front, and there were several trees with flowers planted around their bases.

Dottie felt herself exhale in sad relief.

Now, all she had to do was find the nearest bank, and she knew exactly where that was. She turned and walked east on Tenth, turned down West Fourth and stood staring at the construction all along Sheridan Square. The street had been torn up, and there were Con Edison trucks, parked with big markers, all along several of the streets. But Dottie wasn't even looking at the mess. Her eyes were focused on her bank, the one where she had an account.

The Chemical Bank on Sheridan Square.

BY THE TIME Arthur made it to the corner of Seventh and Fourth, she'd vanished. He cursed himself for walking so slowly. He straightened up and walked to the edge of what was left of the sidewalk and stared past the construction workers and into Sheridan Square Park. He looked over at the small island shaped like a triangle. It jutted out onto Seventh Avenue and held a newsstand. He looked down West Fourth toward Sixth Avenue.

She was nowhere to be seen.

Goddammit, he cursed himself again.

He was rusty at this. And he was ashamed at the idea he'd lost the trail of a fifty-eight-year-old woman. He walked to the coffee shop and pretended to read a menu that was Scotch-taped to the window. His eyes searched the room inside, to see if maybe she had stopped for breakfast.

He walked to the other corner and looked at the building in front of him.

A bank.

He walked inside and saw her immediately. His eyes darted around the room, looking for the best vantage point from which to observe her. There was a long line of people. He walked over to the counter, made out a deposit slip and got on the line. He took the paper he'd bought out from under his arm and held it up high, as if his vision were bad.

He was puzzled, as he peered over the top of the paper at her. For one thing, her dress seemed oversized and ragged. It was nothing like the neat new outfit she'd shown up in the night before.

He knew before the day was out that he would wind up letting himself into her apartment to see the way she lived, but the shabbiness of the dress and the fact that she lived alone were not good signs.

He felt stupid about selling her the gun now.

On the other hand, maybe Sullivan Street was really dangerous at this point.

He tried that thought on for size, and didn't buy it. From what he'd observed, Sullivan Street was safer than the block they'd grown up on.

He thought the crack about using a gun to shoot mice was cute.

Then there was the fact she only wanted six bullets.

That really didn't sit well.

If only he hadn't let his temper get the better of him . . .

Dottie surveyed the interior of the bank. It was a mess from an ongoing renovation. The room was almost shaped like a shovel with a handle; the end with the tellers was a wide square, and then narrowed into an almost rectangular hallway.

She walked over to the area where the tellers were and picked a charge-card application out of the display, trying to peer over the high counter and into the teller area.

The tellers were separated from the customers by a one-inch-thick sheet of what she was sure was bulletproof glass. The glass went from the top of the counter to several feet below the ceiling. And just over the openings where you slid the transaction sheets through, the glass was two inches thick.

She wasn't tall enough to see through to the other side. She looked over on the left. There was a makeshift wall where the bank officers sat at desks. There were only three of them now, perhaps due to the renovation.

The customer service desk ran from the bank wall to the edge of the makeshift wall to enclose the office area.

Next to customer service was a glass door leading to a small vestibule, and then another glass door which opened onto West Fourth Street.

That was where the room narrowed into a corridor, lined with counters and deposit slips and a quick-deposit box on the right.

At the opposite end of the bank was another set of two glass doors separated by a vestibule, which opened onto Sheridan Square.

To the right of the doors at the far end were steps leading to safety-deposit boxes in the basement.

Other than that, there was nothing extraordinary about the room, except for the noise of construction and the dust from the newly put-up plaster board. Emergency lights had been hung along the walls.

She glanced at the ten people on line and then over to the guard. He was a small man, obviously of Latin descent, and his hands were crossed in front of him, and he was kind of rocking forward onto the balls of his feet and then putting his full weight back onto his heels as he stood. Her eyes slid down his body.

On his right hip was a gun and holster.

It was bigger than the gun she had purchased.

She wondered if that made any difference in the world of guns.

She tried to imagine Friday. She would wait until the afternoon, till almost three o'clock, before she'd do it. That way, she thought, they would have done a lot of transactions during the day and would probably have more money lying around, so they would take the attempt more seriously. She would enter and leave by way of Seventh Avenue.

This, in the event that she actually got that far with it.

She could line the people up against the wall, or maybe huddle them next to customer service, while the tellers handed over the money.

That way they could be close to the phone lines, and it would merely look like either incompetence or naïveté on her part.

So she figured if she hit the bank by ten of three, it would be her best shot to be caught. She felt tough. These were tough thoughts.

She looked up and the toughness dwindled as the guard approached her.

Arthur peered over the top of his paper at her.

What the hell was she doing? That was the only thing that kept going through Arthur's mind as he watched her standing still in the middle of the floor, looking around as if she didn't know where she was or why she was here.

It alarmed him.

Maybe her mind was not right?

He watched the guard walk over to her and say something he couldn't hear, because just at that moment a table saw was turned on in the basement, and there was the sound of riflelike explosions from an air gun that was shooting nails into the walls, somewhere on the floor beneath them. He watched Dottie walk over to the counter and make out a withdrawal slip, and she got on line behind him. He turned slightly sideways, so he could see her and watched her eyes wander about the room, and come to rest again on the guard's gun.

She seemed to be spending an inordinate amount of time staring at it, Arthur thought. She looked directly at him, and he turned back forward and waited.

After a moment he knew she hadn't recognized him. He refolded the paper and put it back under his arm. Arthur began looking around the bank. An amused grin went across his face as his eyes landed on two architectural drawings of what the bank was going to look like when it was all renovated.

A bank that supplied you with its floor plan.

How considerate.

He started speculating about how he would approach pulling off a job here.

Bank buildings just seemed to scream out to Arthur Mac-Gregor, "Case me! Case me!"

He always thought of them in the female sense.

"Come on," they seemed to say seductively, "look at how I'm laid out, see my fancy dress"—he'd always thought of the security measures as hooks on an evening dress.

His job was how to undo them one by one, slowly, so the wearer became seduced and cooperative as she was undressed.

He'd been thinking in very sexual terms all day, he thought.

His eyes focused back on line and he realized there were only two people left in front of him.

But this bank he'd pass over.

Even his time-trusted technique of robbing banks wouldn't work in this one.

For one thing, it was the wrong size.

He favored big, busy main branches, which would provide him with enough time to stand on line with his small memo pad and do the sketches he needed to create accurate floor plans of the space. He could gauge linear space to within half an inch.

It also would acquaint him with the employees with whom he'd be dealing during the crime.

He never pulled jobs at night. He also never took banks during banking hours. That was suicide. There was the unacceptable X factor of the public trying to shuffle in and out while you were trying to get on with it, which had made him cease early on to operate during business hours.

He always robbed banks between 7 and 9 A.M., usually getting away a good fifteen to twenty five minutes before the doors were scheduled to open.

The reasons for that were obvious, at least to him. Number one: why go through the fuss and muss of having to blow through a vault door when someone, or several some-ones, had the *key*? And number two: there would be a set number of people you had to deal with, namely the bank employees.

It was pretty mathematical, once you knew how many employees there'd be.

Arthur always started with the idea he had roughly an hour and a half from the time the first person arrived till opening time. He always added thirty minutes just for screw-ups.

Most banks were opened by a guard or two around 7 A.M.

He would stake out the bank, sometimes for weeks, and would watch what time the guard got there, and any habits he had.

Habits again. That was the most important element in his success as a bank robber.

Did the guy, for example, have a cup of coffee in one hand and a paper in the other, so reaching for his gun in a split second would be impossible? Did the guard always arrive at the same time? How observant was he? Was he half asleep, and more interested in his bagel and coffee and reading the sports section of his paper? How easy would it be to slip behind him as he opened the door and take his gun?

Usually it was a piece of cake.

So, once inside, the clock began ticking. Each bank job had its own timing. Some would take forty-five minutes to rob, some over an hour, if they were big.

The calculation for the time it would take was based on the linear footage. For example, if the vault was located down a flight of stairs, he would add seven to ten minutes. Then he would add, say, three minutes for the arrival of each employee, since they would have to be escorted into a predesignated holding area. If there were ten employees, a half-hour could be spent just shuffling them about. And he could gauge by his watch how the robbery was going—if he was behind schedule and had to step up the pace or if he could linger a little longer in the vault.

So first they would escort the guard into the holding area, usually an executive office. Arthur and a partner would rip the phone line out while a third man would keep a gun trained on the guard. Then Arthur, who would oftentimes disguise himself as a guard, would take the keys and wait by the door for the rest of the employees to arrive.

As each employee arrived they would be walked back to the holding area and politely referred to by name, Mr. So-and-So or Mrs. Somebody, and he would carefully explain what was going to happen and how long it was going to take and that everyone would be just fine if they cooperated.

He found that explaining to people what was going to happen calmed them. Being respectful to human beings reinforced the impression that they were not dealing with a psychopath who would just shoot wild. And most underlings were hardly going to stick their necks out for some bank executive. No, in Arthur's experience, the American bank employee was content to be a passive victim of a well-organized crime, just so long as they weren't going to be physically harmed or held accountable for it.

Once everyone had arrived, the person who could open the vault was separated from the others. It would take about ten minutes to put a good-enough scare into him—or her—to get him to open the vault.

Then he and his two partners—he'd never figured out how to get it below that number—would separate, with two of them keeping an eye on the employees in the holding area while Arthur would clean out the vault.

Once his bags were filled with as much money as time permitted, he'd walk back to the holding area, pretending he hadn't started yet, and announce that he needed help cleaning out the vault. His two partners would make it clear that no one should move and they'd all be back in a minute. Then the three of them would be out the door, with the keys, locking it from behind, and into a nice, clean, untraceable car.

Never once had Arthur been caught in the act.

He was turned in when one partner or another would do something stupid or conspicuous and was picked up.

Then they would immediately roll over on him.

There is no honor among thieves. That is a myth.

Anyway, he thought as he looked around the bank, this one would be out as a possibility.

In addition to being the wrong size, it was also under construction. And that meant just so many more people you had to account for besides the employees. Plus there was all that construction outside, making it impossible to park the getaway car at the curb in front of the doors. Not that crossing the street would blow it if all had gone well, but . . .

Arthur was by this time the next one in line, and he watched the teller finish with the customer and was just about to walk up when all the lights went off. He took the opportunity to slide off the line, and walk right past Dottie.

He waited and watched the emergency lights go on. He watched her walk over to the next available teller.

Dottie had decided to take out the rest of her money— two hundred and twenty dollars—and close the account. She wouldn't need money after today.

She was going back to the thrift shop to buy herself another outfit to go see Arthur in.

And maybe a bottle of wine or something, so she could have a farewell drink. She would toast the jail at the Sixth Precinct. She hoped and prayed that the sentencing would be swift once she pled out.

She stepped up to the teller's window and pushed the withdrawal ticket through.

"That's your entire balance," the teller said loudly, and out of the corner of her eye she saw the fat old man who'd been on the line ahead of her limp by.

"I'm closing my account," she answered back.

The teller shrugged and gave her the money.

She turned, stuffed it into her purse, and walked out toward the doors that opened onto Sheridan Square.

Arthur lagged a good block behind at this point, since she'd already seen him in the bank. Whether it had consciously registered or not, if she kept seeing the same stranger, sooner or later it would ring a bell that she was being followed.

She had closed her account.

This was getting uglier and uglier.

He followed her across Sheridan Square and up Seventh Avenue. He stood and watched her walk into St. Vincent's hospital.

★ ★ ★

TERESA was angry. She'd been stomping around her apartment since she'd dragged herself out of bed at noon. Those bastards at Metropolitan Hospital, they were somehow responsible for this. And this talk about cutting off her breast. No. That was not going to happen. She'd told them hell could freeze over.

And then someone said something about an experimental thing that might save her breast after they biopsied—but she had to get Medicaid to approve the procedure.

And that, Teresa knew, was not going to happen. It seemed almost cruel to wave a medical procedure in front of someone who had no medical insurance except for Medicaid. It made her angry.

She was staring out the window at the street below. She watched a group of teenagers, who ought to be in school, spray-painting graffiti on an abandoned building. God, she hated what this neighborhood had become.

It had been so nice and clean when she was growing up. All little brownstones with yards and trees, and opera playing from record players in open windows. And then the 1972 organized-crime busts came, and everyone went to jail or moved to Howard's Beach or the Bronx or Fort Lee, New Jersey. And then there were the race riots, and they burned the neighborhood down. Never made sense to Teresa. If you're angry about being prejudiced against, why the hell would you set fire to your *own* building? The place you had to live in? Naw, her people would have set fire to the building of the guy who wronged them. Now that made sense.

She felt another wave of fear go through her and she replaced it with anger.

What was she going to do? Tell her kids? That would put her in a weak bargaining position for their meeting next week.

She had the weekend to tell the hospital when she was

114

going in for the biopsy, unless she could find the money for the experimental thing.

There had to be another option.

"WELL, WELL, Mrs. Weist," a corpulent nurse with a heavy Caribbean accent said, as she helped Dottie up on the table. "You looking well. You taking your medication?"

"Yes."

"All the medication, woman?"

"Yes."

"Good, good. The doctor he be right in, and he gonna explain what this machine here does."

She nodded and the nurse left the room. She lay very still on her back, shivering slightly in the open-backed gown. She stared at the huge grayish-pink cylinder at the base of her feet, and she could already tell that she was going to be somehow slid inside the chamber, which was going to do God-knows-what to her.

How much was this going to cost?

And how much was it going to hurt?

These were the two thoughts she always had as she sat for an interminable amount of time each visit. Her appointment was for one, but Dottie knew from experience that she wouldn't even get called to see anyone until at least two-thirty. It wasn't bad enough it broke her financially, but these medical tests also caused physical pain as well. Didn't seem worth it.

And then she felt an odd rush of relief, realizing that after tomorrow she would never have to come back to this hospital again. And they could send her all the threatening mail and threatening phone calls they wanted.

Gin.

Maybe she would buy a bottle of gin and a bottle of vermouth, and some cocktail onions, and make herself a

Gibson. She hadn't had a Gibson in years, and dammit, if she was tough enough to rob a bank, she was tough enough to drink one. She winced at that.

A farewell drink.

She felt her eyes begin to fill as she again focused on that crack by Arthur—that he needed to turn the light off like she was so old and ugly that he couldn't countenance her.

And that wasn't even the worst of having seen him last night.

Robbing banks was not the only thing he'd become expert at.

He'd robbed her of her memories of him.

And as she was lying in this cold, dark, morgue-like room she began to feel so alone, and wondered, why me? Why?

Maybe she was being punished for not giving herself to Arthur, because deep down she knew she'd never loved anyone the way she loved him, and that was part of what was ripping her up inside. His coldness and cruelty.

Maybe she was responsible for that too. Maybe he'd been really crushed by her insistence that he choose between her and the one thing he loved to do on this planet. Even though robbing banks was pretty bad, it was still the only thing that excited him. It was like breathing to him. And she had denied them both a whole life. Maybe she was the one who'd been cold and cruel.

Her mind skipped a beat.

Wait a second, wait a second, she thought, pulling herself together.

She'd asked him to give up armed robbery, not brain surgery.

God, she'd only spent ten minutes with the man, and look how he'd already turned her morals upside down.

That was why Arthur was so dangerous. She lost all perspective in his presence. He could somehow turn anything one hundred and eighty degrees, and make bad things seem good and the good things seem bad, till her mind spun around trying to figure out why his arguments for doing the wrong thing seemed so . . . right.

Look at how long it had taken him to get her to sleep with him again, all those years ago. She was a married woman with a child, he'd just done twenty-four months in jail, and had no rights to her.

Took him one hour. And there she was, in a room in the Ambassador Hotel, sweating and hanging all over him.

It was crazy. Where had her morals been?

Morals. That was a joke, she thought, and even now found herself cringing over her behavior with this man. The way she'd run to his room after work and wait for Arthur to make love to her, without benefit of ceremony or ring or anything.

As old-fashioned as it seemed these days, Dottie'd been brought up as a strict Catholic. There was only one activity Dottie and her mother did together, and that was going to church. Her mother proudly enrolled her in parochial school, even though it meant everyone had to work doubly hard to afford the tuition. She went out of her way to make sure Dottie spent as much time as she could learning from the nuns and the priests. Lord, the months the woman spent hand-stitching lace on her confirmation dress, saving money out of a barely adequate household allowance for a corsage. How proud she was at the ceremony. And when they went back to their apartment, there was a party with cake and lemonade, and her mother had smiled for days.

Unmarried sex was simply out of the question. And certainly adultery was just unthinkable. Both sins Dottie had managed to commit. And she felt sincerely bad about this. She was ashamed of the fact that she enjoyed it immensely, Arthur's touching her and loving her. She couldn't stop herself from what she considered was utter perversion.

She chuckled to herself.

These days Dottie would turn on the television and see people talking about all sorts of truly perverted things right out loud, and it always struck her as funny that she'd been so ashamed of what now seemed like a healthy relationship. But then, no, she couldn't cross the boundaries and run away with him.

A doctor appeared, and in a heavy Portuguese accent explained that they were going to put her inside the machine so they could get a clearer picture of whether her bones had improved over the past months.

She lay on the table as the thing whirred around her, and began to shake with absolute fear. She felt a small current running through her, as if she were on the verge of being electrocuted.

Maybe she was just reacting to the sound.

She was in the thing a good ten minutes before she was slid out again, and told to dress and wait in the waiting room.

She looked at all the damaged young people and all the old people who were just sick from living.

"Mrs. Weist?" the nurse said, and she got up and dutifully followed her into the office.

There it was, the black-and-white of her bones.

"Ah, Mrs. Weist, you having very good news. Your bones are much, much stronger," the doctor said.

She nodded.

"Not I'm saying you go ice-skating next winter, but there is much more bone mass. You have been lifting the weights?"

She nodded.

"And using the ankle weights?"

She nodded.

"We are going to add swimming to your routine. Do you have access to a pool?"

"Oh, sure."

"Good. Excellent. I want you to swim twice a week, if you can."

"All right."

For some reason he felt the need to write that down, as if her memory were faulty. He handed it to her.

She hated being patronized.

"See you in a month," he yelled after her as she left.

In your dreams, she thought.

In one month she was going to be sitting in a nice infirmary.

And yes, if there was a pool, she would swim in it.

It was three-thirty when she left the hospital.

Arthur was sitting against a parked car reading the sports section of the *News* when she came out of the same door she'd gone in through.

Creatures of habit.

He lagged back as she walked along Eleventh Street toward Sixth Avenue. She crossed diagonally to the downtown side of the street. And kept walking.

She didn't like the fact that this fat guy from the bank was behind her.

With her luck he was some kind of creep.

She continued down Sixth Avenue, stopping every so often to pretend to look in windows, and glance back at this guy, who she was now sure was following her.

Arthur hung back very far.

He'd been made.

He could tell from the way she was acting. All the way over to the bank that morning she hadn't stopped to look in one window. Now she was suddenly interested in window shopping?

He had to give her more leeway.

He watched her turn on Third Street and he slowed and looked over a table of used magazines a street guy was selling in front of a video store. By the time he'd gotten to the street she was gone. He crossed over to a McDonald's and looked inside. His stomach began to growl. He was hungry.

She wasn't in there. It was beginning to become clear to him that Dottie either never ate or didn't have the money.

His bet was that she didn't have the money.

He was walking along Third toward Washington Square Park when something caught his eye, and he stopped in front of a thrift-shop window. He exhaled hard as he watched her.

Inside the shop was Dottie, staring at herself in a full-length mirror. She was in a beige-and-white polka-dotted silk dress with a matching belt.

The dress fit so nicely, and made her look tiny and trim, the way she had last night. Jeez, she looked good, he thought. A pang went through him as it sank in that this store was probably where the outfit from last night had been bought.

He began to feel his temper go on him again.

This time it was directed at Nathan. Hadn't he had any brains? Hadn't he put aside anything so if this woman was left alone she would not have to live buying guns in the Bronx and used dresses in thrift stores?

He would've taken so much better care of her. And the life they could have had . . .

All right, it wasn't as if he'd lived the life of a monk, he'd had women, plenty of them. But seeing her last night, and now following her around—it was making him a little crazy. No other woman had ever been allowed to get as near to him as Dottie O'Malley.

He turned away from the shop window and crossed the street and went into some kind of furniture store. He could observe her leaving from this vantage point and not be seen.

Oh, he was married to Moe's mother, but very briefly, and really didn't even live with her. In fact, her pregnancy

120

was the only reason he married her at all. He'd come back from the Midwest to find her out to here. What could he do?

He was a bank robber, not a louse.

But other than the connection of a child, they were two people from different worlds.

At first he'd tried; to appease her he bought the pawnshop. It wasn't so unusual, a bank robber owning a business. One of his partners, Paul Fischbein, had taken his cut from their heists and bought himself a liquor store in Queens and retired wealthy with a whole chain of them. And now the pawnshop gave Arthur a life of ease.

But he knew the first day he walked into that windowless office in the back of the place that in a couple of months he'd get edgy and start looking around for another job to pull.

And that was exactly what happened.

A fortune-teller once told him that there was some activity that he had always done, and which he'd always do because it was a part of his soul.

So that seemed to cinch it. The monkey on his back was robbery.

HER SHOES and bag would be fine with the dress, she wasn't going to sink any more money into this. It was getting late, and she had to go see Teresa on her way up to the Bronx. She was going to wear the dress out of the store.

That made her stomach burn.

Yesterday it had excited her, getting a new outfit. Today she hated it. She paid the money and left the store, pausing in front of the door. She looked up and down the street, and breathed a sigh of relief that the fat man was nowhere to be seen.

She looked at her watch. Well, she might as well get this

visit with Teresa over with, she thought. She turned and headed for the subway.

It made her angry, being followed by that creep.

ARTHUR made sure five or six minutes went by before he made his escape from the furniture store. He hopped up Sixth Avenue and looked at Dottie crossing the next street. He slowly, doing his hobbled walk, made it to the middle of the street. He watched her walk down into the subway. He turned and walked back to Third Street, crossed over to the downtown side of the street, and made his way toward Sullivan Street.

Arthur opened Dottie's door as if he lived there. He walked into the small railroad apartment. He hadn't been in one of these for many years. He remembered how little space there was compared to his house in Rye. He walked into the kitchen, the first room in the apartment.

It was small but neat. Dottie's coffee cup was still sitting on the old white porcelain kitchen table. He ran his hand across it.

His mother had had the same table. She had died young, giving birth to a stillborn sister. He had a memory of a warm smiling face, of her warm arms picking him up out of the kitchen sink and toweling him off on the drainboard. And humming. Low humming. And the smell of clothes and skin washed in Fels-Naptha, and the smell of her sweat, which was not unpleasant to him.

He must have been no more than three, in that memory. And four years later, after she was gone, that was when his father started drinking.

The first beating had occurred not long after the wake.

His father had sat at the kitchen table drinking vodka from a juice glass and Arthur, who hadn't had a meal in a day, was sitting on the couch drawing a picture, trying to not look at him. And when at last he did look up he was startled to see the look on his father's face. There was such hatred in his eyes.

As if he were somehow responsible for his mother's death.

He hated his old man for that.

And his father poured himself some more of the vodka and a look of disgust came across his face.

"Whadda you looking at?"

Arthur had looked back down at his drawing.

"I said, whadda you looking at?"

Arthur cringed and stared hard at the paper.

"You look just like your mother." He glowered.

And Arthur remembered the sound of smashing glass above him on the wall and vodka raining on him from where the bottle had hit the wall and then suddenly being lifted off the couch, and just punched and punched.

So he made himself scarce, living mostly on the streets, stealing what he could to get by.

Once in a while he'd be sent to live in Brooklyn, out near Coney Island, with his mother's mother. That was a treat, usually brought on by the DTs, or a jail term for brawling. So he looked forward to his father being in trouble.

His grandmother was a wonderful woman, too ill to take on the responsibility of a boy full-time, but willing in emergencies. Then, for a few cherished weeks or months, Arthur'd be treated to sunny afternoons at the beach, a quiet, spotless apartment, clean clothes, and wonderful hot food; kreplach and kugels and apple strudel, roasted chicken and golden, crispy caramelized potatoes she called tsimmes or something like that . . .

And then his father would show up again and he'd be dragged back to Rivington Street, to the noise and the filth and days of no food, and living on the streets and stealing to get by.

Those were the hardest times, the first weeks back. He'd get himself to school in the mornings, and there, at least until three o'clock, he'd be preoccupied. Even after school, when the weather was warm, he'd play on the streets and just be a kid—until sunset. Then, longingly, he'd watch his playmates one by one run to their homes for their baths and dinners. Miserably he'd climb up the stairs of his own building, sometimes pausing in front of the Spinozas' door. Silently he'd listen to the sounds of the family and smell the hot food, knowing that he'd go upstairs to his own apartment, and he'd be grateful beyond measure if his old man wasn't there.

For dinner he'd eat a candy bar or a scooter pie he'd pinched from Nicholson's store, and then he'd lie alone in bed, staring out the window into the warm light of other windows across the street and he'd ache to be back with his grandmother . . .

The fact he actually continued to show up at school until the ninth grade was a tribute to his mother. But nine grades was all he could take of living with his old man, and he managed to see him only rarely the last couple of years he lived on Rivington. His father was so far gone at that point, he probably wouldn't have recognized him.

Someone told him once that his father, who had immigrated from Scotland several years before Arthur's birth, had killed a man there. Arthur'd always believed that. He'd heard his father died ten years after Arthur'd left Rivington Street, but he was far away at that point and couldn't have cared less in any event.

All these thoughts from a kitchen table, he thought, and continued his snooping.

The cupboards were poorly stocked.

The contents of the refrigerator nearly broke his heart. She had so little.

He wondered how much of a dent in her money the gun had made.

He opened the kitchen drawers, half hoping to find some sort of bankbook with a nice fat balance. He knew that would make her crazy, but it would lighten his conscience about selling her the gun.

All he found was silverware and expired coupons, cut carefully out of the paper.

And the gun. She'd chosen the metal-utensil drawer for it, he noted with a certain amount of amusement.

The orderliness of women.

He walked out of the kitchen and into the connecting room.

She was sleeping on the couch.

With the television on, he knew it in his heart.

He knew the loneliness that makes you run the television day and night, so it gives the illusion you are not alone.

He knew that trick.

He walked into her bedroom. The king-sized bed, squeezed into the little room so there was barely any floor space left, annoyed him badly.

He turned to the dresser. A snapshot of a skinny, droopy-nosed Nathan smiled back at him. It was in a five-and-dime frame.

You self-centered bastard, Arthur thought. Anytime you were ahead of the game you probably took it all to the track and blew it.

The next photo stopped him.

It was the son in uniform, barely more than a child in the photo. And it was eerie, there was no trace of Dottie in him. He looked around the bedroom and realized that there was no trace of a son, period. So, Arthur concluded, either the kid was dead or he'd turned out to be just like the father. He stared at the boy's face and somehow knew he was dead, and probably had been for a while.

He walked over to the closet, opened it and stared at the ragged old dresses, neatly cleaned and pressed and hung on hangers, and sizes too big.

He closed the door. He'd seen more than enough to give him a clear picture of what had happened to Dottie.

He walked back into the living room and stood for a long time trying to decide if he should just take the gun with him.

If he did, he was afraid she'd be out there again, finding someone else to buy from.

She wouldn't chance buying another gun from him; she was too proud and stubborn for that.

Witness the trouble she must have gone to to get all dolled up to come and see him, to pretend she was fine and everything was all right.

Because it seemed clear to Arthur what was going on now.

Dottie O'Malley was planning to kill herself.

And she was going to do it with the gun he'd sold her.

No, no, no. He needed a plan about the bullets.

He'd hated her for so many years, and deep down he'd always imagined how good he would feel if she came to some miserable end.

And now it didn't give him any comfort.

It made him queasy.

Especially since he seemed to be playing such an unwitting role in her self-destruction.

He needed a plan. He needed her to confess to him what she was up to. Because if she would tell him, then he could jump in and stop her and she'd listen to him, because that would mean she'd been willing to have him save her.

Probably that was the goal of the nice clothes and the hair and the prideful and scared way she'd appeared at his darkened shop door the night before. And he'd just hurt her.

He would go back up to the shop and wait for her again tonight.

He walked to the door, gave one last look at the apartment, and stepped into the hallway.

As he closed Dottie's front door, the sound of people walking up the stairs made his ears itch.

"Molly! Don't run ahead, wait for us."

They were on the landing below.

He turned and walked up the next flight of stairs.

Arthur pressed himself against the opposite wall as he caught sight of a small girl walking up the stairs toward him. The child was walking one riser at a time, and was nearing the top of the stairs.

Come on, come on, he thought silently to himself, realizing there were no more landings in the building for him to escape to.

And that would be a kick in the head. Being caught by a toddler.

"Molly! Come back here this instant. Do not make me come and get you!" The mother's voice sounded annoyed.

His heart fell. That was practically a challenge to a child of her age.

"But I gotta!"

Arthur braced himself for discovery. He saw a tiny arm on the railing, and a face behind it, and he put on as menacing a smile as he could and leaned right into the child's face.

"Get out of here, kid, you bother me," he said gruesomely, and watched the child's face grow pale and startled.

"Ma-a-a-a!" she yelled as she bounced down the steps.

"When I tell you to do something, you damn well do it!"

"But I was going—"

"No!"

A door was opened, and he heard them walk into the apartment.

In a second, he was hopping down the white stone steps,

taking them two at a time, down past the landing and down to the first floor.

He startled a small woman, who was holding an infant, and who had turned in time to see him jump down the last two steps and land on the first floor.

He looked at her, and pasted an odd smile on his face.

"Ah, Nautilus machines, it's a miracle! Afternoon," He said, tipping his hat to her. Arthur walked out onto the street, leaving her there in puzzled silence.

"So let me get this straight," Teresa began. Dottie finished the glass of water and handed it to Teresa. "You went to buy the gun and it turns out it's from a guy you dumped thirty years ago."

Dottie closed her eyes and blew out a breath. "I didn't dump him—"

"You promised to wait till he got out of jail. And instead you got married and had a kid. *That's* dumping."

"No, you're mixing it all up. He came back after I was married—"

"So you dumped him *twice*?"

"I didn't dump him *once*! He lied to me about where he was getting the money." Dottie's voice rose, exasperated.

"Yeah, but he was getting the money."

"So?" Dottie's voice was hostile.

"So, it ain't none of your business where he was getting the money."

"Of course it was. I said—"

"You said," Teresa interrupted, "that you were in his room and you were crying about how you were going to burn in hell because you were sleeping with him and had no wedding ring on your finger, and that he had to get the money to get married. Period." Teresa kept her eyes on her.

Dottie narrowed her eyes and looked at Teresa. "You lead a very simple life, don't you?"

"Aay, don't patronize me. I lead a very complicated life. I live by my words."

"But don't you think it was wrong of him to steal—especially knowing that we were going to get married and that—"

"Excuse me! Excuse me!" Teresa singsonged, and took a puff on her cigarette. "Did you or did you not say, 'Let's get the money to get an apartment of our own and get married'?"

"Yes, but—"

"You did not say, 'Get the money by being a lawyer or get the money by being a goddamn Nobel chemist,' you just said, 'Get the money.' You gave him a goal, he went out and got it. I don't see what the problem was."

"Is this the way you and Fred would talk? This is a semantical nightmare."

"Whatever. You gotta be crystal-clear with men, my mother taught me that when I was a little girl, and I always lived by that. You can't just give them half the instructions and think they're gonna be able to guess the rest. Naw-aw. No, you gotta say, 'I want you to do this, in the order in which I say do this' otherwise, it's up to them and you can't say nothing. And as my mother said, 'I guarantee, you leave it up to a man to try and think it through, he's gonna make the one choice is gonna drive you crazy.' That's when you have trouble. Didn't your mother never tell you this?" Dottie shook her head. "Well, she should have. I was happily married almost forty years with this advice."

Dottie was wincing and shaking her head.

"No. He should have known. You got it all turned around—he was a locksmith, he could have . . . it was just that . . ." The words were getting all tangled up in her throat.

"So maybe locksmithing couldn't bring in enough money fast enough. Maybe he panicked, maybe he thought he was going to lose you."

Dottie took a deep breath. "What he did was wrong, and even though he'd been in prison, he started again—and I don't want to talk about this anymore. It was a long time ago and I don't care."

Teresa took a step back, her eyebrows rose and puckered and she gave Dottie a good look up and down, and then gave her a 'What, are you kidding?' look.

"Well, maybe you're right and it don't matter and you don't care anymore . . . but you got some awful fancy clothes on for buying bullets."

"I just want to . . . to look presentable."

"For some guy who's fencing a gun to you? Like I said, you sure you just going up there for bullets?" She was dragging out the word "bullets" so it almost sounded obscene.

"Why else would I go up there?" Dottie's voice was icy.

"Sex?"

"Why is everybody saying that to me!" Dottie stood up and threw two ten-dollar bills on the table.

"Ah, come on, Dottie, Jeez, you're always so touchy about these things. Look, so what if you're dating a guy who sold you a gun—"

"I'm not dating him. He hates me!" Dottie screamed and burst into tears.

Teresa stopped, and looked at this poor woman. She was falling apart right in front of her. She felt bad now about the jokes.

"Look, I was just having a little fun. Here, let me get you a tissue." She walked over to the refrigerator and reached up into a box and pulled out a tissue, handed it to Dottie, and watched her blow her nose.

"Let me make you a cup of coffee. I got real," Teresa offered.

"I don't know, I don't know." Dottie was sobbing into her arms on the table.

Teresa turned around and began to fill a kettle with water. She waited for Dottie to calm down. She put the kettle on the stove and turned on the fire under it. She turned around and looked at her.

"Look, what are you so upset about?"

"I was in love with him. Maybe you're right, maybe I should have trusted him maybe . . ."

"Look, different people got different things they can live with. I mean, look, you got all bent out of shape because you were sleeping with someone and had no wedding ring—wouldn't have bothered me in the least, and I'm Catholic."

"Did you and Fred . . ."

"Not without a ring and a ceremony—but I would've. And the fencing and hijacking and robbery never bothered me neither, but not everyone's like that . . . So, this guy was trouble and you got away from him."

Dottie gave a sniff and nodded up and down, almost grateful to Teresa for saying it out loud.

"So, what's this guy's name?" Teresa sat down into the chair, pulled out a cigarette and lit it.

"Arthur MacGregor."

Teresa dropped her cigarette, and her eyes bulged.

"The *bank robber*?" she said in an awed tone usually reserved for the likes of Frank Sinatra.

"Yes."

Teresa's eyes narrowed. "You're pulling my leg." She

got up and went over to the cabinet and began taking out the coffee cups.

"No, I'm not. I met him on Rivington Street. I used to be best friends with a girl who lived in his building. He used to repair things for people, he had a job at a repair shop. He used to come to their apartment when Mrs. Spinoza's radio broke down."

There was a silence and a smile drew across Dottie's face. "And that radio would break down every Saturday night."

"Yeah?" Teresa said and grinned at her.

"Remember the old radios with the tubes and wires in them? Well, if you just unscrew one or two of the tubes and loosen up the screws holding the connecting wires, those radios were just worthless. So he'd come down, and he'd take the whole thing apart, like he didn't know Eileen and I had tampered with it . . ."

Teresa was staring straight ahead, thoughts whizzing around her head. Arthur MacGregor, the bank robber, had been Dottie Weist's lover?

That was impossible.

That was going to blow her whole image of him.

He was a legend. He was one of those mythical people, larger than life—the kind of man you read about in expensive magazines. And the stories written about him never made him sound like a low-life criminal. It was as if the press gave him the nod—maybe it was a sideways nod—but it was a nod all the same. They made him sound like a hero. Big, good-looking man, smart, fast, and generous.

Teresa had had a friend whose cousin had been in some kind of construction accident, and Arthur MacGregor had sent money for the hospital. She'd heard of him doing all kinds of things like that with the money he got from the heists. Once Arthur McGregor read an article in the newspapers about a kid with a deformed foot and sent over nine hundred dollars for the operation. She could remember the headline in the *News*: BANK ROBBER BANKROLLS OPERATION.

And he was a funny guy. There was an incident she remembered with an FBI agent, who'd accidentally been shot by his own partner while trying to nab Arthur Mac-Gregor. Shot in the leg. Not fatal, but he was crippled and on his back in the hospital for months and months. There were big articles about his poor family, and how the government compensation wasn't enough. Arthur'd sent five grand along with a note suggesting he get into another line of business, one with better compensation and a more understanding boss.

Boy, the press had a field day with that one.

It was even fun being robbed by him. Teresa had a friend who'd been a teller in a bank in Connecticut when he robbed it and he'd broken into song; nearly put on a whole floor show for the employees.

Teresa turned and looked at Dottie, still staring aimlessly at the kitchen table. This man could have the "Solid Citizen" as a lover?

Naw. That just was too much to believe.

The pot on the stove began to whistle, and Teresa went over to the counter. She dumped some coffee into a drip pot and poured water over it, and then another chilling thought occurred to her.

She'd always heard that rumor. That Arthur MacGregor had been ripped up by some woman early in his life and that was why he never had a woman around him for very long and why he robbed banks with such a vengeance. In some versions of the story she was a Sunday school teacher, and in some she was a housewife, or a minister's daughter. But Teresa discounted that, like all them rumors about Elvis Presley. Once you were famous, people tried to hold you up like that.

"And when I walked in last night he was just cold and mean." Dottie blew her nose one last time and thought about what she'd just said. No, he wasn't the same man. "So I'm going to go get the bullets and tomorrow afternoon at three I'm going to rob the Chemical Bank on Sheridan Square."

"So you could go to the same prison as Leona Helmsley."

"Exactly." Dottie sniffed, and set her jaw tightly.

Teresa looked back at Dottie. For a woman she had always thought of as a snobby bore, the entertainment value she'd been getting from her the last couple of days was a real eye-opener. A grateful twinge went through Teresa; she needed this distraction from her own life.

Miss Solid Citizen and the Bank Robber.

This was much better than those stupid soap operas her daughter always watched. Teresa poured out two cups of coffee, set one in front of Dottie and sat down. She lit another cigarette and grinned wickedly.

"So, you gonna tell me how you're gonna rob this bank?" Teresa asked and Dottie opened her mouth.

"No—first—tell me, Dottie, is Arthur MacGregor good in the sack?"

Dottie closed her eyes and exhaled, shaking her head. "You're a class act, Teresa."

ARTHUR got back to the shop around five. He'd changed in the car, slipping out of his disguise and into the clothes he'd brought along as he sat in bumper-to-bumper traffic.

He ignored the glare from his son as he walked directly to the back of the shop. He slipped the bottle of bourbon out of the bottom drawer and poured himself a shot and sat down.

He had till seven to figure out how to make her talk.

CHAPTER FOUR

ARTHUR shifted in his chair and stared at the sunset along Arthur Avenue. He was edgy as he waited for her, and his mind kept going over memories that were making him angry.

Those weeks after Dottie blew him off were the worst he'd ever known. He went on a five-week drinking binge. When he couldn't stand it anymore, he took to following her. He'd stake out the playground in Washington Square, spending entire afternoons hidden in disguises behind newspapers, watching her every movement. It made him crazy that someone else had her. He'd sit all alone on that bench, eating his heart out as she tended to a son who Arthur felt should have been his.

He'd watch her body move through the park.

A breeze lifting her dress just that much higher on her legs, so he could see the curve of an upper-thigh muscle, was enough to make him bleed inside.

Thoughts of her never ceased. She was all over his brain, and only in extreme inebriation did the sound of her voice speaking or, worse, moaning beneath him silence itself.

Even his dreams were controlled by the fact that she was out there and he couldn't have her. He'd wake up in strange hotel rooms covered with sweat in mangled sheets, sometimes with a body next to him and sometimes not. Sometimes he could remember where the lady had come from and sometimes not.

He bought himself a portable record player and a gun. He would sit for hours listening endlessly to the harmonica honky tonk sound of Jimmy Reed singing, "Baby What Do You Want Me to Do." And playing with a gun he'd bought.

There was the wailing sound of a harmonica. And one afternoon he cocked the gun as he sat on the side of the bed.

And that was when Arthur realized that he was crazy. And that he had to leave this city or die. He took a train to Boston, for no other reason than it was the first one leaving. Boston didn't make any difference. Arthur soon discovered he could be anywhere on the planet and he'd still be eating his heart out in drunken sessions in hotel rooms, with the constant playing of Jimmy Reed.

One little slip-up and she was gone. It just seemed so morally sweeping. He'd done his time. He was ready to turn over a new leaf. Hadn't she believed him?

He'd spent his entire prison sentence taking a correspondence course to become a criminal lawyer. Those were the days when you didn't have to go to a law school, you didn't even need a college or high school degree; all you had to do was pass the bar to practice. And he set it up in his mind. He knew where their apartment was going to be; he knew how many kids he wanted; he'd planned it all sitting in a jail cell.

He was in reach of the life he wanted with a woman he was crazy about, and a career which didn't involve long jail terms—for him at least.

And the letter from Dottie announcing her marriage?

That was a joke.

He completely discounted the possibility that she could be serious. Not with the way they felt about each other.

No.

He was going to get out of prison, rescue his woman, and set up a law practice.

He'd had all those plans, plans that allowed him to live through the high suffocating walls, bad food, beatings, solitary. Nothing could shake his unwavering belief that he was going to have a life with Dottie.

Oh, God, it hurt so bad.

It hurt so bad, he had to do something. Click. Replay Jimmy Reed.

"Got me thieve, hide, hide, thieve, any way you want let it roll . . .
Got me doin' what you want me, baby why you wanna let go?"

He listened to that verse over and over and over, like a madman.

And after a time, he didn't know how long, he thought, screw it. She doesn't trust me? She's not coming back?

And from the spring of 1962 through the fall five years later, Arthur MacGregor took his pain out on the East Coast banking system, and any place with a safe or cash register.

He robbed more banks in five years than anyone in the history of the United States.

He developed a style. His disguises, his politeness became part of the program. But the biggest calling card he left was that song. The first time he did it he was standing at the door of a conference room, looking at twelve frozen, scared faces. And for a moment he felt pity for them, and a brief—very brief—twinge of guilt.

First humming low, and then soon out loud, his voice suddenly rang out as he stared at the crazy faces:

"Got me doing what you want me, baby why you wanna let go?"

His voice rasped, and he did a couple of steps, and sang into the barrel of gun, like a microphone.

He was really losing it.

"You know that song?" he said to a round older woman, and she shook her head no, her eyes bulging with fear.

"No? I'll sing it." His voice rang out again, and he shook his shoulders and his head, rocking forward and back.

"O-oh, stand away from that phone, please, sir? Thank you . . ." he ordered, as he watched the president of the bank inch his way toward the black receiver on his desk. He went back to the song.

He remembered dancing over to a man about his age.

"You ever lost a woman?"

"No."

"You lucky bastard. Stay away from them, they'll drive you crazy and kill you."

The fellow looked at him and nodded, and Arthur knew this man knew exactly how he felt, because he gave Arthur a pitying smile as if to say "You poor bastard." Arthur continued singing out in his Rivington Street voice. He could take their money and give them a floor show, all at the same time, that was how comfortable he was.

The feel of a gun.

Heavy cold metal in his hand was a daily necessity. It calmed him. It meant that for at least two hours he'd be totally preoccupied.

He was compulsive.

He'd finish one job in the morning and spend the afternoon casing the next. On the weekends he'd pull jobs on pharmacies, his favorite, as they always had a good amount of cash and truly laughable security systems. Gas stations were also popular, just to fill up the time.

In the evenings, he'd look for long-legged redheads. Ones with that curve in the muscle on their upper thighs that drove him mad. He'd take them out and spend great amounts of money and treat them special.

Then he'd take them back to hotel rooms and screw them.

And after it was over he'd take pleasure in berating them for the ease with which he'd taken them to bed and he would make them cry and then he would throw them out, as if they were worthless garbage.

That was when he was crazy.

He had so much money he could have retired after one year. He had safety-deposit boxes stuffed with cash in small towns all over New England. His two partners were buying houses in the suburbs, and liquor stores. For his part, he had no interest in owning anything, nor did he have any interest in big fancy hotel rooms or flashy cars. So Arthur began sending money to people. Anyone who was in a fix and whose story caught his fancy, he kicked some to.

He stole ten dollars from a gas station one Sunday afternoon because he needed something to do.

But it wasn't about the money.

That was what no one understood.

The FBI soon pegged him as the number-one wanted man in the country.

Arthur shifted back in his chair, and looked at what was left of the sunset.

The most wanted man.

And that, Arthur thought, was what it was all about, wasn't it?

To be *wanted.*

DOTTIE stood at the corner and stared down the street at the darkened windows of MacGregor Pawn and Repair.

She looked at her silhouetted reflection in a deli window. Her hands smoothed her dress and adjusted her hair.

It was colder out than she had expected; she was shivering a bit and could feel goose bumps on her upper arms.

She wished she had brought a coat, and then realized that she didn't have a coat that would look decent, and that made her momentarily angry.

She hated her life.

A feeling of somehow being on trial, that knot in her stomach, and that nausea overcame her as she took a step. To hell with it.

She walked straight to the door and grabbed the knob and pushed it ferociously. It gave a small amount and then slammed against a bolted lock. It sent a shock wave back through her shoulder, and a small shot of pain.

She grabbed her shoulder and stepped back, trembling and feeling her heart thump so hard inside her rib cage she thought it was trying to burst through the skin.

Breaking a bone, just the very inkling, terrified her.

X rays of her leg haunted her.

Dottie drew in a deep breath and held it, counting slowly in her head as she rubbed her shoulder and calmed herself.

After a moment, she grasped the doorknob again, and with careful force gave another push.

The door was locked.

She stood back, staring at it. Goddammit, she thought. He didn't show up. She'd wasted money on the cab all the way up here, and for what?

Cold-hearted, *lying* bastard.

It was then that her eyes focused on a rolled-up piece of paper stuck into the dusty, rectangular mesh-door guard. She pulled it out of the screen and opened it up.

He was in Gianni's on Arthur Avenue.

What was he trying to pull here?

She took the paper and crumpled it up in her hand, and she looked across the avenue.

Arthur watched her through the large plate-glass window, as she peered at the restaurant from across the street. He watched her look both ways and stand still, as if she were deciding what to do.

A waiter cleared his throat next to the table and Arthur looked up at him.

"A bottle of Gattinara, please, and two menus." Arthur said, and immediately his eyes shifted back to the big window.

Well, he thought, here it is, zero hour.

He gave one last look at the room. It was one of those old-fashioned Italian places with checkered linen tablecloths and candles stuck in empty Chianti bottles on each table. It was quiet and dark and intimate, and no one disturbed you, unless you wanted them to. Due to the early hour it was almost empty except for two couples, who'd been placed at opposite ends of the room for privacy.

The door to the restaurant opened, and a gust of cool air blew in, making the candle on his table flicker.

The beige-and-white polka-dot dress looked even better up close, although why she hadn't worn a coat was beyond him. And then the unpleasant thought that maybe she didn't have a coat hit him, and he lowered his eyes. He kept them lowered as the thought of the thrift shop came into his mind.

"Well, Arthur?" Her voice was harsh, and he'd guessed that she'd psyched herself up for this second visit by becoming good and angry.

He looked up, trying to appear startled.

"You're late," he said.

He watched her mouth move angrily, with no words coming out, and the waiter came up beside her, pardoned himself and put down the bottle of wine and two glasses. From under his arm he took two menus and placed them on the table. Dottie's eyes followed the waiter as he pulled a chair out and stood smiling at her.

It took a beat for it all to sink in—the bottle of wine, the two glasses and menus.

"What the hell is this, Arthur?"

"Dinner."

"I didn't come for dinner. I have companions waiting for me," she began. "We have reservations at the Coach House at . . ." She faltered again, as the word "Lasagna" on the menu hit her eye. "Nine," she snapped.

Her stomach was empty.

"Sit down, so the waiter doesn't have to stand there all night, and he can open the wine?"

She stared at him suspiciously, gave a dignified glance at the waiter, and genteelly sat down.

Well, Arthur thought, he'd won the first round. And he was secure in the fact that there were no companions who were going to be waiting for her at the Coach House. He'd also stacked the deck by choosing Italian. Dottie'd always had a weakness for Italian food.

"All right, I can stay a little while," she muttered, and placed her bag on the table.

They both sat in silence, as the waiter popped the cork and poured them each a glass. Her eyes were darting nervously around the room, and he knew she'd been thrown by this.

That was good. He wanted her off-balance.

The waiter stood still for a moment and they both looked up at him.

"Are you ready to order?"

"Give us a minute," Arthur said and the waiter nodded and moved over to the door.

They both watched him go in silence, and then they both

immediately leaned into to the center of the table and began talking in hushed tones.

"What are you doing here, Arthur?"

"I'm having dinner."

"Yeah, why?"

"I'm hungry," he said in deadly earnest, and grabbed the candle and moved it to the edge of the table, so he could see her entire face.

It was quite lovely in candlelight—if you ignored the sneer, and the overall pissed-off attitude.

He picked up his glass of wine and waited for her to pick up hers.

She waited for a second.

"I'll have one sip, just to be polite," she snapped at him, and he nodded.

She took a sip, and her eyes slid over to the bread basket.

She felt herself begin to swallow and took a gulp.

The wine felt warm in her stomach, and she realized she'd stopped shivering.

"I want to talk to you, Dottie."

"About what?"

"About last night."

"What about it?"

He noticed her eyes kept sliding over to the bread basket, and he conjectured that her pride was not going to let her take so much as a crumb unless he took some first.

Jesus, he'd been such a jerk last night, he thought, and now she was getting even.

He reached over and took a bread stick and began to chew on it. He waited for her to follow.

What she did was stare at his lips. And the harder she stared at his lips, the slower and more elaborately he made his mouth gestures, until she looked almost as if she were in a trance at what he was doing with his mouth. Her mouth began to twitch and she licked her lips and he could see how much she wanted a piece, but was on principle going to refuse the food.

Christ, that blood of hers was stubborn!

Most of the women he'd had in his life would've not only taken the wine but grabbed the bread, ordered, and would be well on their way to finding out if they could get a car or a coat out of the deal. But here this one was starving to death across the table, and would she reach for those bread sticks?

Not Dottie O'Malley.

Stubborn, thickheaded—

"Dottie, would you take a bread stick so I don't have to sit here chewing alone?"

"I'm not hungry."

"Try to choke one back."

She frowned at him and slowly reached into the basket. "I'm just taking this to be polite," she warned.

"Thank you."

"I don't need your food, Arthur MacGregor."

"I know, you have reservations at the Coach House at nine."

"Exactly."

He waited until she bit into it, and he watched her expression turn soft as she chewed and swallowed.

He loved the shape of her mouth.

"They make them here, in the back."

"They're very good," Dottie found herself saying, and took a mouthful of wine. She swallowed and felt her stomach calm down.

The waiter appeared, and Arthur looked up at him.

Dottie sat still, wondering if she could in good conscience take dinner from this man.

Now wouldn't she look foolish? After having lied herself into a corner with that bit about the Coach House?

She watched the waiter pour the wine, and then Dottie

knew he would most likely ask for their order, and then she'd have to turn down dinner. In an Italian restaurant. With wine and candlelight, and she began to feel her resolve fold.

But no, she wouldn't look foolish, she thought, and felt her mouth sag.

And then the solution came to her.

"I need the bathroom."

The waiter gave directions, she smiled and nodded and slowly walked across the floor. Arthur looked at her walk off. Well, bravo, he thought. She'd figured out a way to take his food. And if he played his cards right, she was going to come back with him to his house in Rye, and that would be the end of all this nonsense of guns and bullets and thrift-shop dresses, he thought and grinned, and then looked up at the waiter. He was suddenly very hungry.

"We'll start with a hot antipasto, and a veal piccata, and"—his eyes ran down the pasta side of the menu— "lasagna. And two house salads."

He watched the waiter walk away and Arthur smiled to himself, as lascivious memories swished around in his head and wine swirled around in his mouth, and he lost himself somewhere in a Wednesday afternoon in a room in the Ambassador Hotel.

And he watched her walk back. She stood in front of the table and stared down at him.

"I ordered for you," he said, not taking his eyes off her.

"I'll eat your food," she said, and he exhaled. "After I get my bullets. Otherwise I'll not stay here a minute longer."

Arthur felt his mouth drop, and his face began to harden as it became good and clear to him that she was not going to be commuting up to Rye, New York, or anywhere else with him.

"What are you going to do with the gun, Dottie?"

"Bullets, Arthur, now."

She stared at him, and he pushed his chair back. She was beginning to piss him off. He could only do so much of this dance for so long. The waiter appeared, fearing for his order, and Arthur waved a hand at him.

"We'll be right back, Oscar," Arthur said without looking at him.

He followed Dottie to the front door of the restaurant and opened the door for her. He fumbled with the keys to the front of the shop, and let them both in.

"I'll be out in a minute," he said, walking to the back of the shop.

He stood watching her, reached into his bottom desk drawer, and took out a box of bullets.

Well, if this was the way she wanted it, then he'd oblige her. He turned the box on its side, just to make sure he'd picked up the right one.

He stared at the sticker and the black-and-red words: BULL'S-EYE RIFLE AMMUNITION. God forbid he give her ammo she could actually use. She'd probably shoot herself just trying to load the thing.

Yep, he thought, peeling off the sticker, that should slow her down. He tossed the sticker into the garbage pail next to the desk.

He walked back to the front of the shop. He sat down behind the counter, and he could see her eyes watching his fingers as he drummed them on the top of the box.

"Well?"

"Why do you want a gun, Dottie?" he asked again.

"Why do you care?"

"I just want to know."

"Like I told you, I got mice."

"You're not planning to do something stupid with it, are you?"

She gave him a cold eye.

"Like what?" She was icy. "You never cared one bit

146

about me. All you ever cared about was robbing banks. I was right not to trust you."

That did it. He tossed the box on the counter and watched her sweep it into her handbag.

"And now I'll be going, Arthur. Since I wouldn't want to chance you having to look at me in electric light." Her voice had turned harsh. "And I sure as hell don't want to look at your face either."

He watched her toss her head back and stand straight and, with great grace and dignity, her silhouette opened the door and softly closed it, and she was gone.

And as his heart halfway sank, the other half was busy being angry. He'd had such high hopes that candlelight and lasagna were somehow going to make up for the night before. For a moment there, he thought he was going to get away with it.

That swipe about the lights must have hurt, and hurt badly.

A lot worse than he'd intended.

He sat in the dark for a moment, then picked himself up and walked to the door of the shop to go back across the street and have his dinner. He figured it would take about twenty-four hours, but she'd be back.

He locked the shop and looked up and down the street. There was no one on it.

It would take her most of the night to figure out how to get the bullet chamber on the gun to open so she could load the thing, and then it would take a minute to figure out that she'd been given the wrong bullets. And yes, she'd be back. She'd get it into her thick head that she'd been rooked on top of it, and that would be an opportunity to come back up here and throw the thing in his face.

And he'd have another shot at this mess he'd gotten them both into with his stupid temper. He thought back on his little dream about a home and children with this woman, and somehow it struck him as darkly funny that the only thing their relationship had produced was a substantial robbery record and now perhaps a suicide attempt, although that was beginning to seem less and less plausible to him. Not the way she was acting.

And if he did begin to believe deep down inside that she was going to do away with herself, his last resort would be to report her to the authorities.

Christ, what was she going to do with that gun?

He stood at the corner staring at the big plate-glass windows of Gianni's. All this business chasing her around had really pointed up how lonely he was, and he felt this ache in his stomach as he crossed the avenue.

He'd go back and eat alone and he'd have them wrap up the lasagna, and he'd probably finish the bottle of wine by himself, have some shots of bourbon, maybe, get good and loaded to take the edge off almost having her again. And he'd pass out in the cab going home. In the morning he'd have Eva make him a big strong pot of coffee to soothe his hangover.

And then he'd wait.

DOTTIE held the top of the purse, which wasn't quite big enough for the box of bullets. She didn't know how many came in a box, but it was so large, there must be thousands for the gun he'd sold her.

She knew Arthur was telling the truth about the one-year mandatory if you got caught with an unlicensed gun. A year in a New York City jail.

The thought made her shudder.

She felt the clasp on her purse pop open again and she pushed it closed.

The cab screeched around a corner, and she was literally thrown against the cab door. To her horror Dottie watched the contents of the bag spill out. There was a deafening symphony of noises, as the box of bullets emptied itself onto the floor of the cab. And, as the cab straightened itself out again, the bullets rolled like the tide going out.

Roll, roll, roll, roll, crash. They piled up against the opposite door.

Jesus, Dottie thought, almost wishing that she'd just taken six out and thrown the box back at him.

It was her shopping principles. She'd paid for a whole box and goddammit, she was going to take the whole box!

The cab turned another corner.

Roll, roll, roll, roll, crash.

The tide of bullets rolled back in, and Dottie realized she'd better do something fast.

"What is that noise?"

"My purse just spilled out all over the floor, because of your crazy driving!"

Roll, roll, roll, to a clinking crescendo. It was a nightmare. Dottie sank onto the cab floor, desperately trying to scoop handfuls of bullets back into her bag.

"What did you have in there, lady?"

"You mind your own business!" she yelped at him. "You keep your eyes on that road. And slow down! We're not on our way to the hospital, you know!"

She had, by this time, gotten most of the bullets back into her purse. By the time the cab hit a red light and came to a stop, she was able to scoop up the last handful of bullets. And mercy of mercies, she'd crammed them into her bag just before the nosy eyes of the cabbie could focus on her.

She gave him a glare and daintily pulled herself back up onto the seat.

"Now you slow down and stop this crazy driving or you'll get no tip from me."

When the cab finally did lurch to the front of her building she threw the money at him, with as meager a tip as her conscience could allow her, and, as she opened the door there was the tinkling sound of the leftover bullets hitting the sidewalk. She coughed loudly, trying to cover up the sound, and slammed the door. She watched the cab bump off down the street, and she closed her eyes and said one quick Hail Mary that there were no more bullets on the dirty floor.

Or, if there were, that the cabbie'd somehow not think of her in connection with all this.

She tiredly climbed the stairs to her apartment. She automatically flicked on the television set. She placed her bag on the kitchen table and thought about making herself some toast.

Somehow, after narrowly missing the opportunity of lasagna, the idea of toast was unbearable. She filled a glass with water, unscrewed the bottle of Tums and chomped on her nightly dose of the pills. There was the familiar stiffness in her hip, after the long day. She sank down on the couch and gazed at the television set, not focusing on it.

The ticking of the clock made her think of the nice checkered tablecloths and the candlelight. And the candlelight made her think of Rivington Street.

Her earliest memories were of a cold-water flat and of being quickly changed into warm clothes. She had a lot of early memories, and in them the rooms were always dim, drafty places. And she remembered the smell of a sooty oil lamp that sat on a kitchen table with a cheap checkered tablecloth. Her family used that instead of the electric lights whenever possible. That was before they moved up in the world, and away from Rivington. Her mother had been best friends with Eileen Spinoza's.

Dottie O'Malley was the youngest of three; there were two boys older than she. She was born seventeen years after the younger brother, a fact her mother explained by saying,

"God's always surprising you in life, dear Dorothy. He saves the best for last."

And that was a very nice way to explain that she was obviously an accidental afterthought.

As a child in a household of adults, some bordering on elderly, she was largely left alone. There wasn't enough energy for her parents to deal with her, not that she was a tyrant or hyperactive, but a small child was simply too much for them.

Everybody was tired all the time. Almost all memories of her father were of him asleep in his chair in the living room. He worked as a bricklayer six days a week, week in and week out, and on Sundays he slept.

Every evening he would snooze, head tilted over, chin resting just below his right shoulder, mouth opened, eyes closed, his reading glasses slid down almost to the tip of his nose. She would play around his feet, and hope the glasses would someday drop into his lap. She didn't know why this was so exciting to her; she had no plans for the glasses, and knew there'd be hell to pay if she touched them. But it was just that anticipation of something happening.

The *Daily News* would be held open across his chest by his thick, meaty hands. They always had small scratches or nicks from the shards of brick that would splinter off as he'd stack loads on the trowel, and there'd be bruises too from dropping a brick here or there at the end of day when he was tired. Small dots of dried maroon-colored blood on the paper was evidence her father was home.

Even in the deepest sleep his hands remained magically suspended across his chest. The paper would make a crackling sound as his chest expanded and contracted with the snoring. It was kind of musical in a way.

Dottie doubted her father ever made it past the headlines

without falling asleep. Sometimes he could be roused for dinner and sometimes he couldn't.

Her mother ran the house. She was a big, sturdy woman in body, with beautiful, delicate facial features and flaming red hair. She reminded Dottie of a workhorse. Stern and strong, and efficient and mirthless. The only time she smiled was Sunday in church. Dottie had inherited her hair and looks and long legs from her.

Her mother was a schoolteacher, she taught second grade on the Lower East Side. She loved reading and books. She'd actually gone to college, her mother, which was a source of pride in the family. And she was well-spoken. Dottie was always taught to speak clearly without an accent. It was her mother's theory that proper speech and good manners would take you farther than all the money in the world.

And when Dottie's father was out of work her mother would support them by teaching during the day and taking in sewing and laundry to do at night. She could sew seams with the most delicate stitches Dottie had ever seen. And she could iron anything, from a sheet to a fancy ruffled shirt, with the same expertise.

It was the end of the Depression, and everyone worked and worked and worked, and at the end of each week there was very little money.

Dottie's eyes refocused on the television suddenly as she heard the name Arthur MacGregor.

There it was. That stupid documentary on Arthur. Once in a great while Channel 13 would run a series on "Fame in America," and for some god-awful reason, they'd chosen Arthur for one segment.

It was haunting her.

She leaned over to the set and was about to turn it off when she heard a voice-over of him talking.

His voice sounded very flat on tape. And she found

herself sinking down onto the couch and listening to him. He was talking about how to rob a bank. She felt her eyes close and for a while she let the sound of his voice lull her. He was telling about how dexterously he could remove a gun from a guard's holster.

"And you walk up behind; if you bump them you can reach around, unsnap the holster and pull the gun out while they're distracted, but you have to be fast."

And he was so proud of this.

Dottie shook her head and opened her eyes in time to see a picture of Auburn. And there you have it, she thought. Arthur's entire life.

Tomorrow morning she was going to figure out how to load that gun, and then tomorrow afternoon was going to be the end of this.

TERESA lay in bed staring at the set. She couldn't take her eyes off it. She'd never watched much of Channel 13 in her whole life, but she'd read in a guide they were doing a segment on Arthur MacGregor, and she was glued to the thing.

She was watching in the hopes of tripping Dottie up on that ridiculous story about her and Arthur MacGregor, but as she lay still, smoking cigarette after cigarette, everything seemed to bear out the fact that the Solid Citizen had indeed been involved with him. The pictures of the house on Rivington Street matched perfectly, all the stuff about jail; if she hadn't been involved with him then she was a great liar. Teresa sucked on her cigarette and wondered if she could ask Dottie for an autograph or something.

She looked at the clock. It was almost eleven. She stubbed out the cigarette and gazed at the set. When she was little, she used to have this recurrent dream about becoming a famous person. She'd read movie magazines and the tabloids with a vengeance. It wasn't just being famous, it was that you would get to know other famous people. She watched Arthur's face, and a small tingle went through her. Jeez, what it must be like to be famous, she thought, and felt her face cloud.

Now what was she going to do about those kids, who wanted to make her move down to Florida? Teresa turned off the light and rolled over to go to sleep to the sounds of a war movie.

ARTHUR hadn't been a big drinker for years, and he now remembered why.

He was terrible at being hung over. His eyes looked like two red sunsets. He was lying face down, hanging on to the desk in his claustrophobic little office, as if he were in a hurricane and the desk were his only hope of anchor. He'd gone through two pots of Eva's coffee and a roll, and taken several aspirin.

Nothing was helping. The only reason he'd made it to the store at all was that Moe had insisted on driving.

And had berated him the entire way.

He was up to no good, and Moe could tell by the odd hours and the carrying on with this woman he knew didn't exist.

Arthur had looked over at his pudgy mouth flapping and flapping mercilessly and wondered what would happen if he simply leaned over and threw up in his lap.

"Look at you, Pop, your life is going to hell."

"Aw, God, Moe, shut up. Turn on the radio, anything, but just close your mouth."

"No. I will not. Whatever it is that you're up to is going to get us all in trouble."

"I had a date—"

"Ha! At your age?"

"Why do you say things like that?"

"Because you know and I know there is no woman—"

"There is."

"Okay, what did you do last night on this supposed date?"

"We had dinner at Gianni's."

"Bull."

"All right, you're right. I didn't have dinner at Gianni's with her."

"There, you see?"

Arthur looked over at his son.

"I'll tell you the truth. I sold her the wrong-size bullets to go with a gun I sold her the night before."

"Pop—why would you sell her the wrong-size bullets?"

"Because I think she might be planning to kill herself and I don't know what to do."

There was a silence as Moe chewed this over in his head.

"You see, Pop, you can never be honest with me! Jesus Christ! Well, you're on your own. And if something happens, I'm not going to come to your rescue. I got a wife and kids and—"

"A dog and a cat, I know."

Arthur sank down on the car seat and listened to his son rattle on about the whole thing.

He was still lying face down on his desk thinking about all this when the door to his office was opened.

"I'm going out on a repair, I'll be back before lunch, you want anything?" Moe's voice was gruff.

"No." And with that the louse slammed the door.

Arthur pulled himself up in the chair and rubbed his face. He couldn't just sit here anymore. Sitting here was making him dizzy and nervous. He had to move around out in the sun and the air.

He wondered how Dottie was doing with the gun. He checked his watch. It was ten-thirty. He could slip out now, go back up to his house, get on his disguise and be back down at Dottie's in an hour and a half.

TEARS WERE streaming down her face. It was impossible. She couldn't figure out how to get these big bullets into the tiny little holes. She threw the gun and watched it skate in circles along the linoleum floor.

She'd been had!

And now she had absolutely no money left, and no money coming in, and all she had to show for it was two new outfits and a gun that didn't work.

She was at the end of her rope.

That was the only thing she could think of. She'd been screwed. She couldn't even rob the bank with the gun, bullets or no bullets. She couldn't get the barrel to snap back into place. Every time she thought she'd succeeded, the stupid thing flopped out the side.

How could this happen? She'd gotten so close and now this. So what was the alternative? Taking the train up to the Bronx and throwing the thing in his face came to mind. No, she wasn't going to give him the satisfaction.

She wiped her eyes wondering about what to do when she suddenly got an idea. She stood up and walked over to the kitchen cabinet and pulled out the ragged manila envelope. She pulled out the square of folded magazine pages, of which there were maybe twelve, and she began scanning the page for what she was looking for.

Her eyes landed on a section titled, "How I Did It." She picked up the pages, walked over to the couch, turned off the television set, sat down and began to read.

It was Friday.

It was noon.

She had three hours to learn how to rob a bank without a gun.

"IF THE PROCEDURE is not listed on our list of approved treatments for the condition, then we do not pay for it."

"I don't give a damn! I got this lump they're gonna cut out if I can't get this other thing done! Now, youse people are my only medical insurance. They got a experimental procedure that might save me going in for surgery. And that means youse aren't paying all them hospital costs. Now don't it make sense—"

"I told you. We do not have approval for the procedure—"

"Youse listen to me! I don't give a damn what the hell list you got, this whole program sucks!"

"I'm getting the guard—" the woman screamed at Teresa.

"You go right ahead. I paid my taxes just like everybody else. I got no other form of insurance. You pay for medical procedures and I got one here I wanna use!" Teresa was now screaming at the woman, leaning into her face so she was almost nose-to-nose to the woman.

And that was when she felt a heavy hand on her shoulder and she turned and looked up at a guard.

"You get your goddamn hands off me!" she yelled and in a flash she'd been lifted off the floor and was being carried through the hallway, through the crowded waiting room and out to an elevator.

By the time the guard had taken Teresa down through the lobby she was crying. She was pushed through a revolving door and stood in front of the building.

She couldn't believe it. They'd thrown her out onto the street.

★　★　★

ARTHUR stood in the hallway outside Dottie's door. He'd been standing there for two hours. He could hear her moving around inside under the blare of the television set. He held on to the monogrammed case which contained his picks and again debated letting himself inside.

And then what?

He could grab her and take her up to Rye and try to talk some sense into her. And then Dottie would probably whack him one right across the chin and storm out swearing she wasn't going to commit suicide.

He didn't know what to do, so he was going to wait. The fact that she was still at home maybe was a good sign. And what could she do with a gun with the wrong-sized bullets?

DOTTIE stood in her bedroom looking at herself in the full-length mirror attached to the inside of the closet door. She had made her plan, and now it had taken her an hour to choose an outfit.

She had opted for the little Chanel knock-off and a pair of black pumps with very low heels, which she could walk fast in, even run in, if necessary. She had decided not to wear jewelry on the basis that it would just be stolen from her, so she had taken off her earrings, the pendant her mother had given her that she always wore, and lastly, her wedding ring.

After digging around in her closet she found the large black straw hat she had worn to Nathan's funeral. It had a wide brim and a heavy ribbon circling the center. She'd taken a black chiffon negligee she'd never worn out of her bottom dresser drawer and with a pair of scissors cut the skirt part off. She pushed the fabric into the ribbon on the hat, making a thick veil which covered her face to the shoulders.

Somehow she thought it would be easier if her face was hidden; they wouldn't be able to see how afraid she was.

She had taken great care to put on makeup, and doused herself with what was left of a tiny bottle of My Sin perfume. A scent would be memorable and identifiable, and if the holding cell at the Sixth Precinct was smelly, it would cover it up.

She stood at the mirror giving herself one last look.

Stiffly she walked out into the kitchen, pulled out a green laminated-fabric tote bag, and slung it over her shoulder. That she would use to put the money in.

She took one last look at her apartment and slowly opened the door. In the hallway she could hear the sound of someone running up the stairs.

She locked the door and began down the stairs. It was two-fifteen.

Arthur stood pressed against the wall on the landing above, desperately trying to control his breathing so it didn't seem so loud. He'd made it up the whole flight of stairs in three steps, thanking God he was still in good-enough shape. He listened to the sounds of her footsteps as they got fainter. He waited until he heard the front door open and close, and then he made a dash for it. He ran down the flights of stairs taking the steps two at a time. He couldn't lose her.

Dottie squinted into the bright sunlight as she walked down the street. The sun was going down earlier and earlier, and there was actually a bit of a chill in the air. In the sun it was still hot, and the sky and the air were crystal-clear; it was a beautiful fall day.

She found herself walking faster and faster across Washington Place, toward Sixth Avenue. When she got to Sixth the light turned red and the heavy Friday-afternoon traffic stopped moving altogether up the avenue. She looked up at the clock on the Jefferson Courthouse one last time. She'd always loved that clock and that building.

Nathan, Jr., had always told her it was a castle. "A big magic castle, Mommy," he'd said.

But there were no magic castles or knights errant.

She was alone.

She felt her face begin to crack, and she stared straight ahead. The light turned green and Dottie walked stiffly and quickly across the avenue. Her heart was beginning to pound as she walked up past St. Anthony's Church and saw the Chemical Bank building.

She could see the guard's back and his gun holster as she approached the doors. She stood shaking like a leaf, at the side of the door, breathing deeply. She'd gotten here too early. It was only twenty of. And for some reason she refused to walk inside until exactly ten of three.

Arthur stood staring at her from behind the small planted garden in the triangle where West Fourth and Washington Place split. There she was, standing back in front of that bank.

There was something about that bank.

He darted across the street and up to the corner. He quickly made it across, to the side the bank was on, glancing at her as he ducked around the corner. She was pulling the veil over her face. He stared at the door on the other side of the bank.

He felt his legs propel him inside.

She knew if she stood still one second longer she would begin to panic and then she would lose her nerve, and once she lost her nerve she would never get it back. No, she had to do it now. Today. She thought back on the magazine article and suddenly echoing in her brain was Arthur's voice explaining how you grab a gun from a guard.

She'd fallen asleep listening to his blow-by-blow instructions the night before.

She took a deep breath. She set her jaw tightly and slammed open the glass door. Dottie was standing directly behind the guard. It was five minutes to three. There were five people on line and two tellers, and one visible customer service person. Two construction workers walked down the steps, waved to the guard, and left, apparently for the day. There were no lights on inside, just the temporary ones, meaning that the computers were down as well. The people on line were impatient now, as the tellers were doling out cash by hand.

A woman stared at her, she swallowed and looked at the floor.

Dottie stood frozen, not quite being able to move. The hand on the clock moved. It was four minutes before three now. Dottie began to feel the floor go out from under her. She was sweating and she kept trying to move, to do anything.

Arthur stood at one of the deposit-slip tables and kept his eyes glued to her. She was just standing there in that silly funereal hat with the veil over it. He wished he could see her face through it.

He glanced away for a moment and that was when it happened.

Two women, one with a newborn in a Snugli, walked in, knocking Dottie into the guard.

"What the—" she heard the guard's voice as he began to turn around.

Automatically, with the sound of Arthur's voice on that television show talking her through it, Dottie reached over to the guard's right hip.

Snap.

In a second, her hand was around the gun handle and she had slid it out of its holster with the smoothness and ease of a professional.

She stepped back holding the gun, and as if being led

through it by Arthur's voice she cocked it, just the way he'd shown her in the store two nights ago.

"Step back against the wall, sir. I am robbing this bank."

Behind her she heard a woman gasp, "Oh, my *God!*"

The fat man who'd followed her all the day before looked up and his mouth dropped open. And for a second he looked familiar.

Nobody moved.

"AGAINST THE WALL, NOW!" Dottie screamed out.

The guard's hands were up in the air and he had taken a couple of steps backward. She looked over at the customer service desk and saw a woman pick up the phone.

"Put it down. What's the matter with you? I have a gun," Dottie screamed. "Everyone over in the corner and get over by the tellers' windows!" she ordered.

No one moved.

The woman continued to dial the phone. And Dottie was left with no other alternative. She pointed the gun to the ceiling, closed her eyes and squeezed the trigger.

Bang.

The bullet hit the surveillance camera above the door, knocking it off its stand, and ricocheted with a thunderous *ping.*

All of a sudden the guard was on the floor holding his arm.

"Oh, my God. She shot him!" someone yelled.

The guard began screaming and there was a small pool of blood beginning to collect under his arm.

All five people stared at Dottie, who was openmouthed. She suddenly snapped to. "Anybody else? Against the wall, NOW. You, come out from behind the desk; tellers, out of there or I swear to God I'll shoot somebody else!" she yelled, and in a flash people ran to the corner.

A man in a very expensive suit ducked his head out from

behind a big door behind the Customer Service desk, and Dottie pointed the gun at him.

"You too. Anybody else back there?"

He went pale, shook his head and joined the small group now huddled halfway between the customer service desk and the tellers' cages.

And Arthur MacGregor was still leaning against the deposit desk in utter shock at what he was witnessing.

She wasn't planning to commit suicide.

She'd been planning to rob this bank.

What a jerk he was. He'd even watched her case it the day before.

There was no clear line of thought about what he could do about *this* turn of events. And then it hit; there was nothing *to* do.

She was armed.

She was robbing a bank.

And Arthur, like the other customers and the employees, was going along for the ride. After all these years to be on the receiving end of a bank job, he couldn't help but appreciate the symmetry in that.

Dottie stared over at the fat man who was just standing there, gaping, and she pointed the gun at him with a certain satisfaction.

"You too!" she said harshly and waved the gun toward where the other people were huddled.

So Arthur took out his cane, hobbled over to where all the other victims were and joined the circus watching two women try and bandage the guard's arm.

Dottie took a deep breath and walked over to the small Indian woman who'd closed her account the day before.

"Open the door," she ordered and she watched the teller's eyes slide over to the man in the suit, who nodded, pale. The teller opened the large door to the tellers' area and Dottie stepped inside.

Meanwhile, the two women who had pushed Dottie into the guard were kneeling over the poor man.

"Meg, diaper bag!" one woman ordered. "It's okay, let me look at it," she said, leaning over the guard, who was now shaking and beginning to go into shock. She gently pulled his hand away from his forearm. He'd been grazed, the bullet had gone through cleanly.

"Diaper," she said, holding her hand out, and immediately the second woman placed a Pamper in it.

"What are you going to do?" the second woman asked.

"Wrap it," the first woman said, unfolding the diaper. She gently slid it under the man's arm. He gave a howl.

"Okay, okay," she hushed him.

Arthur's eyes darted over to Dottie. She was pulling this off like clockwork, he thought, and an odd tinge of pride went through him. She'd disarmed the guard spectacularly well and these two women were now creating the diversion as if they were her partners.

She was just doing dandily, he thought proudly, assessing the situation.

The bank employees and customers were busy watching the two women work on the guard as Dottie was busy behind the tellers' area.

The area consisted of a long counter behind the glass, with high stools. Money was laid out carefully in denominations from singles to thousands in rectangular gray steel boxes which were inset in the white counter.

She pointed the gun at the bank teller. The woman was maybe twenty-five, and was definitely a first-generation immigrant from India. Arthur's voice from the night before prompted her to read the name on her teller badge. Her eyes then looked her in the face. She looked as if she was going to be sick. Dottie quickly handed her the laminated tote bag.

"Money, in the bag, please, Ms. Varishnu." And she watched the woman look puzzled at hearing her name said so politely, and for some reason, she seemed to relax. She blinked and nodded, and Dottie and she began working their way from one end of the counter to the other.

And Dottie could not believe the police hadn't gotten there yet.

Arthur, meanwhile, was smiling from ear to ear.

He was quite enjoying this. She'd even remembered to address the woman politely by name. Ah, Dottie O'Malley, you must have kept quite a close eye on me all these years, he thought. His eyes dropped back down to the guard.

"Tape," the first woman demanded and felt a bottle in her hand. She paused and looked at it.

"Bactine?"

"It's an antiseptic," the second woman retorted.

"It's for *minor* cuts and abrasions."

"So?"

"You call a gunshot wound a minor cut or abrasion?"

"It'll help sterilize it."

"Is anyone here a nurse or doctor?" the first woman asked.

"My cousin's a dentist," a man offered and everyone glared at him. There was always one of those during every job, Arthur thought. The kind of jerk all the employees secretly wished would get caught in the crossfire.

Everyone else shook their heads.

The woman looked down at the man. "What do you think?"

"I, I," he gurgled and drooled.

The first woman shrugged, opened the bottle and poured some onto the wound. Arthur winced deeply, and felt the seven people huddled around him all shudder at the same time.

The guard turned a bright shade of green, whispered "Oh no" and promptly passed out. The poor bastard probably was better off, Arthur thought.

"Tape," the first woman ordered, and the second one peeled off the masking tape and handed the piece to her.

At this point Dottie had filled the bag and ordered the teller out from behind the counter. She joined the others, and Dottie walked toward the door to Seventh Avenue.

It was three minutes after three.

She stepped over the guard and looked down.

"I'm sorry," she said to him, and then looked at all the people huddled in the corner.

She stood there and for what seemed like an eternity everyone was quiet inside the building. All of a sudden the lights flicked on, and the whir from the computers began.

And Dottie waited.

And she waited.

And Arthur felt like screaming out to her, "What are you waiting for? Get the hell away!" But he contained himself.

And there was not a sound. No sirens, no screaming police barging in the door, and everybody looked very puzzled.

"Thank you for your cooperation," Dottie said finally.

She dropped the guard's gun into the tote bag and walked out the door. On the corner, maybe two feet in front of her, was a cab about to cross Seventh Avenue. In a second, her hand lifted. The cab screeched his brakes, stopped, and she got inside.

"Where to?" a voice said.

"Sullivan Street." she mumbled.

The cab lurched forward and turned down onto Seventh Avenue, and Dottie stared out the window, stunned.

She'd done it.

She'd gotten away with it—so far. Her eyes went up to

the rearview, looking for police. There was nothing but buses and taxis, and cars on their way to the Lincoln Tunnel.

She couldn't figure it out for the life of her. She'd made every mistake in the book, she'd actually stood there waiting, and no one had shown up. And worse, she'd shot that poor man. She still couldn't believe it. She'd aimed right at the ceiling, she'd had no intention of hurting someone. It was an accident.

Her mind tripped through the last day and that television show came into her head and she suddenly felt oddly admiring of Arthur's prowess as a bank robber.

Thirty years and *he'd* never shot anyone.

Dottie felt this odd wave go through her. It began as nausea, and then became the oddest sensation.

It was almost a tingle, like . . . she felt like giggling.

Dottie felt light-headed. It was too absurd.

The cab came to a stop in front of her building. She dug into the shopping bag and mindlessly put a bill in the fare box of the divider. She slid out and realized her legs felt wobbly. She walked to the front door of the building, and heard the driver behind her.

"Lady, you gave me a hundred."

"Keep the change." Dottie's voice floated back to him and she let herself inside. She climbed the stairs and opened the door to the apartment. It was odd. It was as if she were someplace else and had been for the last hour, and she had simply been watching her body go through the motions, while her mind had hovered above it somewhere.

She put the shopping bag down on the table and mindlessly turned on the television.

Now what was she going to do?

★   ★   ★

"WHAT HAPPENED to the alarm system, goddammit!" the man in the good suit screamed at the teller, who began shaking.

"I pressed the button, Mr. Branington! I pressed it! Maybe the construction men disconnected it again. Nothing happened. There was no electricity again," the woman was shrieking back.

"You moron! You helped her!"

"She had a gun. She shot him!" one of the customers yelled.

Arthur stared at the man, who he figured was a bank executive. The man was berating everyone in sight for not getting between this "stupid old woman" and his money.

And you, he thought, staring at the man in the expensive suit, are the reason I got away with this for so long. Just to see jerks like you sweat.

They watched the branch president run out the door and onto West Fourth Street. And slowly, Arthur walked to the other door and slipped out of the building and onto Seventh Avenue. He looked around.

She was gone.

Silently, he walked across Sheridan Square and over and down three steps to a bar.

There were five men at the bar watching the play-offs. Arthur sat down and stared, almost as if in a trance, at the dark wood.

"What'll you have?"

"Bourbon shot," he said slowly.

The youngish bartender poured and placed it in front of him. Arthur downed it in one gulp.

Behind him he could hear the sound of sirens, and he braced himself and motioned to the bartender to refill the shot glass.

He sipped the second one slowly.

Well, she'd done it. And where, he wondered, was she

now? On her way out to the airport? Maybe the bus station or Grand Central, he thought.

Footsteps ran down the steps to the bar, and a man's voice yelled, "Hey, did ya hear? Some woman just held up the Chemical Bank across the square."

There was a chorus of "what?" and the sounds of bar-stools being pushed back against the wooden floor, a rush of bodies and footsteps running up the stairs. Arthur looked around and realized that the entire bar had emptied out. He stared at the bartender, who was leaning on the bar shaking his head.

"They're a nosy lot in this neighborhood, eh?" he asked.

The man smiled and shook his head. "Naw, they're press. Not often they have a story drop in their laps."

"Ah," Arthur said and stood up. "Do you have a phone?" he asked and the bartender pointed to a pay phone on the wall.

He walked over and tossed in a coin. He dialed and waited for the pickup.

Dottie's voice came loud and clear across the line and he hung up. Yup, just as he suspected, she'd gone right back to her apartment and was sitting there like a pigeon. Well, all he had to do was find a way to get her out of the city, and it being rush hour on Friday, that shouldn't be too difficult, he imagined. His car was parked up in Rye, he'd taken a car service down.

He frowned at the phone, hesitating to make the call he knew he was going to have to make; he certainly wasn't going to risk renting a car. Oh, no. He might not have committed the crime, but Arthur MacGregor was not going to have his name pop out of a computer showing he was anywhere near the vicinity of a bank robbery.

No, he was going to have to swallow his pride and make the call.

He picked the phone up and dialed again.

"MacGregor Pawn and Repair," Moe's voice came across the wire.

"Hello, Moe, this is your father," he said stiffly.

"Pop! Pop! Where are you? What's going on? I come back from lunch and you're gone, and Nyles said you didn't tell him where the hell you were going—"

"It was none of Nyles's business," Arthur started, and then realized he didn't have time for this.

"Well, it would have been nice if you could have told me—"

"Moe, shut up and listen to me!" he said sharply and he heard his son quiet down. "Now, I need you to get into your car and come pick me up. I got a little sidetracked, and I'm without my car."

"A little sidetracked; what are you talking about?"

". . . I have a date. She's going to spend the weekend with me and I need someone to drive us up there."

"So rent a car."

"I forgot my credit cards."

"So—aw, Jeez, Pop. I have a dinner to go to tonight, and—"

"This won't take any time at all, and I promise, I'll pay for your sitter. Just close the store now and come get me." There was an exhale on the other end.

"All right; where are you?"

"I'm on Sullivan Street, 156 Sullivan Street."

"Sullivan, where's that?"

"Greenwich Village."

"Aw, Pop! I figured maybe you were in Scarsdale or something."

"See you in about an hour," Arthur said and hung up before he got another lecture.

He stared over at the bartender, and walked back to the bar. He finished his drink and threw some money on the bar.

"Are there any clothing stores around here?"

★ ★ ★

TERESA was sitting in the kitchen of her apartment.

She was thinking of calling Dottie up and volunteering to help her rob the bank. Or at least see when she was going to do this crazy thing.

Actually, Teresa didn't give a damn about the bank, or not much. Right now she needed to be entertained, after the day she'd had. And there was only one person on the planet she could get that level of entertainment out of.

Dottie Weist, the would-be bank robber.

Just as Teresa'd gotten up to go get Fred's address book, the phone rang. She reached across the kitchen table and picked it up.

"Mother?" Tracy's voice nearly shrieked across the wire.

"What?"

"Why didn't you tell us?"

"Tell you what?"

"About what? About the breast cancer, that's what."

Teresa felt her mouth drop open.

"Who told you I had breast cancer?"

"I called your doctor to see what all these tests are that you've been going in for. Jesus, Mother! Why didn't you say anything?"

"They're not sure, and besides, what is there to say?"

"I don't know, but Jesus! There should be something you have to say about this."

"Well, there isn't."

"Now will you stop smoking those things? Now will you?" Tracy's voice was screechingly high.

"What's the point?" Teresa said tersely.

"God, I could just kill you! Listen, I called Fred and he's flying in tomorrow afternoon. He says that there's a good hospital right near him, where they know how to take care of women your age who have this sort of thing—"

171

"I got other plans," Teresa said through clenched teeth and hung up immediately.

Oh Christ, she thought, they're circling the wagons! Tracy'd gotten the whole posse together to force her to go live in Florida now. She couldn't do it. No, she was not going to live there, didn't any of them understand that? She had to call Dottie. As she passed the television set she flicked it on, thinking that it must almost be time for the news.

She walked into the bedroom and searched through the top dresser drawer for the address book. Just as she was taking it out of the drawer she heard a voice on the set announce that there was a "Special Report."

Teresa quickly grabbed the book and sat down obediently in front of the set. She had done this every time since Kennedy had been shot, whenever they had one of those "Special Reports." An anchor came on, and Teresa braced herself.

"Word has just come in that a guard was shot during the robbery of a bank in Greenwich Village. He is in stable condition at St. Vincent's hospital at this hour. The robber has been described as a white woman possibly between the ages of fifty and seventy. She was last seen wearing a pink wool suit, a black wide-brimmed straw hat with a heavy veil over it. She is between five feet four and five six, and weighs between 110 and 120 pounds. She is armed and dangerous. Anyone with information should contact police."

Teresa sat stunned, as the anchorman held his hand up to an ear and paused, listening to something over the headsets.

"Do we have the tape?" he said to no one. And Teresa leaned forward. "Yes, we have the surveillance tape, hang on, all right."

A fuzzy black-and-white videotape snapped onto the

screen and Teresa held her breath. Suddenly she watched Dottie walk into the frame.

Teresa gave a scream and stood up.

It was Dottie all right. In a nice suit and a silly hat. Teresa couldn't believe Goody Two-shoes had actually had the guts to do it. Never in her wildest dreams did Teresa think she was serious.

She stared and stared at the tape, almost as if she were memorizing the moves. A commercial came on, and Teresa sat very still.

Well, she thought, tossing the phone book aside, there goes that idea.

ARTHUR walked through the store and picked out a pair of blue jeans and a shirt. He tipped his cap to the man at the desk, who he noticed was wearing earrings, and slipped into the dressing room.

Within five minutes he had stripped off his disguise and gotten into the jeans and shirt. He walked up to the cashier and watched him do a double-take.

"I'll wear these out, please. And put these in a bag," Arthur said and handed the man the pile of clothing and a credit card, then thought better of it and took out cash. He handed it to the man, who gave him an odd smile.

As he left, the man winked at him.

Well, Arthur thought, every man's entitled to his own way of thinking. And as this was Greenwich Village, he knew people didn't generally go poking their noses into other people's business. That was one of the reasons he knew he could get away with stripping out of his clothes without raising more than an eyebrow. Now that, he ventured, was something he'd hardly have gotten away with on the Upper East Side. He found himself whistling as he

173

walked down the street. His chest naturally leaned just a bit forward when he walked and he always walked powerfully, in strides like a lion.

Well, he thought, in twenty minutes his son would be pulling up in front of Dottie's building and he'd trot up the stairs, and finally, after two days of this silly posturing, he'd take her back home where he definitely decided she belonged.

CHAPTER FIVE

DOTTIE had been sitting on the couch in front of the television, legs folded under her, rocking back and forth and holding herself around the chest with her arms.

The commercial faded off and there it was again, the fuzzy video of her behind the tellers' windows. She began biting her thumbnail and held herself across the chest with her other arm.

This was unbelievable! She got off the couch and started pacing.

She could not believe she'd gotten away with it.

So far she'd been featured on the news at four, five, and now six, and on Channels two, four, five, seven, and eleven.

Channel nine was preoccupied with the play-offs.

And now she sat watching an overly handsome middle-aged anchor again explain what she'd done and give a description.

Channel seven had the staff doctor do an entire insulting segment on how age can affect your brain.

Affect her brain! Her brain was fine. Maybe it was an act of desperation, but she knew exactly what she was doing.

So, while half the channels were busy excusing her behavior because of senility, the other half was busy telling the world in a tongue-in-cheek way that she was armed and dangerous—and then dubbing her the "the Geriatric Ma Barker."

How dare they! Maybe she had intended to get caught, but she'd accomplished a major crime, and—this thought really turned her stomach—she bet if she had been some young black kid, everyone would have taken it very seriously. But here she was, the laughingstock of the six-o'clock news. Was there no end to the humiliation? Dottie had never even imagined anyone in the press would take any interest in it. All she thought of was the way the judge would react.

Those bastards.

The only good it was doing, watching the television, was that she found out about the guard. He'd been already been released from St. Vincent's. Her eyes looked over to the clock in the kitchen. It was almost five-fifteen.

The worst part was now she had an option.

Since it hadn't occurred to her that she might get away with it, she had been prepared to go to jail. She really had. But about the time they started showing the video of her, and laughing at her, Dottie began thinking seriously of getting out of town.

She could keep the money and go live in Florida or California.

On the other hand, then she'd be nothing but a thief.

Just like Arthur MacGregor.

God, why hadn't he done something? No, that wasn't it either. It was that he didn't *care* enough to do something. She had to stop thinking of this. She had gone to Arthur to buy a gun. Period. And he'd sold it to her, just as she'd asked.

The creep.

An ad for an airline came on the television.

She stared at the rosy picture of the plane flying off to the Caribbean and she found herself imagining drifting off into the sunset on the plane. The news came on again, and she watched the weatherman make a joke about the bank robbery.

That cut it.

She was going to keep the money. She stomped into the bedroom and changed into the baggy dress she had been wearing that morning. She was going to get on a plane and go to Florida.

Or maybe she should go by train . . . or bus. God, she didn't know how criminals did all this planning.

She was going to buy herself a little apartment on the beach. She dragged a dusty suitcase out of the closet and put it on the bed.

She began packing, first quickly, then slowing, and tears began to run down her face uncontrollably. She was scared to death of what she'd done. She was going to get lost in some little town in Florida. She would keep to herself, and just stay alone. She wiped her cheeks, shook her head, and sniffled, trying to regain control of the tears.

She walked back into the kitchen. To hell with them all. She grabbed her coat, wiggled her feet into her low heels, and suddenly felt that she should move fast. She'd given the cops over two hours to find her, and that was enough. She turned off the lights and stared around the kitchen for just a moment.

Bang, bang, bang.

The unmistakable sound of a fist against the metal front door of her apartment startled her. Her heart jumped and her chest became so tight she couldn't inhale. She stood staring at the door, unable to move.

Bang, bang, bang.

Aw God.

It was over, the whole nightmarish thing was over. There was a relief in that. She slowly walked to the door, unable to breathe. She realized that tears were again streaming down her face, and suddenly she felt very stupid and very alone and very afraid of going to jail.

And the whole idea now seemed . . .

There was another bang on the door, and she lowered her eyes, weeping uncontrollably. She opened the door.

"Dottie?"

Her eyes flew up to Arthur's face, and she simply collapsed in his arms, crying loudly and shaking.

"I don't know what to do. I don't know what to do," she kept repeating into his lapel as he held her tightly.

"It's all right. It'll be all right, I promise. Come on," he said, gently wrapping his arm around her waist, and he watched her wipe her eyes with the palm of her hand.

"Get your coat," he said and then paused, "and the money. Where's the money?"

She pointed at the green tote bag, still sitting on the table. He nodded. As she pulled on her old coat, he spotted an old sweater hanging on a hook on the wall. Arthur folded it on top of the shopping bag to hide the bills and the gun. He would keep the bag until they got to Rye, then he could dispose of that and the gun.

He looked over at her, picked up the shopping bag and again wrapped his arm around her waist and led her out of the apartment.

"You have to calm down, I want you to count in your head to one hundred. I have my son with me," Arthur MacGregor whispered in her ear, and she nodded and swallowed and quickly began counting.

By the time they'd made it to the car she had counted to almost seventy and she was numb.

"I'll get in back with you," Arthur said loudly.

She nodded and slid into the seat, trying to avoid looking at Arthur's son, who appeared to be gaping at her.

Had he seen the stupid video? Had he put together that she was the woman with the veil and the gun?

Maybe not. She could no longer tell.

They all sat in silence, and Moe started the motor.

Dottie kept her head turned and her eyes looking out the passenger window as Moe began to maneuver the car over to the East Side. After a couple of minutes she felt Arthur slide his hand over onto her lap. It lingered on her thigh just above her knee and then he reached farther and took hold of her hand. He held it gently and she glanced over at him.

He kept looking straight ahead, as his hand began roaming around hers, and he gently caressed the top of her hand, up to her wrist, and slowly pushed his fingers between hers. He stroked up and down in between each finger and she realized that she was beginning to breathe deeply and normally again. It had been so long since someone had touched her and her hand began to feel warm and it was making her relax.

"So," Moe's voice rang out, somewhat startling her, "you're the one Dad sold the gun to, huh?" He let out a deep laugh which sounded exactly like Arthur's.

Her chest tightened. She pulled her hand away from Arthur's, and he immediately grabbed it back and held it tightly. She forced herself not to look shocked, and her eyes focused on Arthur's profile.

"What—"

"Dottie O'Malley, this is my son, Moe MacGregor," Arthur cut her off.

"Nice to meet you," she said, trying to suppress a quiver in her voice. "What did you say about a gun?" she asked.

"It was a joke my father was playing on me for not believing he was dating someone these last two days. Anyway, I'm glad to meet you, Dottie. May I call you Dottie?"

"Yes, Moe, of course . . . A gun! Your father has such a wonderful sense of humor," she said strongly, forced a chuckle, and gave Arthur a sharp jab in the ribs. She saw the corners of Arthur's mouth turn up. She realized she was doing all right; she could see it in his face.

She leaned back on the seat, and he began stroking her hand once more. She breathed out again and let herself get lost in what he was doing.

"Mind if I listen to the radio?"

"Don't turn on the radio!" they both barked at him and Dottie saw Moe glance up into the rearview, puzzled.

"I have a headache," Dottie heard herself say easily.

"All right," Moe said grudgingly.

Arthur continued stroking her hand and she felt herself slide down on the seat and lean her head on his shoulder. He put his arm around her and gave her a squeeze, and she could feel him kiss the top of her head quickly. He took her other hand and began caressing it. The fear began to subside and she suddenly felt very sleepy. He gave a small contented exhale and Dottie looked up at him and saw a smile on his lips and the crease and dimple it made right below his cheekbone and it struck her how handsome he still was after all these years.

Dusk had come and gone and the landscape changed from the glittery night lights of Manhattan to darkness and trees and one-family buildings with front yards. They turned off the highway and onto a smaller road into a residential neighborhood. Windows glowed with warm orangy light and shot elongated rectangles across the lawns. She could hear the sound of wind and the occasional barking of a dog. It calmed her further, the peaceful little houses and the trees, and made her feel that Chemical Bank and Sullivan Street and guns and bags of money were far, far away and she was safe here.

After an amount of time for which she couldn't account, the car slid up in front of a large colonial-style home and came to a stop.

Her eyes stared out at the house and the two slices of

lawn, separated by a brick path. There was a pumpkin sitting on top of the three brick steps, and the large dark-green front door was lit on either side with colonial-type lanterns.

It was the kind of house she'd seen in magazines, and she guessed that in a moment the door would fly open and Moe's children would shoot out of the place.

"Okay," Moe said, and Arthur opened his door and got out, carrying with him the shopping bag.

She waited until Arthur walked around to her door and opened it for her. She gingerly stepped out.

"I'll call you over the weekend, Pop. It was nice meeting you, Dottie," Moe said and waved and immediately pulled the car away from the curb.

Dottie turned and stared at the house as she realized it was Arthur's. She followed him up the walk, amazed that someone could live in a house this big all by themselves, and the odd thought that it must be hard to keep clean when you're alone crossed her mind.

Arthur took out the keys and let them inside.

"Take your coat off, you can hang it in the hall closet," he said and opened the door for her.

"Eva?" he called immediately, and walked off down the hallway.

Eva? There was someone here named Eva? A wife . . . after what he had been doing with her hand? She felt a real lightning bolt of anger, and then realized that she really had no alternative to being here and meeting his wife.

She took her big old coat and carefully hung it beside the half dozen men's coats and jackets. She ran her hand across a large cashmere coat, admiring its softness, and it dawned on her that it looked very expensive. She immediately closed the closet door and walked over and stared into the living room.

There was a fire going in the large fireplace. Silver candlesticks with long white tapers sat on the white-painted mantel, the kind with sedate dentil molding. The candles looked almost like sentries for the painting hung on the wall behind them. It was one of those Early American scenes, where everything had a masculine brownish cast to it. It was painted from the point of view of being high up on a mountain, looking down. There was a valley with autumnal trees lining the slopes leading down to river dotted with tiny boats.

To the right of the fireplace was a large television set, and to the right of that a colonial-style secretary. Delicate Dresden china figurines stood poised on the shelves. Women in lacy dresses, like the kind they wore in the seventeen hundreds, seemed momentarily frozen in the middle of a dance or sitting in poses.

A cream-and-maroon-striped sofa with two big pillows was centered in front of the fireplace, and a large coffee table sat in front of that. Dancing firelight reflected off the highly polished table.

At the far end of the room was a library area, with floor-to-ceiling bookcases filled with expensive-looking hardcover books. A chair that matched the sofa was placed there with a reading lamp and a footrest. The floor was carpeted in beige.

Everything was shiny and clean and restful.

There was a sound behind her and she turned and looked at Arthur. He had taken his coat off, and was carrying the shopping bag of money.

"Would you like to see the rest of the house?" he said and held his hand out to her.

She nodded and avoided taking his hand.

She was led into a formal dining room. A large dark wood table was set with two places. Two candles were lit and separated by a small vase of fresh flowers. Colonial-style china cabinets were filled with fancy plates and etched crystal glasses.

"This is the dining room," he said and she nodded.

He took her through to a country-style kitchen that was nearly the size of her whole apartment. Shiny copper pots hung over a cooking island in the center of the room. She could smell the roast cooking, and she began to get hungry. On top of the stove sat pots with what she guessed were vegetables, and on one counter was a big wooden bowl with a salad in it. Across the floor from the counter was a bay window with a table and chairs pushed in front of it so you could have your meal and look out over the garden. To the right of that was a back door. A rack of hooks was next to the door and there was a large pink sweater hanging off it. Her eyes scanned for Eva, who was nowhere to be seen. Arthur held his hand out to her.

"Let's go upstairs," he said, and she felt herself freeze against the counter.

"Your wife has very good taste."

He cracked a puzzled smile.

"My wife?"

"Eva."

"My housekeeper. You'll meet her tomorrow."

"Am I staying the night?" she asked harshly.

"Why? You got a hot date waiting for you?" he said just as harshly, and she turned to walk out the door. He darted over to her and put his hands on her upper arms.

"That came out wrong," he whispered into her ear. "I don't want to fight with you anymore, Dottie." She felt a ticklish rush go through her as Arthur exhaled hard, as if he were deciding how to say something. "If there's somewhere else you want to go, tell me; I'll take you wherever you want to go."

He waited for her to say something and he watched her lower her head and shake it from side to side.

"I don't have anywhere else to go," she said quietly.

Arthur silently led her back through the hallway near the stairs, and she followed him upstairs. There was a series of guest bedrooms, one converted to some sort of game room with some gym equipment, a television, stereo, and a dart board.

Arthur opened the last door on the floor and flicked on the lights, and she stepped into the master bedroom. It was the corner room and had windows on two walls, as well as two huge French doors that led out to a balcony. A large sleigh bed was covered in expensive sheets. In the corner were a marble-topped table and slipper chair, and next to that was a settee. It was the kind of room she'd seen displayed in Macy's catalog, or run in ads for fancy furniture places. She heard him lock the door behind them and watched him walk over to the desk. He flicked on the radio, and soft jazz filled the room.

Dottie felt overwhelmed by the big house and the fancy furniture, and suspicious of Arthur at the same time.

How did he know? How did he know where she lived? How did he know she was the bank robber?

He dumped the contents of the bag out on the bed and Dottie felt herself tense up as the gun dropped onto the quilt. She stared at all the cash.

He picked up the gun, deftly took the bullets out and the firing pin. She listened to the clink of them as they dropped on the bed. "We have to get rid of this," he said matter-of-factly, and then placed it on the nightstand.

He turned his attention to the money. He shuffled through it with a speed and expertise she had never seen before, and she stood silently. She felt another wave of fear, and there was something sad about watching Arthur Mac-

Gregor joyously pounce on the money and begin to count it with such speed and accuracy.

She felt herself begin to get a little dizzy. She stared at the table and chair and slowly walked over and sank down onto the chair. She placed her elbows on the cool marble top, and found herself almost crumpling up, until her face was leaning on the tops of her arms and she was crying.

"Looks like close to one hundred grand here."

"Oh, God," she moaned.

"Well," he chuckled and she shot him a glare. He wiped the grin off his face. "Here we are."

"Oh, please! Don't gloat, Arthur." Her voice was angry.

"Well, what are you going to do now? I retire and you turn into Ma Barker."

She shot him a glare, and then her look turned suspicious. "How did you know it was me? I waited for two hours for the police, I waited in the bank for them to come and get me."

"I was in the bank when you robbed it."

He swung his legs over and walked over to the dresser, where he'd placed the shopping bag from the clothing store. He dug his hand into the plastic bag and pulled out the cap and the eyeglasses. He put them on and turned around.

She let out a small cry deep in her throat.

"Aw, God! I thought you looked familiar, it . . ." She was stammering and then her eyes narrowed. "You've been following me."

"For two days now."

"Aw, God! So you let me make an idiot out of myself last night? How could you? What? Were you laughing at me? Did you think this was some sort of a game?"

Her eyes were looking at him almost horrified. The hurt on her face was painful.

"No, no—I didn't know what it was. I thought you were

desperate . . ." He took off the cap and the glasses and took a step toward her.

"So you felt sorry for me." She held the back of her hand up to her lips and turned to the door. "I have to go."

She began turning the lock, and he came up behind her; he gently put his hand on her shoulder.

"Where, Dottie? Where are you going?"

"Why should it matter to you? You don't care about me, remember?"

He slid his hand down her back to her waist and pulled her into him. She felt him warm her back, and hold her firmly around her waist.

"Now, that's the biggest crock ever to come out of my mouth and you know it. Now talk to me. Why were you trying to get caught robbing that bank?"

She stared straight ahead, trying to think of a way to explain her reasoning—which now seemed utterly insane to her.

Words began spilling from her mouth, and he kept his arm around her waist, and she kept herself pressed up against him.

"Oh God, I'm just so tired . . . After Nathan died, they cut off his Social Security. I don't get anything until I'm sixty—but it was all right, I had a job at a coffee shop and I could just about make it, you know? Until I fell. I broke my ankle and my wrist. I don't have any medical insurance— my last job was off the books. I had to use all my savings . . . And by the time I came out of the hospital, I'd lost my job. And things just got worse and worse, and no one would hire me. Just a lousy secretarial job . . . I saw this thing on the news about this guy in Minnesota who'd robbed a gas station to get sent to jail because, hell, they spend all this money to keep people clothed and fed and their health taken care of in jail that I—I just thought . . . I didn't know what to do, Arthur. They're going to evict me. I can't afford to eat, I can't afford clean clothes, I went on job interview after job interview this summer and they—goddammit! They laughed at me . . . and I'm just so tired." She turned, and cried a good long time against his chest. He held her strongly, and rocked her gently back and forth. Finally, she looked up at him.

He stared down at her lips.

He reached a hand out and turned off the lights. And he slowly leaned down to give her a gentle kiss on the lips because he couldn't stand it anymore, and he because he wanted to see if she'd let him.

In a moment her arms were wrapped around him and he could feel how soft her mouth was. He found he was shaking, and they were both hanging on to one another as if the other person were going to melt away if they let go.

He began hungrily kissing her neck and up to her ear.

"Oh, Jesus, Dottie. You came to me for protection and the only thing I did was sell you a gun." She pulled her face away to look at him.

"Don't let go of me. Don't. I should have gone with you, Arthur MacGregor, when you came back for me. I just couldn't go through another trial. I couldn't stand the thought of you . . ."

"Ssh. I don't care anymore. You're here now."

She heard a little moan deep in his throat and then she wrapped herself up in him as his hands rubbed up and down her back and across her hips, down her thighs, lifting her skirt. His hands slid off her underwear, which floated down somewhere to the floor.

She leaned her head back and felt herself being backed to his bed.

He felt her drop down onto the mattress, and he stopped touching her. He was so hard that if she didn't touch him soon . . .

187

He was pulled on top of her with such strength it almost seemed to throw him in the air.

Ah, God, that was what he had been waiting for.

The words "in me" traveled along her exhaled breath, and he was rolled onto his back and she was on top of him. She fumbled with his belt and they both pulled his pants off and in a second he was there, inside her, and she was biting his neck and earlobes, and sliding up and down with almost a violence and whispering her demands of exactly what she wanted of him and how, and how much and how often . . .

And Arthur came.

As he had not come since 1962. She was back. She was all his.

WHAT THE hell am I going to do about my kids? Teresa lay back in bed, shaking her head and staring at the ceiling.

Florida. A hellhole, as far as she was concerned.

Her eyes darted over to the clock next to her bed.

And that stinking hospital. They couldn't tell her what the tests were but they had no problem blurting out her business to Tracy. And by ten o'clock in the morning, Fred, Jr., would be on his way in from the airport, and the two of them—she didn't even count that fool Tracy was married to—they were gonna throw her out, like some kind of garbage, to some geriatric hospital in Florida.

She was fifty-seven!

She didn't belong in some home. And she knew, no matter what they said to her, that was what was going to happen. The wife would get tired of her, and then they'd wait until she was weak enough and they'd move her into a home.

And suddenly the peculiar thought that the one person

she could see trading places with right now was Dottie O'Malley Weist hit Teresa deep inside.

She wondered where Dottie was and what she was doing.

Probably on a plane halfway across the world by now. That's what Teresa would do. And now that she thought of it, she thought it was very laughable that Dottie'd duped her entirely with that cockamamy story about trying to get caught. Jeez, for all she knew Arthur MacGregor helped her plan the whole thing.

All that crap about Medicaid. That was just stupid. So maybe they were both on a plane somewhere together.

Well, good for her. After the last couple of discussions with her, Teresa could see she was a woman in need of a little happiness. And the fact she got it robbing a bank, well, God has a funny sense of humor.

So, she thought, staring at the clock, what the hell am I gonna do about this crap of moving me down to Florida?

BRIGHT moonlight was streaming in through the windows, and a small breeze was lifting the lace curtain up through the windows on one side of the room, and on the opposite wall, the curtains were being pushed outside by the flow of the air.

She lay quietly on the bed, looking across the room to which she'd awakened with a start. For one second she couldn't fathom where she was, and the memory of the dream she had been having, of the guard lying on the floor and the blood, came into her head. A violent shiver went through her.

She felt Arthur's weight shift in the bed next to her and his arm fell across her, almost as if he were reaching out in his sleep to hold her. She exhaled and wrapped her arms around him. A wave came over her of feeling so very safe in the room with him. She'd forgotten that.

Dottie felt herself exhale, and she stood up. She took a small lap blanket off the edge of the bed and wrapped it around her shoulders and walked over to the window. She stared out on the lawn and listened to the alien quiet.

In all her life she'd never woken up to such quiet.

She walked back over and stood in front of the armoire and looked at the back of Arthur's head, and watched how the covers moved up and down with his easy breathing. She stared at the armoire door and silently opened it.

She looked at the neatly hung suits and ran her hand over the sleeves of them. She opened a drawer and looked at the laundered shirts from the cleaner's, fastidiously folded into rectangles and bound with blue strips of paper.

There was the sound of a clearing throat, and she looked in the mirror at the reflection of Arthur standing behind her.

"I was just . . ."

"Snooping," he said and wrapped a throw quilt from the bed around them both.

They stood before the mirror admiring the image of the two of them together, and Arthur leaned down and rubbed his cheek against hers. She could feel the sharpness of the stubble on his cheek, and she tilted her head.

"I need a shave," he said and she nodded and he gave a little sigh. "You hungry?"

"Yes."

"So am I. Why don't you get back in bed?"

He walked her over to the bed and she slid beneath the sheets. He tossed the blanket over her and slipped on his pants and a shirt.

"I'll be back in a minute. There's a bathrobe in the armoire."

She watched him walk to the door. She lay back on the pillow and sighed. Arthur watched her face relax into a glow

190

he knew he'd put there, and that was making her breathtakingly beautiful to him.

"I'll make sandwiches."

She watched him leave the room, and she looked up at the ceiling.

Well, here she was. She'd robbed a bank, she'd shot the guard, she was wanted for armed robbery in New York City, and she was on the lam and being hidden by Arthur MacGregor the notorious bank robber.

And Dottie O'Malley Weist hadn't felt so safe in years.

She got up and went back into the armoire and pulled out a silk bathrobe. She tied it around her and found herself running her hands across her upper arms, smiling at the way it felt and smelled of him. She flicked on the lights and dimmed them.

Arthur stood at the top of the stairs dangling his foot off the top riser. In a sudden bolt he hopped down three steps at a time, and hit the hallway running.

He tore through to the kitchen, turned on the lights, and stood breathing deeply. He'd just wanted to see if he could still do it.

After about ten minutes Arthur returned with a tray containing two sandwiches and two bottles of beer.

She felt a smile slide across her face as he placed the tray on the nightstand. He glanced up at her, then turned away. She heard him unbuckle the belt to his pants, and he paused. He was aching to see . . .

"Come here," she said sternly, and he turned and there was a lustrous smile on her face.

He slid in next to her and watched her unbutton his shirt, with that serious, determined look he'd thirsted for. He watched the shirt go flying, and his pants get unzipped, and those get tossed. She glanced up at him, and her serious expression melted away into a big smile, and he slowly rolled her over onto her back and began to caress her.

THE CLINKING of metal against china stirred Dottie back to consciousness. It was morning and the wind had changed. The heavy crocheted lace curtain on the opposite wall was now blowing back through the window and gently hitting a knife balanced on the edge of one of the sandwich plates.

She stretched her arms up, and then pulled them back under the warm bedcovers, and slid down until they covered her, as she used to do when she was a child. The bed linens seemed to be the softest she had ever felt. She heard the door to the bathroom open and she pulled herself back up and peered over at Arthur. She watched him pat his face with a blue towel that was slung around his neck.

She pulled herself up onto the pillows and he sat down on the bed, and they just beamed at each other. He began running his hand alongside her on the quilt, and then up and down from her shoulder to her hip, and he stopped there at her hipbone and rubbed in a circle. There was a gurgle from her throat, and she began sinking back down into the bed, with her eyes closed.

"No, no, you have to get up, Dottie, we have a lot to do."

"I don't want to do anything else."

"Come on, we have to do things."

Her eyes opened and she stared at him. "Like what?"

"We have to get you some clothes, and I have to call Sid."

"Who's Sid?" Her voice was just a bit panicky.

"My lawyer. Listen, I have an errand or two to run. Why don't you get ready?"

It was close to nine when Dottie walked downstairs. There was the whir of a vacuum cleaner in the living room. She could tell by the way it was changing pitch that it was being pushed hard against the carpet. There was the smell of lemon furniture polish and Windex.

Dottie braced herself to meet this housekeeper. She stood at the door to the living room and stared at the very large woman inside. She coughed loudly and the woman looked at her and showed a very broad gap-toothed smile.

"Mrs. MacGregor, congratulations. I am happy for you. I am Eva. Mr. MacGregor said to have breakfast ready when you come down. Come with me."

She held her hand out and gave a hefty shake. Dottie followed her down the hall, and was led into the kitchen. The table near the window was set and there were rolls and jellies and butter. She slid into a seat and Eva brought over a large pot of coffee.

"You want a paper?"

"Oh, yes," Dottie said, lowering her eyes, and immediately a copy of the *Daily News,* with a huge grainy picture of her in her suit and large veiled hat, was placed before her eyes. She immediately placed her arm across it and leaned her chin on her hand.

"Oh, that's fine, Eva. Thank you very much," she said, trying to control her voice.

"You want eggs and bacon or waffles?"

"No, no. The rolls are fine." She flashed a smile up at her.

Eva returned her smile, which vanished immediately, and went over to the sink. She turned on the tap and began rinsing off dishes and putting them in the dishwasher.

Dottie opened the paper and began reading about the police and the guard, and the theories about her. A line reading SEE EDITORIAL, PAGE 28, seemed to leap off the page at her and she immediately turned to the editorial page.

POVERTY AND WOMEN, the headline read.

"Is sad, ya? The woman who robbed the bank," Eva said evenly, turning around.

"Oh? Someone robbed a bank?" Dottie said coolly and then glanced at the paper. "Yes, that is sad," she added nonchalantly, and exhaled as Eva seemed to turn back to her work.

Dottie was just about to read the editorial when there was the sound of Eva clearing her throat. She looked over at Eva, who was sponging down the counter. Her face had a frown-scared look to it, and she kept her eyes on the counter.

"Mrs. MacGregor," she began, and looked at the sponge very seriously. "You have no more need of my services? Maybe?"

"Oh no, Eva."

"Yes, well, if you think I may not be needed, I would like to know as soon as possible."

"I see."

"I have two children. And my husband in construction. He been out of work now and—"

"No, Eva, we'll need you full-time," Dottie assured her.

Eva kept looking seriously at the counter, as if no matter what Dottie said, this was going to end badly for her.

"Eva, my health is not so good," Dottie said after a moment, and she saw Eva's large, flat face relax. With a small exhale, she looked up at her.

"It not serious?"

"Oh, no. But I can't do any heavy work, or a lot of shopping."

"Cooking?"

"I'm a terrible cook."

Eva looked very happy at that.

"I cook good," she boasted and left the room.

Dottie finished the coffee and a roll and was just about to

go back to the editorial when she heard a car horn honk outside.

She quickly walked to the front hall.

"Eva, I'm going," she called out to her, and the vacuuming stopped and Eva appeared at the living room door.

"I make stew?"

"Fine," she said, putting on her old coat. She smiled at her, and Eva disappeared back into the living room, and Dottie hurried out to meet Arthur at the car.

In forty minutes they were at a large mall in Westchester. It stretched over the landscape, large white buildings the size of airplane hangars with logos of store names in letters six feet high.

NEIMAN MARCUS.

MACY'S.

LORD & TAYLOR.

SAKS FIFTH AVENUE.

HARRY WINSTON.

Arthur opened the car door for her, and Dottie got out and looked at all the buildings. She clutched her old coat closed, and they walked inside.

It was even more amazing inside the mall. There were trees and fountains and music. And the air reminded Dottie of some kind of carnival. It smelled of hot dogs and popcorn and fancy perfumes. The people walking around were all very well-dressed, women her age with well-coiffed hair and expensive clothing and makeup, many carrying shopping bags. Dottie kept holding her ratty old coat closed and tried not to look at any of them.

She felt out of place.

Arthur led them into a large department store, and over to an information booth. Dottie stood looking at the glass counters filled with beautiful bags and scarves, or intimidating bottles of scents with fancy stoppers. She watched Arthur walk over to her and pull out his wallet. He leafed through it.

"What are we doing here?"

"We're buying you clothes."

"No."

"Yes."

"These places are too expensive."

"You're the only woman I've ever met whose arm had to be twisted to go on a spending spree," he whispered at her, exasperated.

"It's a waste of money."

"Dottie, you can't go around dressed like that."

"Yes."

"No." He was about to continue the argument when a thought suddenly occurred to him. "Look, if you don't look like you were born in Larchmont, you are just going to draw attention to the both of us. And that could put me in a rather peculiar position."

"Like what?"

"Well, aiding and abetting, sheltering. Now, they may believe I wasn't in on it, but let's face it, I hid you out."

"Is that why you need to talk to Sid?"

He nodded.

"No."

"Am I right?"

"Yes, but—"

"Good. Now, your name is Dorothy MacGregor, you're my wife, you just got out of the hospital and nothing fits. I want you to buy everything you need. I want you to get a good winter coat, and dresses and slacks, and jeans and sneakers, and nightgowns. I want you to have your hair done and buy makeup."

"Arthur, I don't have the money—"

He leaned in and whispered in her ear, "You have almost a hundred grand in my armoire."

196

"That's not mine. I can't touch that!" Her eyes flared at him, and he gave a chuckle.

"All right, you have the limit on my credit cards—"

"I can't afford this."

"Dottie. You have to stop this with the money."

A woman came up beside them with a name badge upon which was written, "Hello, my name is Frieda." Dottie looked at her suspiciously and cleared her throat, smoothed her coat, and looked at her.

"Mr. MacGregor?" she asked.

"Yes."

"You need assistance?"

He darted a glance at Dottie, and immediately said, "Yes. I need you to help Mrs. MacGregor here."

"Arthur!" Dottie wailed, as he handed the woman several credit cards.

"She's to get a complete wardrobe, a haircut, and cosmetics."

"Arthur," Dottie's voice had a warning tone.

"And she's not to look at any totals or any price tags," he said and gave Dottie a quick kiss. "Now I have to go see Sid. I'll be back at five." He took a few steps and turned back, walking backward out of the store. "And nothing from Chanel, you know how I can't stand that."

"Never," Dottie said quickly. "I hate Chanel."

They watched him walk off and Dottie looked at the woman, whose smile faded immediately.

"I don't want expensive things. We're not running up his credit-card bills, so if you think you're going to just sell me anything, think again."

"Yes," the woman said, taken aback.

Dottie took a step, then turned back.

"And I am perfectly capable of picking out my own clothes." She took another step, then turned back.

"Yes, Mrs. MacGregor." Her tone had become icy.

"And I don't need some kid telling me how to dress."

The woman looked entertained by that.

"Just how old are you anyway?" Dottie sneered.

Frieda gave a wide smile. "I'm sixty-three, Mrs. Mac-Gregor."

And Dottie's mouth fell open a bit and she stepped back and looked the woman up and down.

"Should we start with sportswear?" the woman asked.

Dottie coughed and looked at the floor and mumbled, "That would be fine."

"ALL RIGHT Mother, all right!" Tracy's voice was high and raspy.

She darted a glance over to her husband and rolled her eyes.

"We're not talking about some hellhole—"

"Yes, you are."

"Mom, Florida is not a hellhole. It's one of the biggest resort states in America. People fly there from all over the world to vacation . . ." Fred, Jr., was staring at her. He seemed nervous.

Teresa stared at the three of them sitting at her kitchen table. Tracy's jaw, when it wasn't busy flapping at her, was busy loudly snapping a wad of chewing gum. For some reason it made her sunken cheeks look even skinnier and she looked hungry. Her husband was sitting with his arms crossed over his slightly spreading stomach, and he would look away quickly whenever Teresa tried to make eye contact. He'd always done that to her; maybe that was why she never fully trusted him. The man couldn't look you in the eye.

Her eyes turned to Junior. Now, he was a sight. He didn't look a thing like her son. His hair looked as if he'd had some kind of accident with a Clairol bottle; it was about twelve shades too light. It had been cropped very short on the sides and was almost a crew cut on the top. His skin, usually a kind of sallow color from the mix of Teresa's olive skin and Fred's pink, was the color of café au lait. He had on a fussy bright-pink shirt, a pair of khaki shorts, and Top-Siders. A pair of mirrored sunglasses was hanging by strings from around his neck. He looked like some kind of model, but when she looked at his eyes, there was something dead in them.

"Yeah, well, there ain't no accounting for taste." Teresa gave a final drag on her cigarette and smashed it out in the ashtray.

"Look, Mom, we'd love to have you. Annette and the kids are all excited, and we have plenty of room."

Teresa's eyes narrowed. "Of course you got room, half your house got blown down in the hurricane."

"I told you, we have all the walls back up, and the place'll be painted and ready by the time you get on the plane."

"I ain't moving to Florida, and that's final."

"Well, Mom, you can't live here anymore. The neighborhood's gone to hell, and we can't traipse up here twice a week with food because you won't come and live with us on the Island," Tracy snapped, and stood up.

"Now, we're going to start packing up your stuff and we have a plane ticket for you for tomorrow afternoon—"

"I ain't moving!" Teresa felt her eyes begin to fill. "I told you, I like it here, I been here my whole life. If your father was here—"

"Well, he isn't—"

"Yeah, you noticed. Your father's only been dead five and a half weeks, and you're going to move me all over the planet!"

"For your own good."

Teresa let out a damp cackle and coughed.

"This ain't got nothing to do with my good. This is your good. I love this neighborhood. And your father and I swore we'd never leave it till we died, and my life ain't over yet, don't any of youse understand that?" Her voice rose to fever pitch, and Teresa stood up and placed her hands on her hips. "And not you or anyone is gonna order me anywhere, you hear me?"

She watched the three of them exchange glances, and Fred exhaled loudly and stared at the tabletop.

"Mom, we're not paying the rent on this apartment anymore."

"So what?" Teresa snapped at him. "You think I ain't got no other means than the three of youse? To hell with all of youse!" Teresa grabbed her purse, pulled open the apartment door, and walked out, slamming it hard.

She walked quickly to the top of the stairs and stopped. Now what? She didn't know what to do, she just had to get out of there. She felt like running away. Trying to get control of herself, she stared down the empty flight of stairs. Inside the apartment she could hear their voices.

"Let her go."

"But it's dangerous out there."

"Fred, you been in the sun too long." Tracy's voice snapped. "Just let her run off some steam, she'll be back as soon as she realizes she doesn't have any choice. It's not like she has some secret bank account hidden somewhere."

"You sure?" Fred's voice asked.

"Like I told ya, she don't got enough to loan you to get your house fixed and we don't got enough to loan you for the house. At least this way Annette can go back to work and there'll be someone there to look after the kids."

"Yeah, but what about this breast thing?"

"It's just a biopsy, they don't really know anything. And if something happens, she has Medicaid."

Teresa wiped her cheeks with the back of her hand, and began descending the stairs. She was still crying when she got to the second-floor landing. She didn't know where to go, or what to do, but she was sure as hell not going to be shipped down to Florida.

AT A QUARTER to six Dottie went to the information booth. Her hair had been restyled and was now brushed forward with bangs, so that it framed her face and cheekbones. She wore makeup of peach tones and a light red shade of lipstick that made her face glow. She was dressed in a green silk blouse and black wool pants which seemed to state that this was a woman who had always taken good care of herself.

She had on earrings and a matching gold necklace and pretty black shoes, and Arthur stood holding his coat with his mouth open as she approached. The happiness on her face was exactly what he had been hoping for on his drive back to the mall.

It was either this or he figured she'd still be wearing the same dress and coat he left her off with, and there would be at least one saleswoman in this mall who would eternally curse Arthur MacGregor.

Behind her were several people carrying boxes and shopping bags, and Frieda looked as if Christmas had just come to her house.

"Well, Arthur," Dottie said, "ready to go home?"

"Yes, ma'am," he said and watched a man hold out a flaming red coat, and she slipped into it.

He watched the small group of men with boxes and bags follow her out like a small parade, and he turned to Frieda.

"Thank you. This was better than I hoped for."

"No trouble, Mr. MacGregor," She answered and handed him the bill.

He laughed out loud at the number and thought that it was going to be time soon to travel up to Poughkeepsie to make a withdrawal from one of his safety-deposit boxes. He handed Frieda a two-hundred-dollar tip and left.

She had filled the trunk and the backseat with boxes, and sat next to Arthur smiling and looking out the window at the houses and the sunset.

"So," she said, and flicked on the radio. "How was your meeting with Sid?"

"Fine; he's at the house." Her smile drooped. "He'll have dinner with us," Arthur added.

She shifted uncomfortably in the seat. "Does he know?"

"Oh, yes."

She put her hand on the armrest and covered her eyes with it.

"You look beautiful," he said, and she looked over at him.

"I do?" A smile went across her face.

"Yes, and I'm very proud of you. You actually spent money. That tight fist of yours actually opened."

"I'm going to pay you back every cent—now stop teasing me."

"I can't help it. And I don't know what I'm going to say to Sid."

"What do you mean?"

"I spent the entire afternoon telling him what a poverty-stricken, weak old woman you are."

SIDNEY ARNOWITZ was sitting in the living room when they entered, drinking a diet soda and watching the news. He got up and gaped at Dottie.

"This is the woman?" he said to Arthur, as he dropped

202

an armful of shopping bags on the hall floor. "This is the weak, old woman?"

"We went shopping."

"Yes," he said and stared at the plethora of bags on the floor. His face became even longer as Arthur left and reappeared with more bags.

"You bought out the mall?"

"Now, Sid," Arthur said and helped Dottie off with her coat. Eva appeared from nowhere and took both their coats.

Arthur asked Eva to open a bottle of wine, and she nodded and told Dottie how nice she looked and that it was a great improvement from that morning. And then she tripped over her words trying to say that she didn't mean that she hadn't looked good that morning. She quickly excused herself and tromped off down the hall.

Sid seemed to be frowning at Dottie when she looked up at him, and they both looked away.

The video of Dottie was playing on the television, and she froze in front of the screen.

"So this is the problem." Sid's voice rang out behind them, and he waved.

Dottie had sunk down onto the couch and was staring at the video.

"Why don't I give myself up now?"

"You could do that," Sid said, and looked at her, "but I say you do it Monday morning; that way we could get you out on bail."

"So you think they'll post bail?" Arthur asked, sitting next to Dottie.

"I'd be surprised if they didn't. The only reason they might not—and this is where you come in, Arthur—is if they found some kind of connection with you."

Dottie felt her jaw drop and she looked at Arthur, who had a scowl on his face and kept his eyes steady on Sid.

"Come on, Sid, you don't have to scare her like this—"

"I'm not scaring her, I'm being honest."

"I haven't gotten so much as a parking ticket in seven years—"

"Look, the press gets ahold of this, they'll have a field day. First, it'll make her look even worse, because they can say you talked her into it."

"But I hadn't seen Arthur for thirty years when I decided to do this . . ."

"It doesn't matter. Guilt by association. And you are guilty, and this isn't some joke. And the criminal justice system, they aren't going to be so charitable as to look upon you as a starving poor old woman, you got it? You are a felon who shot someone, got it?" His voice was harsh.

"Sid . . ." Arthur's voice rose in warning.

"No. Let's get things straight right now. That statue of American Justice—the *blindfolded* woman with the scales— is blindfolded for a reason. The jury is told, we are told, in deciding a verdict, is there a reasonable doubt of guilt? Period. Did you commit the crime as described in the law books? In your case the answer is yes. You did. The police have a tape showing that. And so does Channel seven, two, four, and five, and for all I know, CNN and the BBC at this point. Now I would be a fool if I walked into the courtroom and planned to defend you any less seriously than that. And I do take what you did seriously. There is a good chance you're going to jail for fifteen years as it is. You want his name brought into this? Even if a judge gave you the benefit of the doubt. . . ." Sid's voice was loud, and his arm shot out and pointed to Arthur.

Dottie couldn't take her eyes off this man in front of her. She was shaking, and spine-withering fear went through her as the image of him doing this in front of a judge and jury came into her head, making the whole thing frighteningly and immediately real after her day of cheery shopping in White Plains.

"You connect her to the name of a known repeat offender, the bench is not going to ignore that. And even if they say, aw, it's okay, he's probably harmless and she just had a bad day, then the press is going to pounce on them. You could get a mess of editorials about the privilege of being white and old; then you'll get the racial debate . . ."

"That's ridiculous—"

"Yeah, but it'll sell more papers longer, it's called building up the story. And I'd say you already have enough press."

They were all quiet for a moment.

"I should leave here—"

"No," Arthur said quickly.

"Yes."

"No! I am not leaving you alone—"

"Arthur, listen to reason," Sid began. "She can stay till Monday—providing you don't pull another stunt like this shopping trip, okay? No one can know who Dottie is. And after she turns herself in, you have to keep your distance. I'm not going to have to deal with the issue of you in the press—"

"But—"

"No buts, or you get another lawyer," Sid said sharply, and they were all quiet for a moment. Arthur walked over to the fireplace mantel and rubbed his jaw, and glared at Sid.

"All right, but I don't like it," he said at last.

"Good."

"So what happens now?" Arthur shot back at him.

"I do two things. I go to my contacts in the press and give

them as much sympathetic information as I can. How desperate you were, how you've been screwed by the system, that you have a disease—"

"Oh, God, no . . ." Dottie covered her face with her hands.

"I want to arm us with as much embarrassing stuff for the cops as I can, so when I go to negotiate for the bail and the charges, they'll want to get it over with as quickly as possible."

"So you're going to take this to trial?" Arthur asked.

"No. I don't think so. I think you'll be better off pleading out."

Dottie watched Sid and Arthur stare at each other in that kind of silence there is when two people are mentally arguing.

Eva appeared with a tray with the bottle of wine and some glasses, and that seemed to break the tension between the two men. They were all silent as they watched Eva pour it. Dottie had to stop herself from grabbing the glass and slugging it down.

It was really happening. How she could have possibly thought this was a good idea again seemed to elude her. She watched Arthur take a sip, and she did the same, and they both looked up at Sid, who waited until Eva left the room.

"What did you tell her?" he asked.

"That she was my wife."

"All of a sudden you have a wife?" Sid asked testily.

"That she was an old flame and I'd been seeing her for the past couple of months and we suddenly decided to get married."

Sid grimaced and twitched his lips back and forth.

"Anyone else know she's here?"

"No," Arthur said, and Dottie looked at him, and they

both thought about Moe. And Dottie thought about Teresa.

"Good. Now, I want to take a statement from you. I want to know every last detail. I want to know when you planned it, and why. I want to know what gave you the idea. Was anyone else involved?"

"No, no one else was involved. It was only me."

Sid nodded and went into his briefcase on the table. He took out a pad and a pen, and a small tape recorder. Arthur was frowning in the corner as they watched him flick the tape on, take the pad up, and sit poised. Dottie knew he didn't like the idea of her pleading out, and by the way they had both stared down one another, she knew they'd been arguing about it.

"Let's start from the beginning. How did you decide to rob a bank?"

TERESA sat on the bench and stared out over what once had been a baseball field and was now a dust bowl. She'd been sitting on the bench for over two hours, looking at the park on 114th Street. Twilight had come, and she knew she'd better start back home. It was not a good thing to be out past nightfall anymore. She felt another wave of sadness come over her.

They were going to win, she knew that, and she hated it.

Okay, she hated what the neighborhood had become. But to leave it, well, that was like giving up, and Teresa was no quitter.

She slowly stood up and, clutching her bag, she began walking toward First Avenue. When she was a little girl, she used to look out over this park, with all her friends playing in it, and she always imagined the day that she would leave the neighborhood. But it wasn't to go and be a baby-sitter in Florida. No. When she left the neighborhood it was gonna be because she was moving up in the world, not down.

There would be a big black limousine that would slide right up to the front of the building, and for one small moment, all the kids and the mothers and the wise guys on the corner would stop, and they would strain their necks out just to catch a glimpse of her when she passed from the building to the car. And people would call to her and tell her that they loved her and they would ask for her autograph. And her car would drive off, to some fancy house some-where, and maybe she'd come back for visits from time to time to the neighborhood.

A small chill went through her, and she realized how old that fantasy was.

And as odd as it seemed, that was the thing that stuck most in her craw about being shipped off down to Florida. To be driven in a beat-up old car to the airport, and then where?

Oblivion.

She turned down First Avenue and walked unseeing to-ward 106th street. It was always safer not to see too much of what went on on these streets.

Her eyes stopped at a television in the window of an appliance shop. Even though the shop was closed and a heavy gate was across the windows, she could still see a big color television set that had been left on. She stared at a picture of an anchorman, his lips moving silently. She stopped in front of it.

The videotape of Dottie rolled onto the screen.

Now *she* was famous and no one even knew it, Teresa thought. And it seemed odd that she, Teresa, who had always dreamed about fame, should stand here and actu-ally, secretly, know someone who was famous.

She watched Dottie hold the gun up to the guard, the way she'd said she was gonna, and for some reason it suddenly seemed like a waste that no one would ever know it was Dottie who pulled the job.

No, Dottie was probably a million miles from this lousy city, and all the cops knew was that they had another unsolved crime on their hands.

Teresa exhaled loudly and began walking again.

And she couldn't even tell anyone it was Dottie, that was worse. She couldn't even brag that she knew all the details and she knew all the circumstances and she knew . . . Teresa stopped short.

Oh, God! That was it. It had been staring her right in the face all this time! It was the answer to everything. She let out a loud laugh, set her sights down First Avenue and began walking quickly.

She climbed the stairs of her tenement building, gasping by the last flight. She heard people moving around inside her apartment and pushed the door open, which was unlocked, and stood gaping at her children.

Cardboard boxes were sitting on all the surfaces, and her things were being packed. No one noticed her for a moment, and then suddenly Tracy yelled out.

"Mom!" Where the hell have you been? You had us scared to death—"

"Are you all right? We have the cops out looking for you everywhere."

Teresa softened her face, and looked tired. She shuffled over to the chair at the kitchen table and sank down into it.

"Honey, get Mom some water! Are you all right?"

"I'm fine. I'm fine," she said in a weak voice.

"Now will you listen to us?" Tracy said, and placed the glass of water on the tabletop so forcefully it slopped over the top.

Teresa took a long drink of the water.

"Now do you see that you're going to Florida?"

Teresa sat still and looked over at them and a big screw-you grin eased itself across her face.

CHAPTER SIX

A<small>RTHUR</small> rolled over and stared at Dottie. Her eyes were open and she was looking at the ceiling. He crossed his hands on top of the blanket and lay there listening to the sound of her breathing.

Everything Sid had said kept running through his head, and he guessed it was running through hers as well, the way she was staring up at the ceiling. There was the press problem, and the videotape problem and the jail-term problem—about the only problem Sid didn't have with the whole thing was his fee. His eyes slid back over to Dottie.

This legal nonsense was not going to work. Pleading out.

He knew what that meant. The press was already going crazy with this. The minute she gave herself up it was going to be like a feeding frenzy; the pushing and the shoving and the twenty zillion stupid, embarrassing questions, and even after all of that, a quick conviction and then what? He knew what. Sentencing. If there was more than a fifty-fifty chance Sid could get her off on probation, Arthur MacGregor would have gone along with it. But Sid wasn't saying there was more than a fifty-fifty chance of that.

If only she hadn't grazed the guard.

"What?" her voice asked, as though she had been reading his thoughts.

"There is another choice," he said.

He could feel her body next to his. She turned sideways, propped her head up on the pillow, and looked at him.

"What if we took the money and ran?"

"Oh, don't be ridiculous."

"Why not?"

"I'm too old to spend the rest of my life running from the police. Moving every couple of weeks—what an absurd idea."

"You've been seeing too many movies. It's not as complicated as you think."

"Arthur, that's not even the point. It's that—"

"You don't have to move all that often—unless, of course, you're planning on sticking up more banks."

Dottie pursed her lips and gave him a wry smile.

"No, I didn't think so. Anyway, it's really not complicated. I know guys stayed at the same address for years, and the cops never found them. Look, we get on a plane—"

"No. Why should I compound it with more lies?" she asked and he stared up at the ceiling and exhaled loudly.

"But what if we leave and you never get caught?"

"I'll get caught. I know me. And besides, what about your business and your son?"

"I don't give a damn about the business, and my son—well, it's not like he needs me around. He'd probably like the fact I was gone. I know his wife would."

"She doesn't like you?"

"She doesn't trust me with her children."

"What?"

He shrugged and exhaled.

"It's a long story. I say we get outta here. I say we take the next plane for Hawaii, and try it."

"I can't live a lie."

"Why?"

She sat up and glared at him.

"This is what I was talking about in 1962! You have the morals of, of—"

"You know how many people are out there living lies? You lived honestly. So what? You did everything right, Dottie. And now look at you. You live on broth."

"That's not fair. I did what I had to do, and living honestly is worth something."

"What?"

"It's . . . it's . . ." She stumbled, trying to figure out what she could say to him.

"There, you see, you can't give me any good reason not to take the money and run."

"It's for peace of mind you live honestly. So when you're dead—"

"Ah, here it comes. So when you're dead what? You're dead."

"You don't get into heaven by lying—"

"What if there is no heaven?"

"Shame on you, Arthur MacGregor."

"You and your Catholic upbringing—"

"That's right. It is a sin to steal."

"Yeah, well, I'd rather laugh with sinners than cry with saints. Like I said, why is it a sin to try and feed yourself?"

"What if everybody went around robbing banks?"

"Then we wouldn't have need of the fucking things! And people wouldn't be out there starving and everyone would have to learn to share."

"I can't have this discussion with you." She rolled away from him, and felt his hand on her shoulder after a moment.

"Are you telling me, Dottie O'Malley, that you never thought of saying, 'Screw it,' and taking the money? The money you robbed, fair and square, whether you meant it or not, and the money that they're all laughing at you over . . ." She turned around and looked at him, and he knew he'd struck a nerve. "Are you telling me that it hasn't even crossed your mind?"

She felt her cheeks get flushed as she thought of standing in her kitchen yesterday afternoon reaching for her coat, ready to get away. Yes, it was true, she had thought of it. Hell, she'd have been out the door. She felt him nibble on her shoulder gently and then he began to kiss her neck.

"Hawaii," he whispered so close to her ear it sent tingles through her. "We could take what you have, and I could empty out my safety-deposit boxes and we could go to the airport—"

"Stop it, Arthur."

"And we could get on a plane going anywhere—"

"And what about Sid?"

"Sid's a lawyer. You think he's going to volunteer the information? There's client/lawyer confidence."

"But—"

"We could just disappear somewhere."

She closed her eyes and let him kiss her neck.

"Well?"

Her eyes snapped open. "I don't . . . you're mixing me all up."

He exhaled and looked up at the ceiling.

"Dottie, do you understand what Sid is saying?"

"Yes."

"I don't think you do. I don't think you understand that he's telling you to go in there and plead out. To say that you are guilty."

"I am guilty."

"Once you do that, you're at their mercy, don't you understand? You could get the whole fifteen years. And it would be wherever they choose to send you. You don't have a chance . . ." His voice was getting shaky. "Prison is—" His voice stopped and he was shaking his head back and forth and staring straight up with a look on his face that scared her. "When they first close that gate"—she felt a shiver go through him—"it's like you've died. You no longer have a name. You are a number. And once they've taken away your identity, they take away you. You don't matter, your very existence is insignificant. You are nothing more than some piece of meat, Dottie. And if something happens to you . . ." He stopped, realizing that if he didn't talk her out of this madness he was going to go crazy.

"Think about it?"

She was silent, and slowly he felt her nod. He felt a relieved smile go across his face. If he could just work on her some more . . .

TERESA lay in bed with her eyes wide open.

All right, she thought, what the hell was she going to wear tomorrow? There was that bag in the cedar chest, still had some of her old dresses. She wondered if she had kept that Chanel suit Fred had come home with one night when they were first married, before the kids and the weight? He'd gotten it off the back of a truck, but no one could tell that it wasn't real. Yeah, maybe she didn't have all the first-rate items, and the first-rate house and clothes she thought she might have in the beginning, but . . .

Fred.

She suddenly realized that with all this craziness, she'd barely thought about him for the whole afternoon and the whole evening.

And Christ, was she grateful to crazy Dottie Weist for that! It was like a vacation having something else to focus on. She'd been through the mill the last year and a half; nothing but months of bad news and crying fits, and hospitals and funeral arrangements; how many times had she decided she was going to give up?

Hell, that day Dottie called out of the blue, Teresa'd been

whimpering around like some sort of manic depressive, feeling that her life was over. And then, listening to Dottie and all the details of sticking up the bank, and all the crazy plans, then all that dirt about Arthur MacGregor, it was as if she was being pulled back into existence. Yep, Dottie might be a nut, but she was a nut who was at least still out there fighting for her life.

She was, in an odd way, a kind of role model, Teresa felt.

She'd probably never see her again, but Teresa resolved that if she ever did come across Dottie Weist again, she was gonna thank her.

Well, tomorrow was going to fix everything, she thought, and rolled over in bed. Yes, and she'd definitely wear that Chanel suit.

GRAY-BLUE light of morning was peeking through the window curtains. Dottie lay in bed in a state between waking and sleeping. Arthur moved next to her, and she pulled the covers down and felt the cool air around her face and neck. There was a sudden bang on the door, and it flew open and Dottie's heart nearly stopped as she dipped under the covers, hiding her head.

Arthur twisted around and glared.

"Pop!" Moe's voice echoed off the walls.

"Didn't your mother teach you to knock?"

"Pop." Arthur watched Moe's eyes narrow and he stared at the lump of Dottie under the covers.

"Go out in the hall," Arthur ordered, and Moe's mouth opened but nothing came out.

"Now."

He watched his son turn and stomp back into the hallway and he closed the door.

"Oh, God!" he heard Dottie's muffled voice from under the covers.

"Pop, I have to talk to you *now*." Moe's voice came through loudly from behind the door.

Dottie felt Arthur's weight leave the bed and she could hear him muttering. She half-pulled the covers off her face in time to see him pull the sleeve of his bathrobe over his arm. He opened and closed the door behind him.

Dottie threw off the covers and tiptoed to the door. She stood as still as she could and strained to hear what was being said in the hallway.

Arthur finished tying the sash and stared angrily at his son. Moe was still in his blue down coat and wearing one of the ugly ski caps Doreen knitted for him every year. In his arms was a stack of newspapers.

"What do you mean, barging into my house at the crack of dawn?" he demanded.

"Pop, that woman—"

"That woman's name is Dottie. You almost scared her to death."

"Oh, don't give me that!"

"You damn well respect my privacy—"

Moe lowered his voice. "I think she was the one who robbed that bank Friday."

Dottie took in a breath and waited to exhale.

There was silence. Arthur stared evenly at Moe.

"Oh, come on . . ." Arthur said finally.

"She matches the description. And that bag you were carrying, the green tote bag. It's just like the one in the video."

There was another silence. "It's her, Pop."

Arthur paced across the hallway and back, glancing at Moe. Moe was nearly Arthur's height, not in great shape, but still, he was in his thirties. Arthur began assessing his son's strength. Sid's warnings were ringing in his ears as he paced, and finally Arthur stopped and looked at Moe, realizing that getting into a fistfight with his son was not going to help, except to make Arthur feel a little better, since he sincerely felt Moe had always needed a good kick in the rear. He was going to have to level with him.

"What if she is?" Arthur's voice said quietly.

"This is serious."

"I know."

"Pop, she's dangerous."

"I *know*." Arthur chuckled.

"Be serious. She shot someone. She is *armed*."

"No, she's not."

"How do you know?"

"I disarmed her," Arthur said and gave a laugh.

"Jesus, you never take me seriously. They say she might be crazy or senile or both. How do you know she's not going to take out a gun—"

"I told you, I disarmed her the night she got here."

"Pop—"

"Frisked her head to foot every inch. Over and over . . ." Arthur winked at his son.

"Oh, Christ, Pop! I don't want to know—"

"Well, then you shouldn't go barging into people's bedrooms at seven-thirty in the morning," Arthur cut him off.

"With all the diseases . . . I mean, you can't be serious that you, that you . . ."

"Yes, I certainly did."

There was another silence.

"Look, I mean, did you take advantage of this woman?"

"Now that's enough." Arthur stopped and stared at him, appalled by the insinuation.

"No, it's not. They say she's senile."

"She's not senile, for God's sake."

"Then she's crazy."

"No."

"She robbed a bank."

"You have to be crazy to rob a bank?"

Moe pursed his lips, smugly.

"Well, she's not crazy or senile. She had her reasons."

"I'll bet. What if the police find her here? You have a record. What are you going to do about that? What about our business?"

"I don't know."

"Look, she can't stay here."

"You're stepping over the line. This is my house. No one is going to find out about this."

"Oh, yeah?"

There was the sound of something being dropped on the floor, and Dottie pressed her ear against the door, as if that were going to do anything.

Arthur shifted his weight onto one leg and looked down at the pile. Fuzzy black-and-white stills from the video graced the front pages of all the papers he could see.

"These are the New York papers and the Jersey papers, Connecticut, and Pennsylvania—she knocked the president off the front pages of the London *Financial Times,* for Christ's sake. Now, Pop, I think we better talk."

There was another silence.

"Come downstairs," Arthur ordered and Dottie heard the two of them stomp to the landing and down the stairs.

She turned and peeled off the new nightgown and shakily walked over to the table. She scrambled and pulled on her bra and underwear. She stared at the new clothes she'd gotten the day before. No. He could return all of them, and she felt a lump in her throat. She opened the armoire and pulled out the baggy dress she'd come in and slid it over her head. She looked around for her hose and cursed herself under her breath that she was wasting time. She had to get out of there. She wiggled her feet into her shoes.

If his kid knew, probably everyone knew. And Arthur had a record and she was putting him and herself in jeopardy by being there, just as Sid had said. What was she going to do? Could she run away all by herself? Or should she go back and give herself up?

She slowly turned the doorknob and peeked out into the hallway.

She could hear the sound of their voices below and she got to the top of the stairs and stared down it. She began to feel a bit dizzy again and she placed one foot on the first step.

Money. Bring the money. She tiptoed back down the hall to the bedroom and opened the armoire. In the bottom she felt for the bag. She began to feel panicky as her hands probed and found nothing.

She stood up and realized she was shaking hard. Where had Arthur put it? She opened the other side of the armoire and began opening the drawers. She stood back after closing the last one, and looked around the room, dismayed.

Had he . . . taken it?

She didn't know what to do now. Her eyes began darting around the room and she suddenly dropped to the floor. Under the bed she saw a lump. She reached in as far as she could and her fingers brushed the bag. She strained farther and farther. Her fingers wrapped around the soft handle, and she pulled the bag out from under the bed. All right. She took a deep breath and returned to the hallway.

She could hear them arguing in the living room as she placed a foot on the first step, and a tiny twinge of guilt went through her. Her old suspicions of Arthur MacGregor were still there.

If she could just get her old coat out of the closet, and leave the house without being seen or heard. That was all she was asking for. Just once, God should make something easy for her. She slowly and carefully descended.

"Because she needs my help. And I love her." Arthur's voice echoed out into the hallway from the living room.

"Love her, Pop? You've never loved a woman in your whole life."

"That's not fair."

"Oh, right. So where has this love of your life been for thirty-some odd years, huh?"

"She . . . was married to somebody else."

"Classic Arthur MacGregor. So, you had an affair with a married woman?"

"I knew her first—yes, for a very brief time. So you can add adultery to the sin pile stacked up against me as well. But, Junior, if you can find a man my age who has not ever done anything wrong in his whole life, I'll show you a man who has been in a coma."

"Bank robbery is not something to be proud of."

"Neither is adultery." He stared at his son's eyes, and they shifted uneasily away.

"She is going to send you back to jail."

"Well, then you'll have the business all to yourself and you won't have to worry about me fencing on the side."

Moe shook his head and looked back at him. "I prefer the fencing."

"And besides, why do you care so much all of a sudden? I'll sign the whole bloody thing over to you, if that's what you're worried about."

"I'm not worried about owning the business." Moe's voice dropped.

Dottie put her hand on the hall closet doorknob and as quietly and, as slowly as she could, turned it. She opened it a crack, trying to remember if it creaked. She could just reach her coat sleeve. She placed her hand on the shoulder and pulled it off the hanger. She pulled it around her shoulders and then, closing the closet, reached for the front door.

She began to feel the growing lump ache in her throat, and it was in direct proportion as to how far the door was opening. She was going back out there alone. She didn't know if she was going to give herself up; she just needed to get on a train or a bus someplace and think it through. She felt the rush of air, and then the words, "Did you hear something?"

Dottie's legs took off under her, and she was running and running, and to her horror she looked down and realized she was leaving a trail of money.

"Hey! Wait a minute. Dottie! Moe, go after her," she heard Arthur shout, and almost immediately there was the heavy weight of a hand on her shoulder and she was pulled back by Moe.

"Let me go."

"Wait," Moe said.

"No, no, you're right and he's wrong. I can't stay around him."

"Wait."

"Let me go, won't you? He'll just talk me into coming back, and you're right, I don't want him to have to do any more jail time."

"Dottie—" She heard Arthur behind her.

"But Arthur, he's right. You shouldn't be in jeopardy because I want to go to jail."

"You *want* to go to jail?" Moe asked.

"Dottie, be quiet."

"Great, so she's senile *and* crazy. I told you," Moe tossed off, and Dottie suddenly turned and gaped at him.

She felt herself begin to breathe hotly. There was a tightness in her chest, and the thought "How dare you!" was shrieking through her head.

"Senile? That's what you think? I'm senile! You listen to me. I'm a not some crazy old woman like they said on television. I am angry." Dottie took a step toward him, and felt his anger explode. "I finally got sick and tired of settling for nothing because that's what they told me I had to do.

And I did it. I settled for nothing, the way I have every day for thirty lousy years. Your father was one of those things I settled myself out of. I have wasted my own life. And if I had to think back on all the things in life I've cheated myself out of and been cheated out of, I wouldn't have robbed a bank. I'd have taken a machine gun and let her rip in the middle of Times Square! Do you hear me, child? So I settled for robbing a bank. And do you know what? I did a good job. I got away with it. And the hell with them all for the tongue-in-cheek remarks and laughing at me because I'm not some kid. I took something back. I took back my dignity, and I did it alone. I'm not crazy, I'm fed up!"

"Dottie," Arthur whispered, and he pulled her into him and gave her a long deep kiss.

When Arthur finally let go of her she stared up at him and then at his lips and a small smile spread across her lips, and her eyes had that same serious thoughtful expression that they'd had the night before.

"Arthur MacGregor, will you run away with me?"

"Oh, my God," she heard Moe mutter behind her.

"Dottie O'Malley, I will run wherever you want to go."

She turned and the three of them silently walked up the brick path.

Moe slammed the door. "Just great, just goddamn great."

"The first thing I have to do is get dressed," Arthur was saying and Dottie began to go up the stairs.

"Are you kidding? You can't be serious," Moe began. They both stopped on the stairs and turned with raised eyebrows. "This is not going to work," Moe said, his hands on his hips.

"Nobody can see her face in those photos. The only reason you figured it out was the shopping bag, and that you picked her up in the village on Friday."

"You can't just leave—"

223

"Why? You can't run that god-awful business by yourself? Now, you are going to go back and sit in your house and not say a word about this to anybody, do you hear me, Moe?" Arthur cut him off and took a step down, toward him.

Moe crossed his arms over his chest. "No, I won't just go back and sit in my house."

"What are you going to do? Turn me in? If you are, it's me alone," Dottie said, and took a step down as well.

They both stood in silence, staring at Moe, waiting.

"I know you never liked me, Pop. I know we're different people and I could never live up to the great Arthur MacGregor."

"Aw, Christ, here it comes, another lecture. For God's sake, be a man. Be a human being."

"I'm trying to, if you'd let me finish." Moe stared evenly at them.

They stood silently again.

"You can't just leave . . . without money."

"We have money." Arthur began.

"Where are you going?"

"The airport."

"How are you going to take that bag of cash on an airplane? You can't carry it on. It has to go through the metal detector."

"Well . . ." Arthur began to explain it and then stopped himself, and looked curiously at his son.

"You trust enough to send it through with the luggage? Not to mention the fact that your name will appear in their computers. How would that look? There's a robbery and Arthur MacGregor and some woman who matches the description leaves town?" Moe asked and looked at them both. "We'll put the tickets on my card. Nobody's looking for Moe MacGregor."

Dottie looked down at him, and nodded. "Thank you."

224

She turned and walked up the stairs. She took one step toward the bedroom and then stopped, turned around and leaned on the railing just to the right above the stairs, and listened.

They both watched her go, and Arthur turned back to Moe, and for the first time in a long time, looked at his son with a bit of admiration.

"I couldn't live the way you chose to, but that doesn't make me nothing, Pop."

"I never said it did. I never wanted you to be in trouble like me. Hell, if I had, I wouldn't have sent your mother money every month, I wouldn't have footed the bills for college."

"But you were never around."

He stared straight into his son's eyes, incredulous. "What? Do you think being on the run from the FBI is a leisurely activity? They were watching your mother for years. I wasn't around because we, your mother and I, agreed that you shouldn't go through life with little men in unmarked cars all around you. Now, I'm not saying I'm a shining example of fatherhood by any stretch of the imagination, but I never lied to you, I never beat you, I never let you starve, and that's a damn sight better than a lot of so-called fathers who are around all the time. Are you the perfect father and husband?"

"I try," Moe said uneasily.

"Well, isn't that all we can do? We're only human, as little as that counts in this day and age when we're all supposed to march around like kindergarteners in naive perfection. Well, I'm not a child, I'm an adult, and we sometimes screw up."

"Did you cheat with her on my mother?"

"I hadn't seen Dottie in years when I was with your mother and, no. I never cheated on your mother. I just robbed banks . . . Dottie and I were very young and we were going to get married, and I went to jail. When I got out I went to find her, because I believed that even though she'd gotten married she would leave her husband. And she didn't. Maybe it was the best choice she could have made and maybe it wasn't."

Moe's eyes lowered. "She was the one, wasn't she?"

"The one?"

"Mom . . . sometimes late at night used to talk about a woman. She used to tell me that no one was ever going to have you, because you belonged to someone else. She was the one, wasn't she?"

Arthur kept his eyes on him until Moe raised them. He nodded slowly.

"You make choices in your life, and sometimes they're worth it, and sometimes they're not. The trick is not regretting any of it. And, with the exception of her, I don't."

Dottie clasped her hands together and straightened up. That was all she wanted to hear.

Moe nodded, and gave a slight smile. Arthur watched him walk into the living room and return with his coat. He put it on, and wrapped a muffler around himself. His hat fell down over his eyes, and he winced and pulled it off.

"God, I hate these things she knits." He shook his head, and Arthur found himself nodding in agreement.

"I'll be back in an hour, then let me drive you to the airport."

TERESA opened the old cedar trunk that had sat at the foot of the bed in her bedroom since she'd been married. She could hear Tracy's husband moving about in the kitchen, and the clink of metal utensils as he emptied the silverware into a box.

They had wasted no time packing up her things; her apartment looked like the inside of a moving van. Brown

226

cardboard boxes covered the bed, pictures had been stripped off the walls; the whole place was a mess. And now, as Teresa gingerly pulled a large old garment bag out of the trunk, she could hear Tracy on the phone.

"She finally came to her senses about Florida . . . Yeah, I know, it's such a relief . . ."

Teresa laid the gray garment bag out on the bed and unzipped it slowly, so as not to make much noise. She took out Fred's tuxedo, then thumbed through several layers of dresses and suits, until she got to the black one.

Carefully she laid the Chanel suit across the bed. She picked up the jacket and looked at it carefully. It looked brand-new. The skirt was a little worn at the top, but with a blouse no one would even look at it. She opened the closet door and took out a white blouse that looked like the one Dottie had worn for the robbery. She pulled off her house-dress and put on the blouse, carefully buttoning it. She inhaled deeply and looked at the skirt.

This was the real test, D-Day.

As she unzipped the skirt, the tag displaying the size eight became visible. As she carefully stepped into the skirt and slid it up to her hips she automatically inhaled, sucked in her stomach and did not exhale. She zipped up the back.

Only then did she exhale. Sharply and gratefully she let the breath out. This was the outfit. The very expensive outfit that she'd worn maybe three times, before she got pregnant. Afterward, she could never fit back into it. Every woman, Teresa thought, has one of these. What she called the too-expensive-to-throw-out outfit. She'd always kept it in the hope that she would lose enough weight to get back into it one day.

This was the day.

Teresa quickly pulled the jacket over the blouse, opened up the closet door, and stared at herself in the mirror.

She always felt like Jackie Kennedy when she wore this

outfit. All she needed was a pillbox hat, some white gloves and a handbag. She pushed her feet into her pumps and stared again at herself in the mirror.

Jeez, she thought, maybe I should scrap my plans and find someone to date.

She gave an odd chuckle. She wasn't interested in dating. Christ, the very thought made her skin crawl. She'd had Fred. He'd been the match for her, the right man. And once you found that perfect person, nobody else is ever gonna come close. Naw. She didn't need a man, she needed to do what she was about to do. She grabbed her handbag and slowly and silently walked out of the bedroom.

Tracy was still on the phone as Teresa passed without looking at her.

"And so I said—Ma! Ma, look at you. What're you all dressed up for?"

Teresa opened the front door to the apartment and stared at Tracy. Behind her she could hear Fred, Jr., stop moving about.

"Church," she snapped.

"You ain't been to a Sunday church service since we were kids," Tracy said suspiciously.

"Well, I think I better go say good-bye to Father Dominick, then," Teresa said.

For just one second she thought Tracy was going to give her a hard time or, worse, offer to go with her. But she watched Tracy shrug after a moment, and place the phone back up to her ear.

"Have a good time," Teresa heard her say as she descended the stairs.

Yeah, she thought, I'm gonna have a hell of a time where I'm going.

★ ★ ★

DOTTIE stared out the car window. The sun was low in the sky. She heard the continual sounds of planes taking off, and watched them rise in the smoggy air, as the car got off the ramp at Kennedy Airport. The sky was yellow and the sunset had a layer of blue-red, and reminded her, grotesquely of the center of a raw piece of meat.

She stared at the back of Moe's head as he drove, and listened to Arthur go over the business accounts—bills due, the taxes, et cetera—and she thought about sitting in the kitchen of Arthur's house and looking back over the garden. She wondered what it would be like in the peak of summer. And for a brief moment she had a vision of a warm afternoon, and kneeling in a vegetable patch, and listening to Arthur's grandchildren run under a sprinkler on the lawn. And she'd look up at him sitting on the porch reading the Sunday papers, and drinking iced tea . . . and the thing was, it was a vision she'd had a long long time ago.

Her eyes refocused on the terminal signs for Kennedy Airport. Well, there weren't going to be any vegetable gardens or lazy afternoons with grandchildren. And she wondered, would anyone care for the garden? And the house. It was a wonderful house. Such a waste. She looked at Arthur. To her it was a waste to leave such a lovely house. To him it didn't seem to matter in the least.

They had driven to the Bronx, first to the pawnshop and then to a bank, where she watched Arthur and Moe deposit a bagful of money in the special business deposit box, and then they had driven out here.

The car stopped in front of the terminal and Moe and Arthur got out. She followed slowly. She stood very still and watched Arthur and Moe unload the suitcases on a cart.

No, she did not want to go to jail.

No, she did not want to go to court.

No, she didn't want to leave Arthur.

And this was the only answer. Arthur was right. No one was going to find out. They couldn't tell from the tapes it was Dottie. Sid wasn't going to tell them. And Moe was going to feed them money as soon as they wired from Hawaii.

So here they were. On their way, to begin the long flight to Los Angeles and then on to Hawaii. And everything Arthur had said was true.

But . . .

Arthur came up and took her arm and together they walked into the terminal, and all the time she was conscious of the bulges in his coat from the money he was carrying.

They stood on a very short line and in almost no time Moe stood in front of the ticket counter, buying the tickets.

It was odd, but she almost felt that it was some kind of movie she was watching. She went through the paces all right. Filling out their names on the luggage tags, watching them get placed on the conveyor belt.

And she let Arthur lead her back by the arm through the terminal to the metal detector. Moe handed Arthur a small carry-on bag, and he began to button his coat.

"And don't let Rob tell you it's okay to underpay the quarterlies—"

"I know, Pop, we been over it—"

"I know there's things I'm forgetting—"

"It'll be okay. I know the business, and it's not like I'm never going to talk to you again."

"My will. It's in the deposit box, along with a small green book. Inside the book are all the banks I have safety-deposit boxes in. Close them all and put every cent into your account, otherwise the bastards in the government will take it all—"

"You're not going to die, Pop, you're going to Hawaii."

"Yes, yes . . ." Arthur said and looked as if he was pondering exactly what else he needed to say.

Moe leaned down and gave Dottie a peck on the cheek.

"Take care of him," he said.

"I just wish I'd made a list . . ." Arthur murmured as Moe led him to the metal detector.

"Call me tomorrow and tell me where you are," he said, and stopped.

Arthur stared at him and suddenly threw his arms around him, and gave him a hefty quick hug, then let go.

"I love you, Pop."

"Come see us," Arthur said, and nodded. He turned and walked through the metal detector.

Dottie followed and they waved back at Moe.

"Take Doreen out for a nice dinner somewhere," Arthur yelled after him, and then took Dottie's arm.

They walked silently toward their gate.

She sat staring numbly through a large plate-glass window at their plane being readied for takeoff. And it was odd. It was as if there was a deadness covering a deep sense of doom.

Arthur sat down next to her and smiled and handed her a hot dog.

"To Hawaii." He winked and took a large bite.

She stared at him and nodded. She looked down at the hot dog. She didn't feel like eating. She didn't feel like anything.

She felt . . . ashamed of herself. And stupid. Very, very stupid. And afraid again.

"Are you all right?" he asked and she saw a look of concern cross his face.

"I don't know," she said honestly. "I need to find a bathroom."

They both stood up and walked over to the information booth.

Arthur hooked his arm through hers, and they walked slowly.

"Think about a nice warm beach all year, and palm trees, and warm water," he whispered to her.

She looked up at him, at his smile, and thought about wrapping herself around him, and slowly the fear began to ebb.

What was wrong with her? She was going to *Hawaii*.

She'd once been to Atlantic City, but that was the only place outside of New York City she'd ever seen. Hawaii. It was farther than she'd ever been in her whole life. She was with a man she'd dreamed about being with her whole life, and she was going to enjoy it.

She slowly slid her arms around him and looked up. "Arthur," she began and then stopped when something behind him caught her eyes.

A small television set attached to the arm of a chair in the terminal had been swiveled around so it did not face the chair back but faced Dottie.

It was the face of someone she recognized. Dottie dropped her arms and Arthur instantly turned around and looked at the set. He followed her over and they both stood in front of the small screen. A reporter came on and behind him were the words: "Special Report."

"We have word at this time that the woman who robbed the bank in Greenwich Village has surrendered to authorities at the Sixth Precinct."

"WHAT!" Dottie's voice echoed through the terminal.

"Who . . ." Arthur began quickly.

She watched the reporter in front of the Sixth Precinct police station. "The woman has just been transferred into the custody of the FBI. There has been no official statement, and we do not have word yet on the identity of the woman who surrendered. To recap: The woman who robbed the Chemical Bank in Greenwich Village on Friday has surrendered to authorities."

The video showed a woman in a black Chanel suit being

232

whisked into a brown car. Her back was to the camera, until they closed the car door. The woman was looking down and away, and suddenly there was a flash and Dottie watched her look up and smile through the glass window.

"OH, MY GOD, IT'S TERESA!"

Arthur sank into the chair. He rested his elbows on the arms of the chair, and with his hands made a fist that he pressed against his lips. He looked up at Dottie and watched her mouth drop open in dismay. He began to shake his head.

"Dottie," he began as slowly and evenly as he could, "did someone else know about this?"

She nodded slowly.

"A woman?"

She nodded again.

"Who?"

"Teresa Newhouse," she said barely above a whisper. "She was the one I got your number from."

He sat still, shaking his head. The scratchy sound of the intercom echoed about, as a woman's voice announced that their flight to L.A. was going to begin boarding shortly.

Arthur glanced up at her, set his jaw, and stood up. He took her arm firmly, and as quickly as he could began walking her through the terminal.

"Well, let's get on the plane."

"Arthur," she said softly.

"No. Don't—"

"Arthur," she repeated.

"No—"

"I can't leave her there," she said gently.

She watched him shake his head, and he let go of her. Then she watched him walk over and slam the wall with his fist and glare at her.

"Why didn't you tell me she knew?" he choked.

"I didn't want to worry you," Dottie offered weakly.

233

"Worry me! Worry me! You have a woman who can identify you and you didn't want to worry me?" His eyes slid around and he dropped his voice. "Aw, Christ, Dottie."

He exhaled and placed his hands on his hips.

"What do you want to do?"

"I have to go back." She watched his jaw get tight, and he was furious.

"For God's sake, why?"

"Oh, come on."

"Why? She's going to take the rap; now let's go."

"Don't you want to know why?"

"No. I don't care. I want to spend the next couple of weeks on a beach."

"No. You heard Sid. He can't guarantee anything. She's in trouble because of me."

"That's a lot of crap. She's not in trouble because of you, she turned herself in."

"She doesn't understand what she's done."

"Dottie, the woman walked into a police station and surrendered. You can't do that accidentally. She wants to go to jail. Do you want to go to jail? Let her! Say thank you! Take my arm, and let's get on the goddamned plane and go to Hawaii."

"I can't just leave her there. Arthur, she doesn't even have money for an attorney. Arthur, I have to."

His eyes narrowed.

"Then you do it without me."

Her jaw dropped at she stared at him, puzzled.

"What do you mean?" she asked slowly.

"I'm not sitting by and watch you throw your life away. They'll release her as soon as she's questioned. They'll know immediately she didn't do it. Now, Dottie O'Malley, you are going to"—his teeth were clenched—"get on that plane, or, or"—his voice was shaking—"or I'm going to Hawaii alone. You hear me? You can't promise to go with me every thirty years and go back on it! Now, she's going to be released. She doesn't know what happened."

She looked at him, and frowned and shook her head.

"I told her everything, except for the gun, but that was all over the news yesterday. Arthur, I have to go back and at least get her a lawyer. It's the only decent thing to do," she said and crossed her hands over her chest and stared at him.

He shook his head and cursed under his breath. After a moment he glared at her, took her hand and they began to walk quickly, with him almost dragging her, through the airport back to the ticket area. He didn't say a word the entire walk and she could tell he was angry. But whether he was angry at her or just at the situation she couldn't tell.

He stood her next to him at a pay phone on the wall, and she watched him dial a number. Arthur put one hand against the wall and leaned on it, his head hanging down, his eyes closed, and he was breathing hard through his nose.

"Sid Arnowitz, please," he said, and Dottie felt herself breathe out.

"Sid—no, it's not Dottie . . . yeah, I watched it. Yeah, she's a friend who knew about the whole thing . . . Maybe she forgot about the woman, Sid, I don't know. Remember, they all think she's senile," he nearly yelled into the phone.

"Arthur, don't yell at Sid," Dottie snapped, and pulled on his coat sleeve.

"I don't know what to do either," Arthur was saying, and Dottie whacked him on the arm.

"Tell him to bail her out! For God's sake, Arthur!"

"Okay, *she'll* meet you downtown in an hour and a half . . . Yes, she'll be alone," Arthur said and slammed the phone down. He stared at her furiously, and then began to walk away from her. She followed him, and pulled him back.

"What are you so angry about? That I can't let her confess to this?" She stared at him hotly, and he rolled his eyes and began to say something but couldn't get the words out.

"What?" she demanded.

"I can't watch it, I can't stand the idea of you . . ." His voice withered away and he turned from her.

"Of sitting by and watching them sentence me to jail," she finished the sentence for him.

They were both quiet as they both remembered the same words of this same conversation almost word-for-word from some thirty-odd years before.

Only this time Arthur was saying them.

"Well . . . I couldn't do it for you." Her voice was hard.

"Dottie, I can't—"

"I know what it feels like. Now, give me the bag," she said softly.

He began to shake his head and then, looking at the floor, he slowly handed it over to her. Her hand tightened around the handle and she had to pull it away from his hand. She swallowed hard, then grabbed him and gave him a deep kiss.

"I love you. Good-bye, Arthur," she said, and quickly walked away from him and down the long corridor, back toward the metal detector.

TERESA couldn't believe how stupid Dottie Weist was; she'd cursed herself under her breath for the last half-hour for listening to her about this whole robbery thing. So far, she'd been wrong about everything. She wasn't going to get to spend the night in some nice clean little cell in the Sixth Precinct, for starters.

They didn't take female prisoners.

As a matter of fact, it turned out there were only two precincts in the entirety of Manhattan that did house female prisoners, and they were in lousy neighborhoods. Even when it came to jail, the women were short-changed, she thought grumpily.

And then she'd found out that she wasn't even going to spend any time in those sewers, oh, no, now the FBI had to get into the act. So they explained that they were going to take her downtown to be interrogated at 26 Federal Plaza.

Interrogated.

That word didn't sit well with Teresa either.

She watched this woman, in a black cotton suit, come in with these two guys in olive-green suits. She first thought the two men were twins; she swore they had on the same exact outfit. They signed for her as if she were some kind of package, and they cuffed her hands in front, in cuffs so big they were nearly falling off anyway, and they walked her outside.

That was the only fun part.

Teresa had always imagined what it would be like to be dogged by the press. It was great. All the lights, and the cameras and the stupid questions, and the pushing and shoving, just as if she were the hottest thing since Shirley Maclaine.

But she'd played it discreet, kept her eyes low, as if she were guilty and embarrassed; only once did she look up at the press.

And they went crazy. They started screaming questions at her, and deep down inside Teresa knew she was going to talk a lot to these idiots. And she also knew—whether she was going to spend her time in some FBI jail instead of the Sixth, and no matter whether it was a Federal crime instead of just a city crime—she knew that this was going to beat the hell out of sitting inside some hot, unpainted shack in Florida.

The three agents they'd sent, two men and a woman, as though they were afraid she was going to escape or something, had driven the car way downtown, and up to a big building and around the back into a fenced-in parking lot, avoiding more of the press. They'd walked her, still cuffed, through the back of the big building, which looked like corrugated cardboard on the outside, and had uneven white stone walls on the inside. The female agent took her arm as they walked over to an enclosed bank of elevators. Large stainless-steel beams, with meshed glass windows so thick they appeared green, separated these elevators from the regular elevators. Inside was a desk with two armed guards and a sign attached over the door that read: "Floors 22–29 Only." The agent held up the plastic identity card to the guard inside. The buzzer went off and the heavy door opened.

They rode the elevator up in silence, got off at the twenty-sixth floor, and led her down a long carpeted hallway. She was taken into a room with a long light wood table and several chairs of the same color.

And that was where what they referred to as the "Interrogation of Teresa DeNunzio Newhouse" began.

"I DON'T believe this, where the hell could she be?" Tracy's voice rang out.

Her husband watched his wife put her hands on her bony hips and shake her head. Fred had just put the last box in the back of the van.

Tracy's eyes darted down to her watch.

"The flight's in less than two hours, Tray. Where did she say she was going?"

"Church," Tracy spat out through clenched teeth. "I'll get her."

Tracy clacked down the stone steps of her mother's building, mumbling angrily. She walked outside and turned up First Avenue, ignoring the throngs of kids and the old

238

men sitting in front of the stores. She turned up 114th Street and began to walk toward the beat-up old red brick church building. She stomped up the rectory stairs and pressed on the bell. A small nun opened the door. Tracy walked inside, and down the hall toward a room. The sound of a television echoed on the stone floor. Father Dominick, a stout man of about sixty, was sitting in a lounge chair in front of the set. His collar was open at the top, and he was frowning, disturbed, at the screen. His eyes lifted to Tracy as she entered, and he slowly, but firmly rose from the chair and held both arms out to her.

"Father Dominick? My mother . . ." Tracy began, but before she could say anything, the priest's arms were around her, and she felt him give a heavy exhale.

"Oh, my dear, I had no idea of the trouble in your house," he began, and she stepped back.

"Yeah, well, it ain't so bad where she's going, no matter what she says about it."

"What?" He blanched at that, and Tracy crossed her arms over her chest.

"Oh, come on, Father, wouldn't you rather see her there than living all alone in this neighborhood—"

"But you can't mean this. Where your mother's going is . . . is horrible."

Tracy stepped back, and felt her mouth drop open; she whipped the large sunglasses off her nose and stared at him, her thin lips twitching.

"I resent that! You didn't actually tell her that, did you? Don't you think that's a bit of an exaggeration? I mean, I assumed you were going to reassure her; help her get used to the idea."

The priest took one step back and looked at her, horrified. Tracy's eyes darted around the room, and landed on a door.

"Tracy, I don't think this is an idea you get used to. I mean, she needs a lawyer."

Tracy's eyes darted back to him, and they narrowed.

"You told her to get a lawyer? What kind of a priest are you? She doesn't need a lawyer. She needs a plane ticket and a bathing suit."

"What?" Father Dominick asked, gaping at her.

Tracy looked at her watch again, and then at the door.

"What do you mean, 'What?' Where is she?"

"She's not here," he said, and he blinked, and a look of concern came over his face.

"Oh, great! Just great! She has to be on a plane for Florida in less than two hours and—"

"Tracy, when was the last time you saw your mother?"

"This morning. She said she was coming here to church to say good-bye. She's going to Florida to live with my brother and his wife."

She watched him wince, and slowly shake his head.

"I don't think your mother's going to Florida today."

"Why not?"

TERESA sat in the chair chain-smoking and staring narrowly at the woman with a plastic laminated card pinned to her which read FBI. She blew out the smoke hard and the woman grimaced disapprovingly.

A man the other two called Ted, wearing an olive lightweight suit was sitting on the table, dangling one leg.

"You should talk to us."

"I ain't got nothing to say."

"It'll be better if you cooperate."

"Give me a break."

"Again, did you have an accomplice or not? We know you did it, we just want the details."

"Yeah, yeah."

Teresa watched them glance, frustrated, at one another, and the female agent looked at her and smiled.

"Let's go back to the timing here. What time did you rob the bank?" she asked, studying Teresa grimly.

"Ain't you looked at the tape? It's right there in little numbers on the bottom left-hand side of it, and that's all I'm saying."

"You have to give us more details than that. We have been at this for three hours now—"

"Yeah, and you're beginning to whine like my kids—you tell 'em what's gonna happen and they ignore you and keep pesterin' you. I told you, I ain't saying anything," she said, stubbed out her cigarette, and crossed her arms over her chest.

Ted glared at her and came close to her face, snarling. "We're gonna keep at this. As long as it takes, maybe another three hours, how about that?"

Teresa's eyes narrowed. "Three hours? Buddy, I was trapped for four months in an apartment during winter with a three-year-old and a two-year-old in diapers . . . Three hours? Give it your best shot."

The man stood up and exhaled. He put his hands on his hips and suddenly screamed out, "You're in a hell of a lot of trouble here, lady! You better talk, NOW."

The other agent, in an identical suit, came up to the first agent, and Teresa narrowed her eyes at him sternly.

"Ted, calm down, she's an old woman," he said, and then looked unsympathetically at Teresa. "Look, just tell him something, unless you'd like to sit here for the rest of your life, huh? Never see your grandchildren."

Teresa let out a cackle, and pulled out another cigarette.

"Who the hell are youse kidding? What? You gonna make me disappear? Some 'old' woman? You think they gonna like that?"

"Who?"

"Them newspapers, the television, the Gray Panthers . . . Cut the crap, boys. I ain't sayin' one word to nobody until I talk to a lawyer. Period. Now take Mr. I-Can't-Control-Him, and get the hell outta my face."

ARTHUR MACGREGOR stood in the main terminal just inside the doors. He watched Dottie standing on the platform outside, on a long line waiting for a cab. He found himself cursing.

They'd missed the plane.

So close. They'd almost made it. He turned and his eyes landed on the newsstand. He marched inside and pointed to a box of Partagas cigars, which was the only smokable brand in the whole case, as far as Arthur was concerned. He bought one and a cheap lighter. He bit off the end of a cigar and spit it into a garbage can, and watched a guard stare at him and clear his throat, pointing to a NO SMOKING sign on the wall right near where Arthur was standing.

Why the hell do they still sell smokes when you can't smoke anywhere on the planet anymore? he thought and stuck the cigar in his mouth anyway. He turned and stared across the terminal. He took the tickets out of his pocket and tried to resist the urge to rip them into confetti.

Christ, what a martyr she was. What a martyr she'd always been. How the hell had he ever gotten mixed up with her in the first place?

Stupid. That's what she was. And that's what *he* was too. Getting all out of breath over her again, only to have to watch her throw it all away.

Yeah, he thought to himself. Throw it all away, see if he cared. It wasn't as if she'd stuck around for him all those years ago. He was in for what, a trifling twenty-four months, and what had she done for him? Mailed him care packages of cookies and cakes and love letters professing her undying love for him? Was she standing at the gate along with the other women when he walked out a free man?

Hell, no. She'd gone out and gotten married and pregnant. And even that he'd been willing to overlook. But this . . .

Well, to hell with her! he thought, and chomped down hard on the cigar. He ought to be happy to be rid of her. He was going without her.

He looked at both the tickets.

Hell, he was going first-class to Hawaii. He was going to cash in her ticket and go in style. Then he was going to sit on a beach in Hawaii and order as many of those fruity drinks with all the toys in them that he could and drink toasts to what a sap she was.

He went back to the ticket line and stood behind a woman and two small boys. He took out the lighter and was just about to light the end of his cigar when the woman in front of him turned around and glared.

"Secondhand smoke is a killer, you know. There's no smoking in this area," she huffed.

"Mind your own goddamned business and look after those kids like you're supposed to," he said, being as insulting as he could.

He kept his eyes on hers until she finally turned her back on him.

He knew Dottie was going to confess to the whole thing, and then they'd have her. And Sid was going to take care of the whole thing. Sure, he'd still pay the bill. He wasn't inhuman. Why, he was downright generous. Hadn't he bought her all those clothes? Hadn't he hidden her? Hell, he'd been better to her than to most of his partners. But she'd really crossed the line. Going in to confess to a crime. Surrendering to them! No, that was the bottom line to Arthur MacGregor. Christ, in love with some jerk who was going to go turn herself in for a crime she could've happily gotten away with. And now he was going to pay so she could be a martyr, Arthur thought.

Nope. Hawaii, that's where he was going.

A pang went through him.

It wasn't as if he could even go to the trial anyway. He couldn't be seen around Dottie. No contact with her. Because Arthur MacGregor would be a liability. The ticket taker he'd bought the tickets from just a half hour before motioned Arthur to come forward.

"Something wrong, sir?"

"We had a family emergency. My—other son has been hospitalized, so my wife . . ." Arthur's voice stopped cold on the word "wife."

And the vision of Dottie standing in the mall all dressed up and pretty, and with her hair done and glowing at him, well, it just popped into his head.

"Sir?"

And her head, lying back on the pillow and beaming at him, the way her body felt in bed next to his, the way she laughed and the sounds when she made love to him—it was making his chest tingle. He'd laughed more in two days than in ten years, just having her around.

And then there were all those clothes of hers in the house.

"And, sir?" the man prompted.

Arthur looked at the young man's face.

"Your wife, sir?" his voice prodded and Arthur winced at the word.

Aw, Jesus! No. He was going, he thought, and placed the tickets on the counter.

"She's going to the hospital and I'm canceling hers and I'm going on alone. Make the ticket first class," he barked at the young man, who looked incredulous at this old man who was not going to see his son in the hospital but was going on vacation, first class now.

"Very good, sir," the man muttered.

Arthur MacGregor puffed hard on the unlit cigar as the clerk typed numbers into the computer.

Arthur MacGregor, the liability, he thought. And just what did she expect him to do now? Just sit up in his house and watch them crucify her? Like a goddamned patsy?

Christ, she'd probably starve before they actually got to court. Hell, that was if she didn't have a heart attack when the press got to her. He remembered his last trial, how they pushed you and shoved you and treated you like game on a hunt, those animals. Only she, being all alone and naive the way she was . . . God, she'd be so . . . scared and confused . . . That's what did it, the confusion. Jeez, he hoped Sid would be able to calm her down. If he were there he'd know exactly what—hey, wait a minute, Arthur thought. Just stop right there.

And then Arthur felt something horrible. Something he'd never considered would happen to him.

He was having an attack of the Responsible Morals.

Just in time, the man handed him back an upgraded ticket and Arthur nodded and walked away. He stared at his lone reflection in the large sliding glass door.

Could he sit in Hawaii knowing what was going on?

He stared down at the ticket and gave himself one last going-over about what an ass he was, and what he was going to do in Hawaii and . . .

He cursed again, threw the cigar on the floor, and went back onto the ticket line. He could still see her through the glass. She was holding the collar of that ragged coat of hers closed, as she waited in line for a cab.

All right, he'd given his word that he was not going to be

seen around Dottie or the trial. But he was not about to let her starve or get pushed around.

He got back up to the ticket booth to the same man, and he placed the ticket on the counter.

"I decided not to go. Cancel it."

"Very good, sir," the young man said earnestly, as though he'd won some sort of moral victory. "I'm sure it's for the best."

"Yeah?" Arthur said, frowning at him. "For who?"

"Ma'am?" the driver prodded after a minute.

She sat still, unable to answer.

She was all alone and was facing jail. And if being alone in jail weren't bad enough, the thought that now there was not going to be a single soul on the planet outside who was going to give a damn that she was in prison had sunk in. There was not going to be anyone waiting for her letters or for her release, and the horror of it hit home.

Was this what he had felt all those years ago?

"Ma'am?"

"Vesey Street in Lower Manhattan," she said barely above a whisper.

She slid down onto the backseat and was just about to close the door when it was pulled back open and Arthur swung into the backseat beside her.

The car lurched away from the curb, and she sat still and quiet, glancing over at him.

"Don't say I never did anything for you," he grunted, and sat chewing on an unlit cigar.

After a moment she slid her arm through his and leaned against him. Her eyes looked forward, and she watched the skyline of Manhattan appear on the horizon.

By the time the cab pulled up to the address Sid had

246

given her the day before, Dottie was a shaky mess. Arthur handed the driver a hundred-dollar bill and got out. She stared at the granite building and walked inside.

"Arnowitz," Arthur said to the guard, and stared at the granite table.

The guard picked up a phone and called up to the office. He nodded to Arthur.

He slipped his arm through Dottie's easily and they rode the elevator up to the Thirty-third floor.

Sid was waiting at the elevator bank. He silently walked them down the corridor to the law-firm offices. It was quiet in the office. The air was motionless and stuffy from a lack of circulation. He led them into a large corner office and shut the door.

"Well, it seems we have a situation here that I need to be filled in on," he said, sinking into a large leather chair. Behind him was a view of Lower Manhattan and New Jersey.

"Who is this woman?" he began and stared at Dottie.

CLACK, clack, clack. The sound of Tracy's heels pounding up the stone stairs of the building echoed through the hallways. She threw open the door to the apartment, and ignoring her husband and brother, marched over to the telephone.

"Did you find Mom?" Fred asked, and she glared at him as she dialed the phone.

"Hello, I need to speak to Don Goldstein," Tracy barked into the phone, and she watched her husband stand up and look worried. She placed the palm of her hand over the receiver.

"Turn on the television," she ordered.

"Where's Mom?" Fred repeated, as he flicked on the set.

"Why are you calling our lawyer?" Brian asked.

"Because," she began, looked at the television, and pointed to it.

She turned away as Fred and Brian walked over and stood in front of the screen. She put her finger in her other ear and strained to hear.

"I don't care where he is, this is an emergency. I need him on the phone, right away."

Behind her she heard Brian whistle low and say, "Oh, my God, it's your mother."

"WELL, we can't do anything today."

"What do you mean?"

"It's Sunday at five. No one's going to hear this today. I'm afraid your friend is going to spend the night in MCC," Sid said and looked at her.

"Are you sure this is all you have to tell me? There are no other surprises?"

Dottie grimaced at him. "No, I told you everything," she snapped.

Sid stood up and walked over to a coat rack. He took a black raincoat off it and put it on.

"Well, there's nothing to be done until morning. I'll find out where the arraignment is and when and"—he glanced at Arthur—"I guess we'll post bail."

"Of course we'll post bail. Honestly—" Dottie shook her head.

TERESA followed a guard down a long noisy hallway. On each side were cells. Women moved about inside the cells, some hollered out as she passed. Blaring sounds of television sets and music fought for attention as they echoed off the tiled walls, intensifying the din.

For the first time she was afraid. This was not the picture Dottie had painted for her. Teresa began to curse her, as she came to a cell, and the guard punched in a number and the door unlatched. She carried her blanket, sheets, and pillowcase inside the empty room, and heard the guard push the door closed behind her.

Teresa sank down on her cot and listened to the springs heave and squeak under her. Well, at least she'd been given her own cell, she thought, and looked at the barren walls.

She was very tired all of a sudden. She'd spread an angry scowl across her face just before she'd entered the building, and all her energy seemed to have gone to keeping it there, as she walked through the cesspool of the floor she was on.

Never let anybody think they can get over on you or take advantage of you; that was what Teresa had been taught her whole life. And in an odd way, it was as if she'd been in preparation for this.

She couldn't imagine Dottie holding up under the pressure.

Dottie.

She wondered where she was, and what she was doing. Probably in another country somewhere. Boy, would she get a laugh out of this . . .

Teresa slowly stood up, gave a large yawn, and began to go about making up her bed. Well, it could be worse, she thought, she could've been stuck with some loudmouth roommate, or some kind of loony, but they'd given her her own room.

She smoothed the fitted sheet over the blue-striped mattress.

It was probably because of her age, or maybe they didn't think a fifty-seven-year-old was going to fit in. Or maybe Dottie was going to turn out to be right about this whole thing, and she was going to wind up holding all the cards.

Whatever it was, Teresa thought as she tucked the top

sheet under, making neat hospital corners as she went, all she had to do was survive one bad meal and one night's sleep until nine 'clock tomorrow morning. Then there'd be the arraignment, and then it was going to be her turn.

CHAPTER SEVEN

T ERESA'D slept like a baby.

It was the last thing she'd thought would happen when they had brought her in the evening before, but she'd slept. Maybe there was something about the noise and the music and the jail sounds which sounded as if she'd left the television on, but for the first time in almost a year she'd gotten twelve complete hours of pure rest. She'd been woken by a buzzer or bell kind of sound at six in the morning; the crack of dawn, and she didn't even feel tired. She ate an enormous breakfast, instead of the tiny bowl of cornflakes that was usually the only thing she had the energy to make for herself. She had three cups of lousy coffee, showered, and dressed. She wore the same suit.

There were crowds lining the hallways in the court building as they brought Teresa, now in small plastic handcuffs which almost looked like Hefty bag ties, into the courtroom. Her eyes scanned the room, and then, dazed from the photographers' flashes, she closed them for a moment, and felt them fill with soothing tears.

As she opened her eyes again, and wiped them with the back of both her hands, the thin, twitchy face of her daughter suddenly materialized in the middle of the crowd. Her eyes were still shaded by her big sunglasses, but her mouth was moving back and forth in overdrive. Teresa knew she was glaring beneath those glasses. Tracy's hair was all disheveled, and Teresa wondered who was watching the kids so she could be there.

Behind Tracy was the emotionless face of her husband, who looked more stunned than anything by this, and lastly, her youngest, Fred, who looked just plain worried. Teresa felt a brief wave of guilt for worrying them, but that vanished immediately and was replaced by what she had felt coursing through her veins for twenty-four straight hours, and that was *excitement*. It was as if someone had given her a shot of Adrenalin; she loved this, and she kept her head high and dignified and smiled at every reporter or anyone with a microphone or camera.

She was led to the front of the courtroom. A guard held open the low swinging gate that separated the players from the spectators, as Teresa smugly thought. She kept her eyes straight ahead, staring at the light oak-paneled walls, the matching judge's chair, and the guards who stood motionless in front of a door on the right. A large American flag hung limply on a staff next to the judge's bench.

Behind her she could hear the strange clicking of fingers on laptop keys, and the indistinguishable din of voices all talking at the same time. Flashes of light bounced off the paneling in front of her.

Jeez, the amount of film they were wasting on the back of her head, she thought for a moment, and then suddenly turned around and faced the courtroom. She gave them all a smile, slowly turning her head from one side to the other. Click, click, click, and they went crazy.

People started shouting questions right and left, lights, held by news camera crews, went off, creating an unpleasant blinding glare, and still Teresa DeNunzio Newhouse kept smiling. Behind her there was the sound of a gavel hitting whatever that thing is that they put up there and Teresa turned around to see a youngish man with jet-black hair who was the judge. One of the guards started yelling for order, and quickly everyone quieted and then they all sat.

There was all sorts of echoey mumbo-jumbo from the judge, to which Teresa didn't pay the slightest bit of attention, but kept her chair at an angle so she could keep an eye on the spectators.

Tracy looked as if she was either going to be sick or blow her top at any minute.

"Mrs. Newhouse? Mrs. Newhouse! You may be interested in what I'm saying up here!" A voice rang out and Teresa turned around and squinted at the judge.

"Good, now the question was, do you have legal counsel?" he asked crisply.

Teresa stood up and was just about to say no, when she heard not one but two voices ring out behind her.

"Yes, your honor! He'll be here in—" Tracy's voice rang out, and was interrupted by another, a man's voice.

"I have been retained as legal counsel to Mrs. Newhouse." A man, heavyset, balding on top, but impeccably dressed, pushed his way through.

Teresa's eyes darted over to Tracy, who looked as stunned as she was, and they both looked at the lawyer. But it was who was behind the lawyer who made Teresa's mouth drop open.

It was Dottie.

Dottie Weist, her lips pursed sideways into a half-frown, half-grin, which said, "When I get my hands on you . . ." and her arms crossed over her chest, was staring straight into her eyes, and Teresa felt a slight chill go across her. She was wearing pants and a silk blouse, and her hair and makeup were different, but it was Dottie. Teresa turned around quickly and let a thousand thoughts and questions, and some half-thoughts, whiz through her head, and she suddenly felt that she was trapped.

Her eyes slid suspiciously over to this lawyer, who was busy unpacking his briefcase on the table next to her.

Dottie. Here in the courtroom. What was she going to do? Teresa's heart was beginning to pound, she felt hot and sweaty all of a sudden.

Was Dottie going to confess? Or had Teresa unwittingly tripped up their big plan? Was she going to . . . she turned her head around, almost against her will, and again stared at Dottie. Behind her was a tall, very fat man in a windbreaker, with thick glasses and a cap, and Dottie was whispering to him.

Teresa turned back quickly, and she felt her chest begin to tense. It had to be *him*. Arthur MacGregor. She felt herself begin to panic as the thought that she had actually screwed up a perfectly executed robbery occurred to her. She looked at the man behind Dottie again.

Jeez, if that was Arthur MacGregor, he'd let himself go, she thought, and turned back around. So what was Dottie here for? What were they here for? She bet it was to find out what she'd told the FBI. And if that was the case, then Teresa was in the catbird seat; she exhaled and relaxed. And then she thought, but if it wasn't, she could be in big trouble. Teresa looked back at the judge.

"You are credentialed to practice law in the state of New York?" the kid judge was saying.

"I am, Your Honor."

"Are you prepared to enter a plea?"

"Not at this time. I am requesting that bail be waived as my client has no known priors—"

"Your Honor," the district attorney interrupted, "this woman is accused of holding up a bank with a gun, and shooting a guard."

"Yes, yes," the judge mumbled, and then they all mumbled some more, but all Teresa could think of was Dottie and Arthur MacGregor standing silently behind her, ready, it seemed, to blow her whole story.

"Bail is set at a hundred and twenty-five thousand dollars; next court date will be in three weeks"—the judge thumbed through a roster—"at ten A.M." And with that he hit the gavel.

Teresa looked at Sid and blinked.

"Mrs. Newhouse, I am Sidney Arnowitz; I have been retained by Mrs. Dorothy Weist and a third party as your attorney." He held out his hand, and she slowly took it. He gave a relaxed shake and immediately dropped her hand. "It should take half an hour or so to post bail, and then I suggest we go back to my office so I may take your statement."

She nodded up and down, and felt herself sinking into the chair.

"MOTHER, do you realize what you've done? Do you realize everyone knows about this now? I mean, what were you thinking of!" Tracy's voice was high and raspy, and she was pacing back and forth, her hands on her hips. She almost reminded Teresa of a caged lion, the way her permed black hair framed her face.

They had been waiting in this room in this fancy law office for what seemed like an eternity. A long, dark conference table dominated the room, whose walls were lined with bookcases of matching dark wood that were filled with thick, expensively bound legal books. There were two doors, one on each side of the conference room. They had entered the room through one door, and Teresa figured that Dottie was behind the other. Through her mind flashed the ending of that movie, *The African Queen,* when the camera focused on this torpedo, just lying in wait for the big German ship, to ram it and blow it to smithereens.

Only Dottie was the torpedo and she, Teresa, was the German ship.

She shifted uneasily in her chair and stared ahead. A pair of beige draperies was pulled open, revealing a breathtaking view of New York Harbor. Out in the hazy bay, Teresa could just make out the Statue of Liberty. She kept staring at it and staring at it, and wondering when she was going to come face-to-face with Dottie.

"Maybe your mother had a reason, Tracy," Brian's voice droned on.

"Oh, I know the reason, I know the reason. You did this because you thought that it would stop us from moving you down to Florida. Do you know that there have been reporters camped out on my lawn since early this morning? I'm not talking about one or two, Mother, there're so many people sitting on our lawn, it looks like pictures of Woodstock after the rains. Everything is trashed, the new azaleas and the roses we just had landscaped. There is a petition to make us sell the house. My neighbors are all screaming about the noise and the garbage. We have to get an unlisted telephone number, for Christ's sake." Tracy walked back and forth, taking short jittery steps.

Teresa took a lazy drag on her cigarette, and blew the smoke out at a thin angle.

"And that lawyer, who the hell is he? Huh? Where did he come from? Do you realize we were going to mortgage our house to cover your bail?"

"Then ain't it a good thing that you don't have to go through with it, Tracy?"

"Whose lawyer is that?"

"It's my partner's," Teresa joked and tossed her head back.

"Oh, please—"

"You heard of the Hemlock Society? Well, we're the Larceny Association."

"I've never heard of that," Tracy snapped sarcastically.

"It's a secret. It's me, and that guy a while back who robbed that bank in Nassau County—"

"He was a gambler, Mother, he did it because he was in debt."

"Naw, when they interrogated him, instead of spilling the beans on us, he gave them that cock-and-bull story." Teresa watched Tracy momentarily take it seriously. She straightened up and shook her head.

"When that lawyer, whoever the hell he is, comes back in this room, you are going to tell him the truth."

"I told him the truth."

"Stop it, just stop it! You and I both know that there is no way you held up that bank on Friday."

"How do you know?"

"Because you were at the doctor's," Tracy said triumphantly and placed her hands on her hips. "You had a doctor's appointment! Now tell him the truth, or I will."

"I am telling the truth."

"You were at the doctor's," Tracy said harshly.

"That," Teresa said, leaning forward, "was Thursday. Friday, I was robbing a bank."

"Oh, GOD!" Tracy screeched and whirled around, shaking her head and raising her fists toward the ceiling.

She was taking this worse than even Teresa imagined she would.

"I have to get a glass of water," Tracy roared and swept out of the room.

Brian shrugged and followed her. Fred, Jr., looked at her wearily.

"Look, Mom, it wasn't a bad idea, your going to Florida to live with us. Maybe Tracy didn't say it right when she told you about it, but really, it wasn't a bad thing."

Teresa's eyes narrowed, and she looked at him.

"Tell me, you got a roof on that house of yours yet?"

"Of course."

"You got walls inside?"

"Yes."

"Are they painted?"

He shifted in his chair. "Well"—his voice faltered—"we're still taping them. But the house is fine . . . You know the hurricane hit pretty badly—"

"Yeah, so what makes you think I'd be all excited to move down to someplace been devastated by a hurricane? Did anyone ask me where I wanted to live? Or what I wanted to do? I ain't ninety, you know."

"It was just a way to get you out of this neighborhood that everyone could afford instead of some—"

"Home, right? And then what? Do you think I'm stupid? I read all them articles, like that one in *Life* magazine: 'How Long Can We Keep Mom Home?' I seen what the next step is gonna be. And I ain't ready for this yet. I am fifty-seven years old, for God's sake. I could live another thirty years, and I ain't gonna do it in some home because the two of youse decided I am too old to live on my own." She looked at him. He blew out a breath and looked away from her.

The door to the room opened and Sidney Arnowitz walked in, followed by Tracy and Brian. They all watched him in uneasy silence as he took a chair at the head of the table. They all sat down.

"Now, Mrs. Newhouse, it seems—"

"Tell him the truth, Mother. Tell him that you didn't rob the bank."

"I robbed it," Teresa said flatly.

"She didn't," Tracy interrupted.

"I did, I robbed the bank, and I shot the guard," Teresa said quietly.

"She was home—"

"Mrs. Newhouse," he said sharply, and stood up, "I need to take a statement now. Would you all please clear the room?"

Tracy glared at him and then stood up and grabbed her bag. She gave Teresa one last evil eye and swept out of the room, followed by Brian and Fred, Jr. The door was closed, and Sid looked over at Teresa.

"I robbed the bank, I threw my clothes into the Hudson river, and I stashed the money." She repeated the sentences she'd been rehearsing in her head for two days now.

Sid drew a broad smile across his face and clasped his hands on the desktop and then looked at her.

"Mrs. Newhouse, you and I both know that Dottie Weist held up that bank. You and I also know that she came to you to provide her with the number of a fence so she could buy a gun and rob the bank. We also all know that in doing so, she told you, over the course of two visits, exactly how she was going to go about robbing the bank."

"Yeah?" Teresa said, and stubbed her cigarette out in the ashtray.

Sid stared at her, frowned a moment, and then stood up. He walked over to the door on the opposite wall and opened it. Teresa watched Dottie enter, and her smile slowly dropped. Behind her a man appeared who vaguely looked like the fat man she'd seen behind Dottie in the courtroom. Only he seemed to have dropped about fifty pounds and was not wearing glasses and his face was the handsome face she had seen in newspaper photos over the years.

Now this man she could see falling in love with, and she felt herself exhale with a little sigh as it became obvious that she did indeed now hold all the cards. And Teresa found herself rising slowly and then standing in awe of Arthur MacGregor.

"Hello, Teresa," Dottie said sternly and looked at her.

Teresa didn't take her eyes off Arthur.

"Arthur MacGregor, Teresa DeNunzio Newhouse," Dottie said and Arthur extended his hand, which Teresa shook vigorously.

"Arthur MacGregor . . . My friend was in that bank you held up when you started singing, and you sent my cousin's husband, Georgie Provino, a hundred bucks to get him through when his business failed. This is a honor, Mr. MacGregor, I swear," Teresa began.

"Thank you," Arthur said, somewhat charmed, and shook her hand.

They all sat down in silence, and then looked at Sid.

"It seems we have an interesting situation here. Now the question is—"

"Are you crazy? How could you do this?" Dottie cut in, leaning across the table to Teresa, who did the same.

"What do you mean, how could *I* do this?"

"I mean, are you crazy?"

"Crazier than who? Than you?"

"Well, at least I actually did it."

"And I did what I had to do."

"I don't think you realize what you've done."

"I know exactly what I've done. I confessed to robbing a bank."

"*I* robbed the bank."

"Yeah, so what makes me crazy?"

"You confessed to it!"

"Yeah, I confessed to it, but that don't make me crazy. Hell, you were the one *stunadze* enough to walk into a bank and disarm a guard. You're the one took your life in your hands. You coulda gotten shot! Now, that's crazy."

"What is it? Is it Fred that's made you this way?"

Teresa's eyes narrowed. "Now, you wait one minute. You come up to my house six days ago and tell me you're gonna rob a bank so you could get sent to the same jail as Leona Helmsley." She darted a glance at Arthur and the

260

lawyer. "I ain't making this up. She come up to my house looking for the number of a fence to get a gun to go rob a bank to go to jail. Now, I didn't call you crazy. I didn't tell you you was nuts—"

"I wasn't; I had a damned good reason—"

"So? What makes you think I ain't got a damned good reason too for confessing to this?"

"Because it's insane—"

"No, you coming back here into this city is insane. Why the hell aren't you on a plane to the South Seas or something?"

"I came here to save you—"

"Save *me*?" Teresa looked at Arthur. "Don't you just wanna smack her sometimes? I don't need no saving. And I don't believe that's the reason you're here."

"Why else would I be here?" Dottie was offended.

"To find out if I spilled my guts to the FBI."

"Oh, that's so unfair. How could you think that badly of me? I'm here to get you out of trouble. Because it was the right thing to do."

"It was the wrong thing to do. There you go with all this right or wrong stuff." Teresa leaned even farther into Dottie, and lowered her voice. "I figured out why you do this stuff, why you couldn't go off with him in the first place, why you stayed in the bad marriage."

"Why?" Dottie asked hotly.

"Guilt. You think that by making yourself into some kind of martyr, it's gonna compensate for all these terrible things you think you done."

"Like what terrible things?"

Teresa's eyes slid to Arthur, who seemed somewhat amused. "Like him. Like outta of the seven deadly sins, you got three covered—sex, adultery, and now stealing. So you try to overcompensate for all this and you wind up miserable. If you'd have just followed your heart and stopped listening to everyone else, it would've been okay. You're not so bad that you can't have a little happiness in your life, Dottie. You shouldn't be sitting in this room, you should be off someplace having the time of your life. And that's why it's wrong what you've done here, and this man is now in jeopardy because of you. It is wrong that you're back here."

Dottie sat back in her seat, stunned, and she looked at Arthur, who was nodding. She was silent for a moment.

"What do you want, Teresa?" Dottie's eyes narrowed.

"I want to go to jail, just like you said." Teresa leaned forward.

"But do you understand the ramifications of your actions?" Sid began, and they all looked at Teresa.

She sat back in her chair. "Once again, since none of youse appear to be listening, I confessed to the crime. I understood exactly what I was doing. What, are you all stupid? Or do you think I accidentally got all dressed up to look like Dottie, took two trains outta my neighborhood, walked four blocks so I could accidentally confess to what she did?"

Dottie watched Sid's face get that hard look he'd had the night before in Arthur's living room, and she watched him stand up and she braced herself for the speech. He put his hands in his pockets and paced back and forth, his figure almost silhouetted against the window.

"This isn't some joke. I know all about that nonsense of going to jail to pay your medical bills, and it won't wash. It's been tried before . . . And the criminal justice system, they aren't going to be so charitable as to look upon you as a starving, poor old woman, you got it? You have identified yourself as a felon who shot someone, got it?" His voice was harsh.

"Yeah," Teresa said, waiting for him to get to the point.

"Yeah, so, that statue of American Justice—the *blind-*

folded woman with the scales—is blindfolded for a reason. The jury is told, is there a reasonable doubt of guilt? Period. Did you commit the crime as described in the law books? In your case the answer is yes, you confessed to doing this. The police have a tape showing a woman who you could definitely pass for, holding up a bank and shooting a guard. And so does Channel seven, two, four, and five, and for all I know, CNN and the BBC at this point. Now I would be a fool if I walked into the courtroom and planned to defend you any less seriously than that. And I do take this seriously. There is a good chance you're going to jail for fifteen years as it is. Even if a judge gave you the benefit of the doubt, do you really want to go through with this? I suggest, Mrs. Newhouse, you think again." Sid had walked over to the opposite side of the table and, placing both his palms on the tabletop, he leaned down to face Teresa eye to eye.

Teresa didn't bat an eyelash, and for just a brief second she could see the glimmer of confusion in his eyes, as if he were thinking, "Why isn't she going pale?"

"So, you think I'll probably do some time. This is not news," Teresa said after a moment.

"You don't take any of this seriously, do you? Last night was just a taste, dammit! Now if you choose to continue this, I want some things understood right now."

"Like what?" Teresa's voice had an edge to it, as she stared him down.

"Like, you do as I say, when I say it. First"—Sid straightened up and went back to pacing and counting on his fingers—"we plead out immediately. I don't want you talking to anyone about anything. We'll try and plant something in the press about your plight and—"

"How sick I am, yeah, yeah, yeah. Is that it? Is that all you gotta say?"

He stopped, and now looked openly puzzled. Dottie

stared up at him, wondering what he was going to do. She'd been scared to death by this speech. She glanced at Arthur, who seemed amused.

Arthur's chin was leaning on the palm of his hand, his elbow resting on the table, and he was grinning at this tough woman, trying to remember exactly how he had come to know Fred Newhouse.

"I . . . I just don't understand why you did this, Mrs. Newhouse. Quite frankly, it puts me in a very strange position. I mean, I've been a criminal lawyer in the state of New York for almost twenty-five years now, and I can tell you, I have defended a lot of guilty people and we claimed they were innocent. I have never had to claim someone I knew was innocent, as guilty."

"Yeah, well, now you get to," Teresa began. "Now, sit down and listen." She began and Sid sank down into a chair. Teresa leaned forward.

"First of all, I will cop a plea; I wouldn't want you to look insane or something, because they do have the tape. But if I agree to cop a plea, I want a stipulation in it, is that the right word?" She looked at Sid, who nodded. "Good, I seen that on *L.A. Law*," she said aside to Dottie, who just nodded. Teresa stood up and began walking around the table.

"Okay, the stipulation is, I wanna be sent to that place in Danbury, Connecticut, the one Leona Helmsley got, you know? The one with the garden, and the lawn, and them big color television sets—and . . . I want the same room. You got it?"

"But I can't—"

"Sssh! I ain't finished. Secondly, you tell them district attorneys that if they don't agree to this, I'm gonna do a number on the six-o'clock news gonna fill that courtroom. Next, I wanna call a news conference, as soon as possible . . . and I wanna to be on 'Phil Donahue,' and 'Oprah.' "

"What about 'Geraldo'?" Dottie threw in.

"He's a jerk." Teresa sniffed.

"And what are you going to say?" Arthur asked slowly.

"I'm gonna tell them that my doctor wants to biopsy a lump in my breast for cancer and do a radical mastectomy, but there's another procedure that's experimental that I could try. Then I'm gonna tell them that Medicaid won't pay for the procedure I want 'cause it ain't on some list, even though it would be cheaper for all us honest citizens"—Teresa was looking straight at Dottie, who had gasped at mention of the breast cancer and was now listening seriously to all of her reasons for confessing to the crime. Teresa nodded to her and then began walking around the table.

"And I wouldn't have to be in the hospital, and the recovery could be easier. Then I wanna talk about how Medicaid didn't pay for some procedures that coulda made my husband more comfortable, so we had to spend our whole savings on hospital bills, and how Social Security has now cut me off because they won't give survivors' benefits until a person is sixty, and how I'm gonna lose my apartment—"

"And what does this have to do with bank robbery?" Sid asked.

"These are my motives—what, are you stupid?" Teresa looked incredulous.

"But you didn't even commit the crime!" he yelled.

Sid shook his head, as did Dottie and Arthur, and they all stared transfixed at Teresa.

"So what? Now, I want a news conference, and that should take care of you going to all the trouble of planting stories and all that other bull. You go tell the DA that it's the prison in Danbury, with Leona Helmsley's room, or they ain't got a deal. And tell them that if they don't send me in, I'll rob another bank."

"Why?" Sid's voice was thin now.

"Why? Why? Because they put me and Fred through hell over his cancer treatment, and them bastards in the government are gonna pick up the *whole* bill this time, that's why. And because I could see myself lying in a nice clean infirmary where I don't gotta do no cooking or cleaning for myself, and I could be looking out on trees and grass while I'm recuperating, that's why."

"What if you die? You want to die in jail?" Arthur prodded.

Teresa gave a smug laugh. "I ain't gonna die. I'm too mean."

They were all silent, and Teresa stared at Sid.

"It doesn't seem unreasonable, Sid," Arthur began.

"Ain't it okay? Now, you let me and Dottie come up with the statement, just so I know the fine details of the thing, and I'll confess to the rafters. And that's what I want from you, lawyer."

They were all quiet.

Arthur cleared his throat and leaned forward. "And us, what do you want from us?" he asked firmly.

A slow, sly smile drew across Teresa's face, and she placed her hands on her hips and looked straight at him.

"I want fifty thousand, in cash, in a safety-deposit box for when I get out, and you will never hear it cross my lips she was the one did the crime."

Sid's mouth dropped open, Arthur whistled low, and Dottie kept her stare.

"You're blackmailing them on top of this?"

"Well, I gotta get something outta this, don't I?"

"I can't listen to any more . . ." Sid shook his head.

"Forty-eight," Dottie said evenly.

"Fifty-two," Teresa said quickly.

"You just said fifty," Arthur interjected. "And you already confessed to the crime. What if we turn around and refute your story in the press?"

Teresa tossed her head back and gave a raspy chortle. "You ain't ever gonna do that."

"Why not?" Arthur asked.

"Because she's fallen back in love with you in the past six days, and judging from the fact that you're sitting here like a pigeon, you probably, for reasons I can't begin to understand, have fallen back in love with her. You ain't gonna let her confess to no crime so she can go sit in prison. That's why she didn't come forward two days ago."

Arthur let out a laugh and then conceded with a shrug.

"This is insane," Sid began, and there was a knock and they all silently watched Sid walk to the door. His secretary whispered something, and they heard Sid say, "What?" in an alarmed tone. He turned back to the others and quickly excused himself and left, shutting the door behind him. Outside they could hear the voices of Teresa's children as they descended upon Sid. Dottie and Arthur looked back at Teresa.

"You are just unbelievable—" Dottie began.

"Hey, hey, now, I ain't so bad. I am fully prepared to do time for you so you can go off with him," Teresa said, blinking, and somewhat confused by Dottie not seeing what a golden opportunity she was being handed.

"So what do you get out of this? Besides a jail term?" Arthur asked.

"What do I get? A piece of the money, so when I do get out, I will have a little something. I get that the government will have picked up the tab for this breast thing. I get to be on television, I get to meet people . . . I had my man, and my home and my life, and that made me happy. And now that's over, but I'm too young to just go sit in some home somewhere. I ain't afraid of some jail in Danbury, Connecticut, for Christ's sake, I'm afraid of spending my life sitting in some home in Florida because I ain't got the money to do what I want, and I gave up. I need to find out what I want to do. And as crazy as it sounds, this might give me the chance. Is that so bad?"

Arthur looked at Dottie, who slowly shook her head. They were all silent again.

"So . . . where do you want the fifty grand deposited?" Arthur asked finally.

"Fifty-two." Teresa said.

"Forty-nine," Dottie bid.

"Fifty-one," Teresa said, leaning forward, and waited for Dottie's next bid.

The door opened and Sid walked in stiffly. He shut the door behind the prying eyes of Teresa's children.

"Sid?" Arthur said, looking at him concerned. Dottie stared at his face, a little pale and angry-looking as he stormed over to the bookcase.

"Just be quiet and listen." He snapped on the radio to WINS.

"—at nine forty-five this morning. An FBI spokesman issued the following statement . . ." There was a scant pause and then a voice with a heavy New York accent began.

"In light of these new developments, charges of robbery will be dropped against Mrs. Newhouse until such time as we can either verify Mrs. Newhouse's role, if any, in the robbery on Friday, or until we can prove Mrs. Newhouse is shielding someone else."

"Could the robbery this morning be a copycat crime?" A voice asked.

"With all the press coverage and publicity over the past several days, we cannot rule that out. In either case, we will be keeping a close eye on Mrs. Newhouse."

"Is the federal government planning to file any charges of filing a false report, or, say, obstruction of justice against Mrs. Newhouse?"

"We will consider charges of filing a false report. Unless,

as I said, we find out she's shielding someone; then of course we'll file obstruction charges."

"What is going on?" Dottie asked, and found her eyes darting nervously at the door.

"It seems a woman wearing a blue suit and a large veiled hat held up a Citibank on Flatbush Avenue at nine forty-five this morning, while we were all in the courthouse."

"*What?*"

"You've inspired a protégée," Arthur quipped.

"Oh my God."

Sid turned and furiously slammed his fist on the tabletop. "All right! I've had enough of all of this! Just once, one of you tell me the truth here. Now, who is *this* woman?"

Dottie's shook her head and glanced at Teresa, who was just as dumbfounded.

"I don't know."

"Oh, come off it! You lied to me about her," Sid yelled at Dottie and pointed at Teresa. "And then you lied about committing the robbery to the cops! I look like an idiot here, ladies! Now tell me, who is she?"

"Lower your voice—I don't know." Teresa snapped.

Sid glared at Dottie.

"She's not with *us*." Dottie sniffed.

"What do you think, we've recruited every disgruntled senior citizen in New York, Sid?" Arthur asked.

"It's beginning to seem that way to me. So, none of you knows this woman in Brooklyn?"

Sid looked at Arthur, who shook his head. "Must be an independent bank robber."

The muscles on Sid's jaw tightened. He was not taking this well. "Great! Just great. Okay, that's it then. I guess you can go. There's nothing more to be done today. Where will I be able to get in touch with you, in case they do decide to file charges?"

Teresa was silent. Dottie glanced at Teresa for a second, then, startled, looked back at her face. Teresa's eyes stared blankly at the tabletop. Behind the sadness, Dottie could see the desperation she knew so well. The pain of the thought, How am I going to *live?*

In one sentence, it was as if someone had sucked the life energy out of Teresa.

"You can contact her through me, Sid," Arthur said, as he stood up. "We might as well settle the fees."

"Fine," Sid said stiffly and walked to the door, followed by Arthur. He turned to Dottie and Teresa. In the waiting room they could hear the sounds of Teresa's children—of applause, of anger, jokes—all in reaction to the news on the radio.

"Should I let them in?" Sid asked, his hand on the door-knob.

Teresa stared dully and Dottie could see her eyes beginning to get red.

Dottie looked at him. "Give us a minute."

Sid nodded and left. Dottie kept her eyes silently on her. Teresa tiredly shook her head. At last her eyes rose and met Dottie's.

"Teresa," Dottie said gently, "it's okay, it's good news."

"Yeah," she replied wanly.

"You don't have to go to jail now."

"Yeah," she murmured.

They sat in silence, and Teresa slowly shook her head.

"What am I going to *do?*" she asked, her eyes forlornly searching Dottie's.

"Well, we march down to Medicaid—"

"Aw, Christ! They'll just throw me out again. Nobody gives a damn about some broke woman with a lump in her breast. Nobody gives a good goddamn. You know where I'm gonna wind up? Sitting in some woman's house in

Florida till I can't sit up for myself. And then . . ." Her voice cut off bitterly. She stood up.

"No. No, you won't," Dottie said determinedly.

ARTHUR and Dottie insisted that Teresa go home with them until she decided what she wanted to do. Arthur staved off all objections from her children and, kissing Dottie in the lobby, went off to get the car.

Dottie took Teresa by the arm and led her out of the building. The day was bright and sunny, though it was the first truly chilly day of the season. Dottie shivered in the too-thin coat she'd thrown on, and felt Teresa shiver beside her. They walked to the corner, and Dottie looked for Arthur and the car.

"There she is!" someone yelled, and suddenly newspeople swarmed around them. Lights from cameras blazed, making Dottie squint and hold a hand over her eyes. Questions were shouted, as the press began to push closer and closer. Dottie nervously looked around for Arthur. At last she saw the Ford drive up and she grabbed Teresa's arm and began to pull her through the crowd, trying her best to ignore the shouting men and women.

"Why did you confess?"

"Tell us what went through—"

"Did you think—"

Teresa and Dottie stepped off the curb.

". . . some senile old woman. Who cares . . ." The voice cackled and laughed and came through loud and strong. The end of the snide remark echoed against Dottie's spinal cord. She dropped Teresa's arm and spun around.

"WHO SAID THAT?" she demanded. "Which one of you IMBECILES said that?" she barked, her hands on her hips.

She watched the men and women, so full of bravado a

moment before, stand foolishly silent, hands limply holding pads or microphones or cameras. They all took a gigantic step back, giving Dottie a wide berth and leaving the two women at the hub of the circle of press.

"Come on! Step forward. Step forward, you damned coward!" Dottie challenged.

They were silent. Teresa looked stunned.

After a moment, Dottie grabbed Teresa's hand and turned.

"Who are *you*?" a voice called belligerently.

Dottie turned back.

"I am Dorothy O'Malley Weist, that's who."

"Are you a relative of Mrs. Newhouse?" a female voice shouted from inside the press ranks.

"No," Teresa spoke up. "This woman sent the lawyer for me."

There was a collective "Huh?" And Dottie watched the pads rise, pencils and pens poised.

"You hired the lawyer? Are you a friend?"

"Yes, I am." Teresa looked at Dottie, whose face remained angry.

Scratch, scratch, scratch, went pencils and pens.

"So," a voice began, and Dottie searched for a face to match the voice. "How do you feel, now that it's come out she lied? Do you feel like you've been duped for your generosity, Ms. Weist?"

"No! Absolutely not," Dottie answered, blinking incredulously.

"But she lied—"

"God, is that all you are concerned with? I hired her a lawyer because I knew that she was broke and I knew she wouldn't have the money for one. I also knew that her pride wouldn't let her ask for one. It's like that when you get to be our age and you can't feed yourself. You should think about it sometime, maybe even write about it."

272

"What exactly were your reasons for confessing to this crime, Mrs. Newhouse?"

Teresa stared at Dottie, grimacing.

"I . . . I got a lump in my breast, and I don't have any money or medical insurance."

"Aren't you eligible for Medicaid?" a tall man with curly brown hair challenged.

"Oh, sure!" Teresa smirked. "You ever tried to deal with them? My husband was dying from cancer, and they gave us a hard time about painkillers, for Christ's sake. I couldn't get anyone on the phone—you know, if you have AIDS, Medicaid has seven numbers you could call. You got a lump in your breast, and they don't got one number you can call. So I went to the office. And when I went down there to ask if I could get an experimental procedure for this thing—"

"What procedure?"

"It's a way they can just radiate the lump and not cut your whole breast off. It might not seem like much to you, but it is if you got the breast they're gonna cut off."

"And what happened?"

"They threw me out on the street."

"So, why'd you confess?" another voice asked.

"So I could go to jail. Because they gotta take care of you when you're in jail, they gotta feed you, they gotta clothe you, and they gotta get you good medical care, and you don't have to go and beg. It seems like in this country, except for being in the army, jail is the only time the government *gotta* take care of you. Being honest don't matter, being a good citizen don't matter. But if you're a criminal—"

"But you're not. You didn't do the crime."

"So?" Dottie cut in. "She's like millions of American women in this country today, and whether I committed it or she committed it, or some woman in Brooklyn committed it, it doesn't matter. What matters is that someone wake up. We better start fixing this. And we better start fixing it fast. Because you're *all* going to be this age one day—that means you and you and you—you're all going to be in this position one day, and there are going be even more senior citizens and most of them are going to be women. And maybe, like her, those women didn't work in some fancy job that gave them a nice fat pension and nice expensive medical coverage, and then what? How the hell are they supposed to survive? You think anyone hires people our age? Would your newspaper hire me? Go on, give me a name, I'll call," Dottie said to the tall reporter with the brown hair. He looked down at his pad.

"Oh, no! We don't discriminate, but . . . and if you think she's just going to die soon, or I am going to, think again. We're not dying at sixty-three or sixty-five anymore. I read in your paper I'm most likely to die at seventy-eight. That's twenty more years, and my mother died a full ten years after that! Teresa contributed just as much as the cop on the beat, as the fireman down the block."

"Yeah, like what?" the reporter asked.

"Teresa contributed two full-fledged taxpayers, Charlie, that's what she contributed. That has to be good for at least twenty grand a year for the government. But because that job has no official title or paycheck stub or pension fund, the system can't measure it, so they treat us like we have no value. Well, it doesn't mean that her life has no value. It is the Teresas of this country that keep it going. She raised two good, strong children, she bought from stores in this city, she bought American, she paid her taxes, and she wanted something back. She *deserves* something back. So no, I am not upset because she didn't do it."

There was silence for a moment.

"Is this true?"

Teresa stared at the reporter and her eyes narrowed.

"What? You don't believe that things could get this bad out here for women like me? I saw a straw, I grabbed it, and I'd do it again. I got no money, I got no insurance, and no one out there is listening."

Dottie and Teresa locked arms and began to push their way through the reporters.

"Would you testify in Washington to what you've just said?" a voice asked, and Teresa turned around.

"Testify to who?"

"The Senate's holding hearings on the plight of senior citizens next month in Washington," the tall, curly-haired reporter said.

"Mister, I would tell this to the president's face if I thought any of them in Washington would listen. But they just say it's too complicated for them to do anything about. You know what I think? I think if *their* wives and their daughters and their mothers didn't have no coverage, things would get uncomplicated pretty fast."

Teresa and Dottie, their arms still linked, stared at them all. Silently, the circle opened up, and with great dignity the two women walked through the throng.

Arthur grinned and held the door open, first for Teresa, then for Dottie. They began their drive back to Rye.

"So, how about Hawaii?" Arthur asked, glancing at Dottie.

"After you give me my money," Teresa piped up.

Dottie and Arthur turned around and stared at her.

"But they dropped the charges—"

"Only until they either get that other woman, or"— Teresa gave a big smile—"until they find out if I'm shielding anybody."

Dottie's eyes narrowed. "You are just—"

"Aw, come on! What do I got now? I got nothing. I got no place to live, I got this damn lump—"

"Monday you go to a doctor, a real doctor. We'll take care of that."

"Uh-huh, so you'll help me with this breast thing, get me all cured, and for what? Then what am I gonna do?"

Dottie looked perplexed for a moment and then a grin spread across her face.

"Like the man said: Let's go to Washington, Teresa."